The Reading Comprehension Blueprint Activity Book

The Reading Comprehension Blueprint Activity Book

A Practice & Planning Guide for Teachers

by

Nancy Lewis Hennessy, M.Ed.
The Consulting Network
Kitty Hawk, North Carolina

and

Julia A. Salamone
The Haverford School for Boys
Haverford, Pennsylvania

·P·A·U·L·H·
BROOKES
PUBLISHING CO®

Baltimore • London • Sydney

Paul H. Brookes Publishing Co.
Post Office Box 10624
Baltimore, Maryland 21285-0624
USA

www.brookespublishing.com

Typeset by Progressive Publishing Services Inc., York, Pennsylvania.
Manufactured in the United States of America by
Sheridan Books, Inc.

Case studies are real people or composites based on the authors' experiences. Real names and identifying details are used by permission.

Constructing Meaning drawing used at the start of Chapters 3–8 are used with permission of Will Wagner.

Library of Congress Cataloging-in-Publication Data

Names: Hennessy, Nancy Lewis, author. | Salamone, Julia A., author.
Title: The reading comprehension blueprint activity book : a practice &
    planning guide for teachers / a practice & planning guide for
    teachers / Nancy Lewis Hennessy and Julia A. Salamone.
Description: Baltimore : Paul H. Brookes Publishing Co., Inc., 2024. |
    Includes bibliographical references and index.
Identifiers: LCCN 2023043370 (print) | LCCN 2023043371 (ebook) | ISBN
    9781681257624 (paperback) | ISBN 9781681257631 (epub) | ISBN
    9781681257648 (pdf)
Subjects: LCSH: Reading comprehension—Study and teaching—Activity
    programs. | English language—Composition and exercises—Study and
    teaching. | BISAC: LANGUAGE ARTS & DISCIPLINES / Literacy | EDUCATION /
    Special Education / Learning Disabilities
Classification: LCC LB1050.45 .H463 (print) | LCC LB1050.45 (ebook) | DDC
    372.47—dc23/eng/20231002
LC record available at https://lccn.loc.gov/2023043370
LC ebook record available at https://lccn.loc.gov/2023043371

British Library Cataloguing in Publication data are available from the British Library.

2028   2027   2026   2025   2024

10   9   8   7   6   5   4   3   2   1

Table of Contents

About the Downloads

Purchasers of this book may download, print, and/or photocopy the forms in this book for educational and professional use.

To access the materials that come with this book:

1. Go to the Brookes Publishing Download Hub: http://downloads.brookespublishing.com

2. Register to create an account (or log in with an existing account)

3. Filter or search for the book title *The Reading Comprehension Blueprint Activity Book: A Practice & Planning Guide for Teachers*

About the Authors

Nancy Lewis Hennessy, M.Ed., Literacy Consultant, The Consulting Network, Kitty Hawk, North Carolina

Ms. Hennessy is an experienced K–12 teacher and administrator who currently works as a literacy consultant. While in public schools, she provided leadership for innovative programming for special needs students, a statewide revision of special education code, professional learning opportunities for general and special educators, and district-wide strategic planning.

Nancy has designed and delivered keynote addresses and multiple virtual and live professional learning events including workshops, podcasts, and training courses on dyslexia, the science of reading, and structured literacy. Most recently, Nancy has focused on delivering virtual and in-person professional learning opportunities on reading comprehension.

She is the author of the book *The Reading Comprehension Blueprint: Helping Students Make Meaning of Text*. Nancy has also written the chapter *Working With Word Meaning: Vocabulary Instruction*, in *Multisensory Teaching of Basic Language Skills,* Fourth Edition. While serving as a national trainer for Language Essentials for Teachers of Reading and Spelling, she co-authored LETRS, *Digging for Meaning: Teaching Text Comprehension,* Second Edition, with Louisa Moats.

Nancy has held various positions for the International Dyslexia Association (IDA), including President and Branch Council Chair and currently serves as the Vice-President of the North Carolina Branch of IDA. She has also served on the National Joint Committee for Learning Disabilities. Nancy is an honorary member of the Delta Kappa Gamma Society, was the 2011 recipient of IDA's Margaret Rawson Lifetime Achievement Award, and was recently honored with the North Carolina Department of Public Instruction's 2023 Impact Award.

Julia Salamone, M.Ed., Instructional Specialist, The Haverford School

Ms. Salamone is a lifelong learner with over 20 years of experience as an educator in both independent and public schools. Her background is in special education and literacy, with credentials that include a master's degree in special education from Arcadia University. She currently works as an Instructional Specialist at the Haverford School for Boys where she supports Upper School students in navigating the complexities of reading and writing in the disciplines. Additionally, she consults and collaborates with the teaching faculty to improve student outcomes.

Julia has also designed and delivered numerous virtual and live presentations. She has served as an instructional designer who created various teacher training courses on dyslexia, the science of reading, and structured literacy. This includes the development of the *Pathways to Proficient Reading* course, where she worked under the mentorship of Nancy Hennessy, and *The Pathways to Proficient Writing Course*, where she acted as the co-developer. The former is accredited by the *International Dyslexia Association* (IDA) and offers blended learning opportunities aligned to the IDA's Knowledge and Practice Standards for Teachers of Reading, while the latter is designed to highlight the connection between writing research, theoretical models, and best practices in writing instruction.

Julia's educational interests include reading comprehension, differentiation, student writing, and teacher empowerment. She resides with her husband, Scott, and daughters, Lena, age nine, and Mila, age three, in Blue Bell, Pennsylvania, and in her free time enjoys practicing yoga, spending time with her family, and watching movies, old and new.

Acknowledgments

Good teachers possess a capacity for connectedness. They are able to weave a web of connectedness among themselves, their subjects & students so that their students can weave a world for themselves.

Palmer, 2017, p. 11

I have known so many "good teachers" and my connections with them and in the past, my students, have profoundly influenced my thinking about the teaching/learning process. I have been inspired by the work of my incredible colleagues including my co-author, Julia Salamone, and most recently, the contributions of committed individuals who have joined me in book talks and studies. Most of all, I am grateful to those who have stayed the course, like Louisa Moats, advocating for changes in reading instruction and giving us the courage to share our thoughts and our work with each other. This book would not have been possible if our paths had not crossed and is dedicated to each of them.

Nancy Lewis Hennessy

Teachers create a collective force for improved classroom instruction and serve as support groups for each other's work on their practice.

Darling-Hammond et al., 2017, p. 10

I have had the great fortune to work collectively with many incredible educators throughout my teaching career. This book is a heartfelt tribute to all of you. I would also be remiss if I failed to honor my co-author, Nancy Hennessy, who has served as my mentor, creative partner, and friend. Thank you for always inspiring me and for all that I've learned along the way. Finally, to Scott, Lena, Mila, and Ava: you are my world. I love you to the moon and back.

Julia Ann Salamone

Preface

The road to reading proficiency can be demanding for both the teacher and learner. Comprehension presents its own challenges owing to its complexity. While a knowledge of the science of reading provides guidance, it alone is not sufficient. The educational community has the task of translating and then implementing instruction that supports their students' understanding of text.

My (Nancy's) membership in the educational community, over many years, has taught me multiple lessons. One of the most important is that our learning is never done if our students are to succeed. My book *The Reading Comprehension Blueprint: Helping Students Make Meaning of Text* was a result of my realization that there is always more to learn and then do. At the same time, my continuing interactions with educators consistently remind me that translating and implementing the science is a time-consuming and arduous task. *The Reading Comprehension Blueprint* represented my effort to provide insight into the research and then make connections to informed instruction.

My (Julia's) experiences in the educational community mirror many of Nancy's sentiments. As a self-declared lifelong learner, I've always strived to use my professional learning experiences to help my students grow. I also learned the value of collaboration early on. Throughout the course of my career, I've had the opportunity to work with and learn from some truly talented educators. These interactions have challenged me to deepen my own understanding and then refine my practices. From these collaborations, I realized that we learn best from each other, especially when our collective efforts work to support student learning and achievement.

We recognize that teachers need multiple resources to support their work. This book, *The Reading Comprehension Blueprint Activity Book: A Practice & Planning Guide for Teachers,* represents a collaborative effort to further bring the Blueprint to life. The initial chapter introduces the big ideas of the Blueprint, including the why, what, when, and where of this framework, followed by a chapter that addresses the purpose for reading, including the identification of content and literacy goals. The remainder of the activity book explores the what, why, and how of this instructional framework, providing multiple lessons and activities for developing and using vocabulary, sentence comprehension, text structure, background knowledge, inference, and writing to construct and express meaning of text.

We know that you take your responsibility to your students seriously and we are hopeful that this book will further support your efforts to bring the science of reading to your practice. We appreciate your commitment to learning and all that you continue to teach us!

Nancy & Julia

Introduction

Purpose of the Activity Book

The science of reading includes both word recognition and reading comprehension. Understanding the nature of comprehension, its contributors, and informed instructional approaches is critical knowledge for those educators working with students to achieve reading proficiency. These topics are directly addressed in the text, *The Reading Comprehension Blueprint: Helping Students Make Meaning of Text* (Hennessy, 2020).

Viewing Link: An Introductory Video https://brookes publishing.com/ blueprint-activity -book/

This *Activity Book* is designed to accompany and supplement the information provided in the *Blueprint* text. We have included references to related pages in the text. At the same time, it does briefly revisit foundational knowledge based in the science of reading including the why and what of comprehension in Chapter 1 and similar information for topics featured in the remaining chapters for those who need a review or are new to the information. However, the primary focus is on implementation of the Blueprint, an instructional framework that identifies necessary processes, skills, and knowledge and the instructional activities and skills for making meaning of text. The *Activity Book*, not surprisingly, provides additional instructional plans, activities, and resources focusing on content and literacy goals including the development of vocabulary, sentence comprehension, knowledge, inference, and ability to express understanding.

This book is designed as a professional learning resource for practitioners including classroom teachers, interventionists, coaches, specialists, and instructional leaders. It is intended for those working with students in kindergarten through eighth grade but can be adapted for older students with comprehension challenges or those working with disciplinary text. Additional recommendations and resources are provided for these purposes. The book lends itself to varied learning experiences including individual learning, small-group discussions, and professional learning communities. Opportunities for reflection and connection to application are built in throughout the book for this purpose. As your read, note specific features we have included to support your learning:

- Check In: Connect to current knowledge and practices

- Lexicon Checks

- Reflect & Connect

- Tips for Success!

- Listening/Viewing Links

- Try This!

Tips for Success!

Keep in mind change takes time. Consider your current curriculum and specific context. A little bit at a time may be the best approach!

The Big Ideas of the Reading Comprehension Blueprint

The Big Ideas: The Why, What, When, & Where of the Blueprint

This chapter explores the big ideas of the Blueprint by posing a series of questions and providing responses. It addresses the foundational knowledge for understanding and eventually using the Blueprint itself. As you read this and the following sections, reflect on connections to your practice.

CHECK IN: Connect to current knowledge and practices!

Our understanding of how the reader extracts and constructs meaning from text is foundational to how we think about instruction. How do you define or describe comprehension? Script a brief response.

> "Reading comprehension is not a single entity that can be explained by a unified cognitive model. Instead, it is the orchestrated product of a set of linguistic and cognitive processes operating on text and interacting with background knowledge, features of the text, and the purpose and goals of the reading situation."
> Castles et al., 2018, p. 28

Why: The Science of Reading Comprehension

This science-based description of reading comprehension from Castles et al. (2018) tells us that making meaning of text is neither simple nor straightforward. Ann Castles and colleagues, as well as others, inform us that comprehension is not a single skill; rather, it is a multidimensional process that requires a variety of skills and knowledge. Now, consider Hugh Catts' comments on comprehension:

> Reading comprehension is not a skill someone learns and then can then apply in different reading contexts. It is one of the most complex behaviors that we engage in on a regular basis and our ability to comprehend is dependent upon a wide range of skills and knowledge. (Catts, 2021–2022, p. 27)

Additionally, others remind us that comprehension for skilled readers, "usually feels pretty effortless . . . but this sense of ease is misleading, however, as it belies the complexity of what we do as we read, even when a text is simple and straightforward" (Nation, 2019, p. 47).

These descriptions and multiple theoretical models of skilled reading and reading comprehension can and should inform practitioners' thinking when teaching reading. They collectively reflect the complexity of the comprehension construct by identifying varied contributors to proficient reading. For example, Hoover and Tunmer's Cognitive Foundations for Reading Acquisition (see Figure 1.1), an elaboration of the Simple View of Reading, not only identifies the two essential factors of word recognition and language comprehension, originally represented in the model, but also articulates the processes and knowledge that comprise these two contributors.

Lexicon Check: Processes & Products

The products of comprehension are indicators of what the reader knows and understands after reading is completed, whereas the processes of comprehension are those cognitive activities by which the reader arrives at those products (Rapp et al., 2007, p. 291).

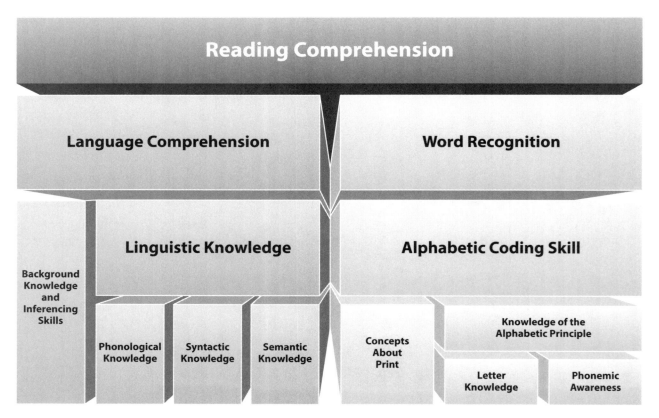

Figure 1.1. Cognitive foundations of reading. (From Hoover, W. A. & Tunmer, W.E. [2020]. Summary of the cognitive foundations framework. In *The cognitive foundations of reading and its acquisition: A framework with applications connecting teaching and learning.* [pp. 89]. Springer Cham.)

Castles and colleagues' description reminds us that comprehension is the "orchestrated product of a set of linguistic and cognitive processes" (2018, p. 28). This is reflected in Hollis Scarborough's Reading Rope (2001) and the work of Cain and Oakhill (2007) that further articulate the importance of language processes and skills and connections to instruction.

Scarborough's Reading Rope (see Figure 1.2) surfaces the contribution of oral language and related language processes to skilled reading. The language comprehension strands of the rope represent critical contributors that work in concert with one another to support reading comprehension.

Cain and Oakhill (2007) further describe levels of language processing that align with the strands of the rope and provide instructional direction. Consider the following and see what connections you make to instruction:

> At the word level, the reader must decode individual words [and]...access meaning of the words they hear or read.
>
> At the sentence level, the comprehender needs to work out the syntactic structure and sense of each sentence. Simply deriving the meanings of individual words and sentences is insufficient.
>
> In order to construct a mental model of the text, the comprehender needs to integrate information from different sentences to establish local coherence and to incorporate background knowledge and ideas (retrieved from long term memory) to make sense of details that are only implicitly mentioned. (Cain and Oakhill, 2007, p. xii)

Research tells us that the proficient reader simultaneously engages in different levels of cognitive processing (see Figure 1.3) that complement one another and

THE MANY STRANDS THAT ARE WOVEN INTO SKILLED READING

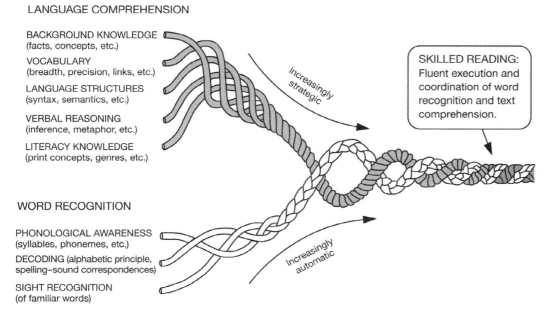

Figure 1.2. The many strands that are woven into skilled reading. (Republished with permission of Guilford Publications, Inc., from Connecting Early Language and Literacy to Later Reading [Dis]abilities: Evidence, Theory, and Practice, by H.S. Scarborough, in Handbook of *Early Literacy Research*, vol. 1 [p. 98], S. B. Neuman & D. K. Dickinson [Eds.], copyright Guilford Press, 2001; permission conveyed through Copyright Clearance Center, Inc.)

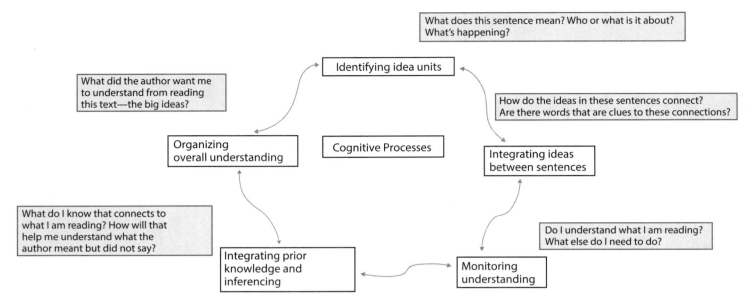

Figure 1.3. The mind of the reader. Hennessy, 2020. Based on Irwin, 2007.

Tips for Success!

The science of reading addresses not only word recognition but also reading comprehension. Informed comprehension instruction reflects this knowledge and includes the development of instructional approaches that align with the science.

depend on the language processes and knowledge just described. The reader works with the words and sentences of the text (surface code) to identify the idea units that the author has explicitly scripted. At the same time, readers connect the ideas within and between the sentences and integrate their knowledge with what is implied within the text (text base). In this way, the skilled comprehender uses what the author has provided—coupled with their language processes, skills, and knowledge—to create an overall understanding and/or mental model of the text that can be used for future applications (Kintsch & Rawson, 2005; Snow, 2002).

It is important to recognize that reading comprehension is a dynamic process that occurs moment by moment as the reader extracts and constructs meaning. The outcome is shaped by the interaction of what the reader brings to the text, the demands of the text itself, and the nature of the task, all of which occur within varied contexts.

This knowledge of the complexity of comprehension provides direction for an instructional guide that reflects what the science has discovered about the construction of meaning, whether reading by ear or eye. It calls for a framework that directly addresses the language and cognitive processes, skills, and knowledge that are necessary for quality products. The ability to demonstrate understanding (products) at different levels of understanding is dependent on the reader's ability to access, apply, and integrate their knowledge of words, sentences, text structures, and background knowledge to express understanding of text.

What: The Reading Comprehension Blueprint

What is the Reading Comprehension Blueprint? In the broadest sense, it serves as a master plan or a guide for action. More specifically, it is an evidence-based framework for delivering instruction that facilitates the student's ability to extract and construct meaning from text. It is not a unit or lesson plan; rather, it is intended to organize and scaffold the teacher's preparation of varied texts for varied purposes. This framework can be used flexibly for reading one passage or multiple texts. Although all components are considered critical to comprehension, the teacher's instructional focus is determined by student needs. The Blueprint calls for the use of evidence-based strategies and activities but allows for the teacher to choose those that are most appropriate to his or her students and the educational context. It also acknowledges the metacognitive nature of teaching by prompting educators to ask and respond to a series of questions related to the design of instruction—questions that address both the process and product demands of comprehension (Hennessy, 2020, p. 43).

How: The Components & Related Questions

Take a moment to review the Blueprint's organization and contents (Figure 1.4). On the left, the focus is on preparing for instruction and for the development of critical competencies for comprehending the text. Note that the Blueprint calls for the identification of critical understandings and purpose—including goals and objectives—and then identifies the instructional components necessary for reading and making meaning of the text. You may have noticed that these components reflect the importance of developing essential language comprehension and cognitive processes, skills, and knowledge.

On the right, the series of related questions, based in science, support the educator in making essential decisions related to the what and how of instruction, while specifically identifying the learning goals, strategies, activities, and routines necessary for acquisition and application of critical contributors to comprehension.

The When & Where: Instructional Considerations

The bidirectional arrow in Figure 1.4 acknowledges the recursive nature of comprehension and the interrelatedness and necessary integration of these skills, while also recognizing the importance of comprehension monitoring while reading. It acknowledges the when and where of instruction and whether it is the individual, small, or whole group that is determined by the educator and dependent on the needs of the student.

Voices From the Field: Comprehension & the Science

I am enjoying putting the science behind literacy practice into the teaching of literacy. It has prompted me to rethink how and why I am teaching in a specific way.

—A Blueprint Book Study Participant

Reflect & Connect: Script a Response

How has this information influenced your thinking about reading comprehension and the implications for instruction?

Viewing Link

Expert Minute—Thinking About Comprehension

https://www.mtsu.edu/dyslexia/expert_minutes.php

Blueprint for Comprehension Instruction

PREPARING FOR INSTRUCTION
CRITICAL UNDERSTANDINGS OF TEXT

What do you want students to know and understand after reading the text? What are the critical concepts and understandings—big ideas you want your students to acquire? What texts will support these understandings?

PURPOSE FOR READING TEXT

What are the content instructional goals and objectives?
What are the literacy instructional goals and objectives?

TEXT READING
VOCABULARY

Which words will your students need to know? Which are worth knowing?
Which ones will you intentionally target and directly teach? Which ones will you incidentally-on-purpose teach? How, when?
Which words will you purposefully discuss and incorporate into expressive language activities?
How and when will you teach and foster the use of independent word learning strategies?

LANGUAGE STRUCTURES
(phrases, clauses, sentence comprehension)

Are there phrases, clauses, and sentence structures that may be difficult for your students?
How and when will you directly teach sentence comprehension? How and when will you teach students to work with challenging sentences?
How will you facilitate the integration of ideas within and between sentences, e.g., the use of cohesive ties and connectives? How and when will you teach students to work with these?

KNOWLEDGE
• Text structure
• Background knowledge

How is the text organized? How and when will you directly teach students the purpose, features, and signal words of different genres? How will you teach students to use the structure to understand purpose? To organize and express their understanding?

What background knowledge is critical to understanding the text? How and when will you teach students to access and build their knowledge and integrate it with the text?

LEVELS OF UNDERSTANDING AND INFERENCE

How will you teach students to construct meaning at different levels of understanding, including the surface code, textbase, and mental model of text? How will you directly teach students to use inference to integrate ideas and connect background knowledge to the text?
How will you support your students' deep comprehension of text?

EXPRESSION OF UNDERSTANDING

What strategies and activities will you use for students to demonstrate understanding at different levels during and after reading?
How will you support their oral and written expression of understanding?

Comprehension Monitoring

Before, During, and After Reading: Strategies and Activities

Figure 1.4. Blueprint for reading comprehension instruction. (From Hennessy, N. L. [2020]. *The reading comprehension blueprint: Helping students make meaning of text.* Paul H. Brookes Publishing, Co.)

2

Implementing the Blueprint

Preparing for Instruction & Text Reading

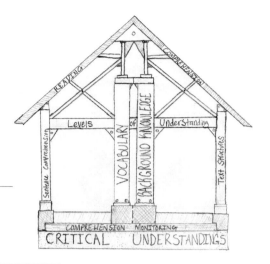

This chapter explores the initial components of the Blueprint that focus on getting ready and preparing for instruction and the "bidirectional arrow" components of the Blueprint. As you read, consider connections to your practice.

 CHECK IN: Connect to current knowledge and practices!

How does your current comprehension instruction address the acquisition of knowledge and critical language processes and skills? Script a brief response.

Preparing for Instruction

Critical Understandings

"Critical Understandings refer to the big ideas, the important understandings, that we want students to 'get inside of' and retain after they've forgotten many of the details. They go beyond discrete facts or skills and focus on larger concepts, principles, or processes" (Wiggins & McTighe, 1998, p. 10).

There is an increasing emphasis on the importance and integration of knowledge-building along with literacy skills during comprehension instruction. Individuals such as Tim Shanahan (2017a) tell us, "Too often the emphasis of a reading lesson is so much on the reading skill or strategy that the opportunity to expand children's understanding of their world is lost." Hugh Catts has written about and supported "concentrated efforts to build rich and integrated ideas about social studies, science, and other subjects during ELA lesson" (2021–2022, p. 30).

The Blueprint calls for the educator to consider the following questions:

What do you want your students to know and understand after reading the texts?

What are the critical concepts and understandings—the big ideas—you want your students to acquire?

Purpose & Goals of Reading Comprehension

Shanahan (2017a) reminds us that reading lessons need to have "double outcomes—an improvement in reading ability and an increased knowledge about whatever was read." The Blueprint recommends that this be accomplished by asking the following questions:

What are the content instructional goals and objectives?

What are the literacy instructional goals and objectives?

Implicit in these recommendations is the choice of texts used for comprehension instruction. While decodable and/or predictable texts provide opportunities for initially building foundations for making meaning, this is not their primary purpose. Regardless of reading levels within a classroom, the use of grade- and age-appropriate texts across content areas provides opportunities for developing the language and knowledge base needed for working with all types of academic texts. Experts tell us that we cannot let the language of print get in the way of student progress (Adams, 2010–2011). Educators need to be purposeful about building academic language, particularly for students at risk of reading difficulties and English language learners (Lesaux & Harris, 2015). Academic language, or the language of schools and workplaces, is different from the language we use every day. It features sophisticated vocabulary, complex syntax, and varied discourse structures. Students who demonstrate proficiency in the use of academic language are better able to acquire new knowledge, participate in the academic tasks of school, and express their understanding and ideas. Thus, students must have access to these challenging texts regardless of their respective reading levels. Teachers can scaffold instruction by providing access to read-alouds and/or high-quality audio versions of texts. These accommodations also provide learners with language-based learning differences or, for those who are English language learners, equitable access to the rich texts necessary for developing academic language.

The following questions can prompt reflection on some necessary considerations when choosing purposeful texts for comprehension instruction:

- Do your readings support the development of knowledge?

- Do your readings provide opportunities to develop necessary language processes and skills?

Tips for Success!

Critical understandings share several characteristics:

- They connect to big ideas that have a lasting impact beyond the classroom.
- They are transferrable to other subject areas and disciplines.
- They go beyond facts and provide a foundation for helping students make deeper connections.
- They are recurring and can be revisited and built upon over time.

The following examples highlight how the critical understanding of "growing up" can be adapted and built upon. Notice how these understandings deepen over time, and how these ideas have lasting value beyond the classroom and school.

- Every day we grow and develop.
- Growing up involves increased responsibility.
- Growing up takes patience and kindness with oneself.
- The reality of growing up isn't always easy.
- Growing up often involves learning important life lessons.
- Moving to adulthood involves looking forward to the future.

- Do your texts provide opportunities to develop and apply academic language skills to text?

- Do your readings represent different genres, disciplines, and the interests and experiences of your readers, and are they culturally responsive?

- Have you considered access issues for struggling readers? (Hennessy, 2020, p. 50)

A Tool for Preparing and Planning for Instruction: The Unit Organizer

The Blueprint provides the framework for informed instruction while the unit organizer provides a tool for making the design and delivery of instruction visible. It serves as an instructional map that helps educators chart and stay the course of instruction by connecting educators' yearly goals with their everyday instructional planning. They provide the foundation for the design of lesson plans necessary for accomplishing these goals. The organizers begin with the identification of critical topics and enduring understandings, which are the big ideas and concepts we want students to hold onto after they've left the classroom. They also provide a vehicle for connecting to the essential questions, overall purpose and goals, purposeful reading, interdisciplinary links, and evidence of learning for the unit. The Blueprint provides the guiding questions, noted in the previous section, which help educators to plan for and craft enduring understandings and identify related content and literacy goals and purposeful texts. The model unit organizer that follows provides potential responses to the Blueprint questions posed while also demonstrating how a common theme (critical understanding) can span different grade levels. The model serves as an example of how to plan for varied themes.

A Model Unit Organizer

The unit organizer in Figure 2.1 compares two instructional units connected with the theme of identity. Notice how the through line of identity is adapted to the developmental needs of each grade level. The concept of one's identity is a theme that should be revisited across grades and disciplines; however, this big idea is explored on different levels of meaning. This allows for elaboration and further construction of the student's mental model as they grow. Additionally, the organizer addresses goals, resources, and evidence of learning.

	First Grade	Eighth Grade
Critical topic	*All About Me!*	*Who Am I?*
Enduring understandings	• I am unique; there is no one else like me. • I have likes and dislikes. • I have strengths and challenges. • I am part of a family and a classroom community. • My family is unique. • All of the people in my class are unique and have their own interests and can do different things.	• Individual identities are complex and show themselves in many ways. • Everyone has multiple identities. • Societal views can influence individual identity. • Our identities have similarities and differences. • It's important to see my identities as well as the identities of others reflected in the world around me.
Essential questions	• What characteristics and traits make me an individual? • What are my likes and dislikes? Strengths and challenges? • What is a community? • What makes my family unique? • What makes my classmates unique?	• What defines our identity? • How is it shaped? • Can we have more than one identity? • Do we keep the same identity throughout our lives? • How do authors develop characters' identities?
Content goals	Students will: • Identify their own likes/dislikes, and strengths/challenges. • Recognize that everyone has similarities and differences. • Describe a community. • Investigate their own family histories and traditions. • Build awareness of others' family histories and traditions.	Students will: • Create a working definition of the word identity. • Describe their own identity and factors that shaped it. • Reflect on the various ways certain social contexts impact our identities. • Examine the topic of identity in a variety of stories.

Figure 2.1. Unit organizer for first grade and eighth grade on the theme of identity.

(continued)

Figure 2.1. *(continued)*

Critical topic	First Grade *All About Me!*	Eighth Grade *Who Am I?*
Literacy goals	Students will: • Identify and discuss story elements (characters, setting, events, conclusion). • State what authors and illustrators do. • Locate the front cover, back cover, and title page of a book. • Identify adjectives and identity terms that describe themselves, their families, and their classmates. • Use new vocabulary words in their speaking and writing with prompting and support.	Students will: • Understand there are many variations of the narrative genre. • Recognize, from reading and writing, the nature of memoir. • Analyze the impact of an author's literary choices in a memoir. • Compare characters and self to create connections and demonstrate understanding of the character within a story. • Compose a personal narrative that develops a real experience or event in their lives.
Resources	• *Leo the Late Bloomer* by Robert Kraus • *Eyes That Kiss the Corner* Joanna Ho • *Chrysanthemum* by Kevin Henkes • *Frederick* by Leo Leoni • *The Proudest Blue* by Ibtihaj Muhammad • *We Are All Wonders* by R. J. Palacio • *The Best Part of Me* by Wendy Ewald • *It's Okay to Be Different* by Todd Parr • *The Day You Begin* by Jacqueline Woodson • *Fry Bread* by Kevin Noble Maillard • *Hair/Pelitos* by Sandra Cisneros • *The Family Book* by Todd Parr • *Last Stop on Market Street* by Matt de la Peña • *All Are Welcome* by Alexandra Penfold	• *Persepolis* by Marjane Satrapi • *American Born Chinese* by Gene Luen Yang • *El Deafo* by Cece Bell • *A Long Way Gone: Memoirs of a Boy Soldier* by Ishmael Beah • *Red Scarf Girl: A Memoir of a Cultural Revolution* by Ji-li Jiang • *I Am Malala: The Girl Who Stood Up for Education and Was Shot by the Taliban* by Malala Yousafzai • *Brown Girl Dreaming* by Jacqueline Woodson • "The Jacket" by Gary Soto • Various chapters from *The House on Mango Street* by Sandra Cisneros • "Fish Cheeks" by Amy Tan • "When I Was Puerto Rican" by Esmeralda Santiago • "Richard" by Allie Brosh • Six Word Memoirs website (www.sixwordmemoirs.com)
Interdisciplinary links	• Art: Students will create a family portrait using precut shapes. • Math: Students will count the number of family members who live in their house and look for similarities and differences with their classmates.	• Art: Students will create a symbolic self-portrait that represents their own unique identity. • Science/Social Studies: Students will discuss the purpose of genealogy and will conduct a series of interviews to collect family information.
Evidence of learning products	• In-class discussions • Small group discussions • Questioning • Completed classroom community quilt square • Completed sentence starters and sentence frames • Completed "Me Book"	• In-class discussions • Small-group discussions • Questioning • Completed six-word memoir • First draft of personal narrative • Google doc comments/feedback • Revisions to draft

The Lesson Organizer

The lesson organizer is focused on accomplishing unit goals, which are typically detailed and specific to a time period. They identify objectives, the sequence of instruction, and strategies and assessment methods specific to the contributors to comprehension. Examples are included in the chapters that follow.

The Bidirectional Arrow

The bidirectional arrow in the Blueprint (see Figure 2.2) serves as a reminder that reading comprehension is not a step-by-step process but dependent on the interaction of multiple skills and sources of knowledge. It also calls attention to the flexibility of the Blueprint. Instruction is determined by the educator, including choice of setting and use of informed strategies and activities.

Blueprint for Comprehension Instruction

PREPARING FOR INSTRUCTION **CRITICAL UNDERSTANDINGS OF TEXT**	What do you want students to know and understand after reading the text? What are the critical concepts and understandings—big ideas you want your students to acquire? What texts will support these understandings?
PURPOSE FOR READING TEXT	What are the content instructional goals and objectives? What are the literacy instructional goals and objectives?
TEXT READING **VOCABULARY**	Which words will your students need to know? Which are worth knowing? Which ones will you intentionally target and directly teach? Which ones will you incidentally-on-purpose teach? How, when? Which words will you purposefully discuss and incorporate into expressive language activities? How and when will you teach and foster the use of independent word learning strategies?
LANGUAGE STRUCTURES (phrases, clauses, sentence comprehension)	Are there phrases, clauses, and sentence structures that may be difficult for your students? How and when will you directly teach sentence comprehension? How and when will you teach students to work with challenging sentences? How will you facilitate the integration of ideas within and between sentences, e.g., the use of cohesive ties and connectives? How and when will you teach students to work with these?
KNOWLEDGE • Text structure • Background knowledge	How is the text organized? How and when will you directly teach students the purpose, features, and signal words of different genres? How will you teach students to use the structure to understand purpose? To organize and express their understanding? What background knowledge is critical to understanding the text? How and when will you teach students to access and build their knowledge and integrate it with the text?
LEVELS OF UNDERSTANDING AND INFERENCE	How will you teach students to construct meaning at different levels of understanding, including the surface code, textbase, and mental model of text? How will you directly teach students to use inference to integrate ideas and connect background knowledge to the text? How will you support your students' deep comprehension of text?
EXPRESSION OF UNDERSTANDING	What strategies and activities will you use for students to demonstrate understanding at different levels during and after reading? How will you support their oral and written expression of understanding?

Before, During, and After Reading: Strategies and Activities

Comprehension Monitoring

Figure 2.2. The bidirectional arrow in the Blueprint. (From Hennessy, N. L. [2020]. The reading comprehension blueprint: Helping students make meaning of text. Paul H. Brookes Publishing, Co.)

The arrow also highlights the importance of comprehension monitoring and teaching students how to check their own understanding. There are varied reasons *why* the reader might encounter a breakdown of understanding. For example, a reader may have inadequate vocabulary knowledge and struggle to grasp the precise vocabulary employed by an author. Others may not have the grammar and syntax skills necessary to unpack sentences of varied lengths and constructions, while some readers fail to possess the background knowledge needed to make meaning on a deeper level. Knowing these sources of difficulty provides opportunities to use strategies that the reader has learned as potential solutions. Skilled readers actively notice their thinking as they read and monitor their comprehension to make sure they understand. If they can't, they can apply strategies to repair inaccuracies or misconceptions. Consider Figure 2.3 for an example of comprehension monitoring in action.

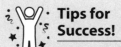

Tips for Success!

Comprehension monitoring is a hallmark of skilled readers. They use this ability to reflect on what they read and process their understanding. Skilled readers monitor their understanding by asking themselves questions like:

- Does this make sense?
- When did I lose track?
- What just happened? Why?
- Does what I just read fit in with the rest of the text?

However, struggling readers may fail to recognize when their comprehension breaks down and/or what to do to fix it. Thus, it is an educator's responsibility to teach all learners ways to monitor their understanding, so that they walk away from the text with its larger meaning overall.

Why	So
Word meaning	Think about using your independent word learning strategies (dictionary, morphemes, context) to figure out what the word means.
Sentence meaning	Reread and ask yourself: • Where is the *who* or *what* and the *do* in the sentence? • What words are standing in or substituting for important words in the sentences?
Knowledge	Think about what you know and make connections. Look up or ask for additional information about the topic.
Paragraph/section meaning	Reread the paragraph and ask yourself: • What is this all about? • What does it tell me?
Engagement	Tell yourself to stop at the end of a section or page to: • summarize • annotate • visualize • question

Figure 2.3. Comprehension monitoring: The why & so.

Planning for Text Reading

Critical Contributors to Comprehension

This section of the Blueprint reflects what science has taught us about critical contributors to comprehension. While these are intentionally named to highlight the importance of developing language processes and skills, each corresponds to an instructional component including the teaching of vocabulary, sentence comprehension, background knowledge, text structures, and inference.

The questions for each component are intended to call attention to the use of routines, strategies, and activities that focus on the development of necessary language skills and knowledge. For example, teachers need to directly teach vocabulary so that the reader has access to word meaning as they build meaning of the text or build the necessary background knowledge to make inferences. Additionally, the Blueprint calls for educators to teach instructional strategies that support students' ability to express or demonstrate their understanding of the text such as directly teaching students how to summarize understanding (orally or in writing).

Keep in mind that comprehension is the "the orchestrated product of a set of linguistic and cognitive processes" (Castles et al., 2018, p. 28). The Blueprint was designed to call attention to the importance of developing the processes and skills necessary to create varied products that demonstrate understanding. It calls for the differentiation and use of instruction that supports both process and product.

Voices From the Field: The Blueprint

The Blueprint emphasizes that comprehension instruction must be thoughtfully planned and explicitly taught. In addition, the bidirectional arrow visually represents the integration of skills throughout the reading process. I found the guiding questions in the Blueprint to be opportunities for us to design instruction that meets the needs of all students.

–A Blueprint Book Study Participant

Reflect & Connect

At this point, what are your thoughts about current instruction and the potential use of the Blueprint?

Listening Link

Glean Education Podcast: Blueprint for Reading Comprehension Instruction
https://www.gleaneducation.com/podcast

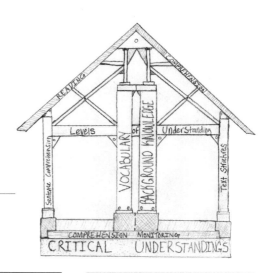

3

Implementing the Blueprint

Vocabulary

Chapters 3 through 8 of the activity book explore the implementation of the critical contributors necessary to constructing comprehension. The focus for this chapter is the contribution of vocabulary or word meaning including the what, why, and how of vocabulary instruction, providing multiple instructional examples based on the instructional framework.

> *"Words are carriers of meaning and are closely tied to text comprehension and knowledge construction."*
> Verhoeven & Perfetti, 2011, p. 2

 CHECK IN: Connect to current knowledge and practices!

Surface and script what comes to mind in the map (Figure 3.1) when you think about the what, why, and how of vocabulary.

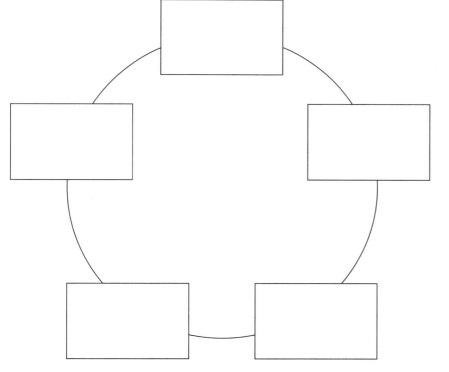

Figure 3.1. Vocabulary mind map.

What: Definition & Description

The focus in this chapter is the acquisition of word meaning or vocabulary, which may be thought of as an individual's lexicon or mental dictionary of words. It includes both receptive and expressive vocabulary. Receptively, word meaning supports our comprehension of information received through listening or reading. Expressively, vocabulary knowledge allows individuals to convey their understanding of content, whether they are speaking or writing. Word meaning is critical to reading comprehension and the student's ability to express understanding, particularly in writing.

Why: The Science

Several theoretical models and research studies reinforce word meaning as both a contributor to word reading and a critical component of language comprehension. Hoover and Tunmer (2020) identify semantics (knowledge of word meanings, phrases, and their relationships) as a component of linguistic knowledge. Scarborough's (2001) metaphor for skilled reading identifies vocabulary knowledge, specifically the breadth, depth, and precision of word meaning, as a key contributor to comprehension.

Research has also indicated that as early as kindergarten, language measures—including vocabulary—add to the prediction of reading comprehension difficulties, over and above other word reading predictors, and are direct measures of word reading performance in second grade (Catts et al., 2014). Research also indicates that vocabulary instruction can improve comprehension, especially when the text includes those word meanings that have been directly taught (Coyne et al., 2022; Elleman et al., 2009).

How: The Design of Instruction

Introduction

Word meaning is acquired over time and in multiple ways. An effective instructional approach reflects both direct and indirect approaches to learning the meaning of words. It also supports the development of both breadth, depth, and fluency of word meaning.

During the creative process of developing effective instruction, educators must also consider and plan for multiple formal and informal word learning opportunities to help address the sheer number of new words students potentially encounter each year. The research recommends a four-part instructional framework to fulfill this need and develop learners' vocabulary knowledge (Graves, 2009; National Institute of Child Health and Human Development, 2000). This framework targets:

- *Intentional instruction*, which focuses on the direct, explicit instruction of targeted words

- *Incidental-on-purpose instruction*, which features indirect, but purposeful, teaching of targeted terminology

- *Intentional independent word learning strategies instruction*, which helps students understand the meaning of words when they read independently

- *Word consciousness*, which is the development of an interest in and awareness of word meanings through direct and indirect learning opportunities

The questions featured in the Blueprint (see Figure 3.2) reflect this framework and are designed to support educators as they plan for the design and delivery of instruction. These reflective queries help educators to plan effective vocabulary instruction by purposeful word selection, organized instruction that delivers the four-part

---

Lexicon Check

Depth refers to the richness of word knowledge an individual possesses about known words. It represents the learner's ability to understand the multiple uses of words determined by context and to use them precisely in speaking and writing.

Breadth usually refers to the size of an individual's mental lexicon. It denotes how many words a learner recognizes at a more general level.

Fluency represents an individual's ability to quickly access the meaning of the word within the context in which it is used.

Blueprint for Comprehension Instruction
TEXT READING
Vocabulary
Which words will your students need to know? Which are worth knowing?   Which ones will you intentionally target and directly teach?   Which ones will you incidentally-on-purpose teach? How, when?   Which words will you purposefully discuss and incorporate into expressive language activities?   How and when will you foster the use of independent word learning strategies?

Figure 3.2. The Blueprint questions: Vocabulary. (*Source:* Hennessy, 2020.)

framework, and incorporation of activities that help learners process and apply word meanings. Thus, these questions serve as a useful reminder and should be considered as one employs the organizer highlighted in this section. Planning focused lessons that align to the Reading Comprehension Blueprint and connect to critical understandings is essential for student vocabulary development.

Thus, the questions in Figure 3.2 serve as a useful reminder for using a structured approach (see Figure 3.3) to implementing this framework. The contents of this organizer provide insight into potential responses to these queries and instructional direction by identifying critical considerations for each component of the framework including instructional focus, strategies, and activities.

Intentional Instruction: Lesson Plans & Activities

Model Lesson Plans

The unit organizer serves as the foundation for the design of the lesson plan. These organizers are designed to address the development of the language processes, skills, and knowledge necessary to demonstrate understanding. The following lessons are connected to the identity unit plans shown previously (see Figure 2.1) and provide models for developing students' vocabulary. As you read through these plans, notice how each lesson connects to its unit's enduring understandings and essential questions to address the overarching goals of the unit, while mapping out specific objectives, activities, and assessments to grow students' vocabulary.

Lessons 1–3 provide examples of two important components of intentional instruction—specifically, instructional routines and opportunities for practice and processing.

Tips for Success!

In the following sections, you will be initially introduced to model lesson plans that focus on specific components of intentional and independent word learning strategies followed by numerous activities that can be incorporated into lesson planning. Consider how you might use/adapt these examples for your practice.

CHECK IN

In what ways does this approach to lesson planning compare or contrast with your current practices?

Intentional instruction	Incidental on purpose instruction	Intentional independent word learning strategies instruction
✔ **Word Choice** ✔ **Simple Instructional Routine: Definitional & Contextual Information** ✔ **Complex Instructional Routine: Processing & Practice Activities**	Structured Point of Contact Teaching Structured Teacher-Student Talk Structured Shared Reading Structured Independent Reading	Using the Dictionary Using Context Clues Using Morphemic Analysis
Word consciousness	**Word consciousness** *Purposeful Activities*	**Word consciousness**

© 2018 Nancy Hennessy

Figure 3.3. A comprehensive instructional framework for vocabulary.

Simple Vocabulary Routine

(textbook pgs. 65–68)

Simple Routine

Teacher:

✔ Pronounces targeted word and discusses structure and/or asks questions about linguistic structure.

✔ Asks students to repeat.

✔ Explains the meaning in everyday language.

✔ Provides examples from context and other situations. Asks students for example.

✔ Says, spells, and writes the word.

This lesson highlights how vocabulary is introduced via the simple vocabulary routine. The simple routine for vocabulary instruction introduces and is designed to teach learners new vocabulary terms. It is interactive, includes teacher modeling, and engages students through response and feedback. Notice how the terminology chosen aligns to the enduring understanding, *All About Me*.

Name: Leo the Late Bloomer: Vocabulary Lesson

Grade: First

Preparation for Instruction

Enduring Understandings:

- I am unique; there is no one else like me.
- I have likes and dislikes.
- I have strengths and challenges.
- I am part of a family and a classroom community.
- My family is unique.
- All of the people in my class are unique and have their own interests and can do different things.

Related Essential Questions:

- Who am I? What are my likes and dislikes?
- What makes me unique?
- What makes my family unique?

- What makes my classroom and classmates unique?

Content Objectives:

- Students will be able to examine the concept of "growing up" and how we all grow at different rates. Explore family relationships.

Literacy Objectives:

- Students will be able to be introduced to new vocabulary via the simple routine.

Resources/Materials

- *Leo the Late Bloomer* by Robert Kraus and Jose Aruego
- Index cards (for student vocabulary rings)
- Vocabulary definitions and examples (preprinted and cut in advance)
- Glue sticks

Sequence of Learning Events

Purpose: Students will learn the following words from *Leo the Late Bloomer* by Robert Kraus and Jose Aruego: bloom/bloomer, patience, neatly, sloppy

Review/Prerequisite Skills: For this activity, with prompting and support, the learner should be able to:

- Participate in discussions about unfamiliar words
- Recognize words or phrases that are unfamiliar to them
- Connect prior understandings to unfamiliar words
- Recognize and count syllables
- Use illustration/dictation to convey meaning

Teacher and Student Instructional Activities:

Lesson opening:

1. Explain to students that today they will be learning some new vocabulary words connected to the book *Leo the Late Bloomer* by Robert Kraus and Jose Aruego.

Teacher modeling: The simple routine

2. Using the instructional routine that follows, the teacher will introduce the targeted words.

<u>Teacher:</u>   Today we are going to learn some words connected to our new story, *Leo the Late Bloomer*. The first word we are going to discuss is right in the title, and that's *bloomer*. Listen as I say the word and get ready to repeat: *bloomer*. Now you try.

<u>Students:</u>   Bloomer.

<u>Teacher:</u>   Excellent. How many syllables do you hear in the word *bloomer*?

<u>Students:</u>   Two

<u>Teacher:</u>   Wonderful. Can someone say *bloomer*, but without the -*er*?

<u>Students:</u>   Bloom.

<u>Teacher:</u>   Excellent work! A bloom is a flower. When we add the word part -er to bloom it changes the meaning to a person who blooms. That's sort of silly because people aren't flowers, right? So, when we describe someone as a bloomer that means they are growing and changing. But in our story, the main character is described as a "late bloomer." This means a person grows or develops later than expected.

<u>Teacher:</u>   Does the word *bloomer* answer the question *who* or *do*?

<u>Students:</u>   Who—it's a person who blooms.

<u>Teacher:</u>   That's right! That makes this word a noun.

<u>Teacher:</u>   Can you think of a time when you bloomed, and grew and developed? Maybe you learned a new skill after practicing it for a while. [Student responses will vary.]

<u>Teacher:</u>   And in our story, the main character, Leo, is a late bloomer. For example, he couldn't write his name even though all of his classmates could write theirs.

<u>Teacher:</u>   Watch and listen as I write this word on the board. The word is *bloomer*. Listen again as I spell the word syllable by syllable.

<u>Teacher:</u>   Repeat *bloomer* to yourself and spell it quietly as you write it on your index card.

3. Repeat the routine with the remaining words identified for instruction (*patience, neatly, sloppy*).
4. Students can be provided with definitional and contextual examples, printed in advance to be pasted on their index cards.

Student-guided practice:

5. As the teacher goes through the routine, students should write each word on their index card. For students who need additional support, the word can be written in highlighter by the teacher first, and the student can trace the letters.
6. The teacher should circulate and support students as they repeat each word and subvocalize for spelling.

Independent work:

7. Once students have written the word on their index card and pasted the definitional and contextual information, they should create an illustration to represent the image.
8. The teacher can circulate and support students as they complete this process for each vocabulary word. The words should be attached to students' vocab rings once complete.

Differentiation/Inclusive Instructional Practices:

• For students who struggle with writing, words can be preprinted on their index card in highlighter. They can then trace over the letters.
• Use mirrors to assist students in their pronunciation of new words.
• Use of visual representations to provide students with concrete images of targeted words.
• Use of cognates to assist English language learners in identifying similarities in meaning, which will help them commit these English words to memory more easily. For instance, the Spanish word for *bloom* is "floración." Connections between this and the word *flower* could be made to assist students in committing the word to memory.

Evidence of Student Learning/Informal Classroom-Based Assessment:

• Participation in vocabulary routine
• Completed index cards with visual representation of targeted words
• Text discussion

Teacher Reflection in Lesson Implementation:

_____

_____

_____

_____

_____

Try This! Now that you have explored the simple routine, select one of the remaining words from the read-aloud, _Leo the Late Bloomer_: _patience, neatly,_ or _sloppy_. Using your chosen word, complete the following script for the simple routine for vocabulary instruction.

The Simple Routine for Vocabulary Instruction

- Listen (teacher says the target word, discuss structure).

- Repeat (student echoes the word).

- Define (teacher explains in everyday language).

- Use (teacher provides an example, students provide an example).

- See, say, write . . . (Teacher writes the word, students say and write, discuss structure/parts of speech.)

Complex Vocabulary Routine

> **Complex Routine**
>
> This model lesson highlights how vocabulary is introduced via the complex vocabulary routine. Note that the terminology chosen aligns to the enduring understanding.

Who Am I?

This lesson recognizes that to develop a depth of word knowledge, students need multiple opportunities for processing and practicing word meanings. Informed strategies and activities focus on making semantic connections, creating visual representations, and using word meanings orally and in writing. The following chart contains categories with some examples that can be included as part of a complex routine. This focus on increased exposures, included in this lesson, supports deeper acquisition of word meaning.

Connect	Represent	Use
Semantic maps	Pictures Drawings Videos	Questions, examples
Semantic feature analysis	Gestures and movement	Conversation prompts
Cognates	Word walls	Writing stems

The complex routine for vocabulary instruction includes components of the simple routine but features additional adaptations.

Name: What Is Identity?: Vocabulary Lesson

Grade: Eighth

Preparation for Instruction

Enduring Understandings:

- Individual identities are complex and show themselves in many ways.
- Everyone has multiple identities.
- Societal views can influence individual identity.
- Our identities have similarities and differences.
- It's important to see my identities as well as the identities of others reflected in the world around me.

Related Essential Questions:

- What defines our identity?
- How is identity shaped?
- Can we have more than one identity?
- Do we keep the same identity throughout our lives?
- How do authors develop a character's identity?

Content Objectives:

- Students will be able to:
  - Create a working definition of the word *identity*.
  - Reflect upon their own identities.

Literacy Objectives:

- Students will be able to be introduced to new vocabulary via the complex routine.

Resources/Materials:

- Word knowledge survey for *identity*—can be printed on paper or electronic
- Adapted four-square template (see Figure 3.12, which is also available as a blank, downloadable worksheet on the Brookes Download Hub; see front matter for instructions to access the downloads that accompany this book)
- Semantic web

Sequence of Learning Events

Purpose: Students will begin to craft a working definition of the term *identity* and begin to describe their own identity.

Review/Prerequisite Skills:

- Participation in discussions about unfamiliar words.
- Connecting prior understandings to unfamiliar words.
- Awareness of the concepts of race, gender, age, class, etc.
- Use and familiarity of vocabulary knowledge surveys
- Use and familiarity of adapted four-square template
- Use and familiarity of concept map

Teacher and Student Instructional Activities:

Lesson opening:

1. Explain to students that today they will be discussing the word *identity* as a class. They will then explore and reflect upon their own identities.

Teacher modeling:

2. Using the instructional routine that follows, the teacher will introduce the targeted words.

Teacher: Today we are going to discuss the word *identity*, which will be the major focus of our next unit. Listen as I say the word and then repeat it: *identity*. Now you try.

Students: Identity.

Teacher: Excellent. Before we begin our discussion, let's rate our current level of understanding. I have distributed a word knowledge survey for the word *identity*. Take a minute to complete the survey by considering the following guidelines: Is this word your BFF, which means you can use in your speaking or writing? Or have you seen or heard this word, but couldn't provide definition? Or perhaps this word is entirely new to you? Either way, take a moment to rate your level of understanding.

**Once this is complete, the teacher can informally poll the students to see where they rated themselves. This could be done using an app like Kahoot or Poll Everywhere, or with a show of hands.

Teacher: So, it's great that so many of you have an existing awareness of this word. Today let's build on that knowledge to expand our thinking. The word *identity* is a noun, and it is the qualities, characteristics, or beliefs that make a person who they are. Because an identity isn't something we can hold or physically touch, it's an abstract noun. This type of noun represents feelings like love or envy or a quality like beauty or determination. This word ultimately comes from the Latin *idem*, which means "sameness," and has many cognates in the Romance languages. For example, in Spanish the word is *identidad*, while in French it's *identité* and in Italian *identità*.

Teacher: Our identities can be impacted by many things, like our race, gender, age, class, and so forth. Can you think of anything else that might help to shape our identities?

Students: ***Answers may vary but might include family, society, location, media, life experiences, ability, etc.*

Teacher: Yes! So many different factors can shape one's identity as we will see as we dive into our readings connected to this unit.

Teacher: Let's add this word to our vocabulary journals. Take out your four-square template and watch and listen as I write this word on the board. The word is *identity*. Listen again as I spell the word syllable by syllable.

Teacher: Repeat *identity* to yourself and spell it to yourself as you copy it down. Once you have that down, you can begin to fill in the parts of your four-square organizer.

**Students can complete the adapted four-square organizer to include: a student-friendly definition (In Your Words) examples (Just the Facts), a visual representation (Paint a Picture), and synonyms and antonyms (Could Be Related But). Once completed, students can be instructed to place the worksheet in their vocabulary notebooks, making sure to file it in the correct section alphabetically.

Teacher: Now we are going to explore the qualities and characteristics that make up our own identities. We are going to do that through concept mapping. Remember that we use concept maps to brainstorm concepts and ideas connected to a given word. Today we are going to brainstorm concepts, characteristics, and qualities that make up our own identities. Take a moment to write your own name in the center of the concept map.

Teacher: Great! Now let's begin to brainstorm some of the qualities that make up our identities.

**The teacher can model adding some qualities to their own concept map. These can vary and include gender, race, class, age, family, society, location, media, life experiences, ability, etc.

Student-guided practice:

3. After modeling some initial qualities and characteristics, the teacher can ask students to generate any additional categories. These categories can be added to the board to help students when generating their own characteristics.
4. Students can now begin to add to their own identity concept maps. Remind them that this will be a process and they will revisit this map throughout the unit to make additions and adaptations.

Independent practice:

5. Students can complete the identity concept map independently, while the teacher circulates and supports as needed. Students can then choose one item on their map to share with a partner.
6. The map should be filed and available for use later. Students will add and adapt their working identity maps throughout the unit.

Differentiation/Inclusive Instructional Practices:

- Use visuals or gestures to provide students with concrete representation of targeted words.
- For students who struggle with copying from the board, definitional information can be printed on the adapted four-square template in advance.
- Students can use drawing in addition to writing to capture their ideas about their identities.
- Create an anchor chart that includes class definition of identity and the categories that impact it including gender, race, class, age, family, society, location, media, life experiences, ability, etc.

Evidence of Student Learning/Informal Classroom-Based Assessment:

- Participation in vocabulary routine
- Completed vocabulary knowledge surveys
- Completed adapted four-square template
- Completed concept map
- Partner share
- Text discussions

Teacher Reflection in Lesson Implementation:

Try This! Now you've explored both the simple and complex routines for vocabulary instruction. Take a moment to compare these two approaches. As you reflect, what similarities and differences do you note? How can you use the vocabulary routine in your own instructional practices?

	Simple Routine	**Complex Routine**
Similarities		
Differences		
Where might I use this in my own practices?		

LESSON 3

Semantic Gradients: Shades of Meaning   (textbook pg. 71)

The use of semantic gradients is a great way to have students explore the subtle differences in words. It also helps show the importance of precise word use and how authors select words carefully to express their intended meanings. In this next lesson, first grade students are asked to broaden their understanding of a pair of opposite adjectives. Students will think critically about the shades of meaning and, through discussion, will place words on a continuum to represent their nuances in meaning. This lesson features vocabulary connected to the unit *All About Me!*

Name: Determining Shades of Meaning: Vocabulary Lesson

Grade: First

Preparation for Instruction

Enduring Understandings:
- I am unique; there is no one else like me.
- I have likes and dislikes.
- I have strengths and challenges.
- I am part of a family and a classroom community.
- My family is unique.
- All of the people in my class are unique and have their own interests and can do different things.

Related Essential Questions:
- What defines our identity?
- How is identity shaped?
- Can we have more than one identity?
- Do we keep the same identity throughout our lives?
- How do authors develop a character's identity?

Content Objectives:

- Students will be able to:
  ○ Identify their own qualities and characteristics, likes/dislikes, and strengths/ challenges.
  ○ Recognize that all humans have similarities and differences.

Literacy Objectives:

- Students will be able to:
  ○ Identify words, adjectives, and identity terms that describe themselves, their families, and their classmates.
  ○ Distinguish between shades of meaning with words and select words with precision.
  ○ Use new vocabulary words in their speaking and writing with prompting and support.

Resources/Materials:

- *It's Okay to Be Different* by Todd Parr
- Semantic gradient organizer (see Figure 3.4, which is also available as a blank, downloadable worksheet on the Brookes Download Hub; see front matter for instructions to access the downloads that accompany this book)
- Opposite pairs of adjectives, including: tall/short, quiet/loud, happy/sad, big/small, weak/strong, fast/slow, pleasant/angry
- Five synonyms for each word pair, preprinted and cut out
- Glue sticks
- Exit ticket

Sequence of Learning Events

Purpose: Students will distinguish between shades of meaning with words through exploration of opposite pairs of adjectives.

Review/Prerequisite Skills: For this activity, with prompting and support, the learner should be able to:

- Have already listened to the read aloud, *It's Okay to Be Different* by Todd Parr
- Understand what an adjective is (describing word)
- Able to sort and organize information

Teacher and Student Instructional Activities:

Lesson opening:

1. Tell students that today we will be building off of our reading of the book *It's Okay to Be Different* by Todd Parr.
2. Remind students that in the book the author, Todd Parr, celebrates all the amazing ways we are unique and that these differences make us who we are. In fact, we all have unique traits that describe us and make us special.
3. Review the word *adjective* with students. Explain that these describing words help us portray ourselves. However, like any good author, we want to make sure to choose the best word possible to do so. Our activity today will help us do this!

Teacher modeling:

4. Display for students the semantic gradient organizer. This can be with a document camera, or the organizer can be recreated on chart paper or drawn on the whiteboard. Display a pair of opposite adjectives (i.e., quiet/loud). Explain to students that we will be working with this pair of words today.
5. Provide students with five synonyms for each word in the pair. For example, quiet/loud might include:
   a. quiet: silent, peaceful, soft, hushed, reserved
   b. loud: talkative, noisy, roaring, boisterous, thundering*
   words like reserved and boisterous may need a quick, point-of-contact definition provided
6. Using the synonyms, model for students how you might organize these words. For example:
7. *"I want to organize these words from <u>most</u> to least <u>extreme</u>. I think 'silent' is the most extreme because there is no sound at all. Then I would put 'reserved' next because someone who is reserved is slow to share their thoughts and ideas. Next, I would put 'hushed' because this is quiet and serious, kind of like a parent talking to a child. Then I would add 'soft' because it's light, but you can still hear it, and finally 'peaceful.' You can hear a peaceful conversation, but it's not overwhelming or distracting."*
8. The teacher can model organizing these words along the continuum.

Student-guided practice:

9. Now have the students help you organize the next set of synonyms for *loud*. Remember to arrange the words from most to least extreme.

10. Once this is complete, have students help you arrange both sets of synonyms from most to least extreme along the gradient.
11. Discuss with the group. Ask students to share their thinking. Do they agree with the order? Why or why not? What might they change?
12. Remind students that they can use this strategy to help them select precise words to communicate their thoughts and ideas. For example, what word on the gradient would they use to describe:
    a. students
    b. lawn mower
    c. fireworks
    d. library
    e. forest
    f. leaves falling
    g. party
13. Collect student responses to the query above. What do they notice when one word is substituted for another? How does this impact the word's intended meaning and impact?

Independent practice:

14. Inform students that it is now their turn to organize different sets of opposite pairs in small groups. Distribute the semantic gradient template and assign opposite adjective pairs.
15. Next, pass out preprinted synonyms for the assigned adjectives to each group. As in the model lesson, students should go through the following steps:
    a. Select an opposite pair of adjectives and their corresponding synonyms.
    b. Organize the first set of synonyms from most to least extreme.
    c. Organize the second set of synonyms from most to least extreme.
    d. Finally, arrange both sets of synonyms from most to least extreme along the gradient.
    e. Discuss with the small group.
16. As students complete this activity, the teacher can circulate and support small groups, asking questions and facilitating discussion as needed. Students should make adjustments to their placement on the gradient prior to gluing.
17. Once all groups have completed their gradients, reconvene and share as a whole group. Groups should share their rationale for placing certain words along the gradient.
18. After the group has debriefed as a whole, each group's gradients can be hung up and students can review in a gallery walk. As an exit ticket, they must complete the prompt *Words that describe me . . .*, by collecting three to five adjectives. These words will be revisited later.

Differentiation/Inclusive Instructional Practices:

- Depending on the students, learners can be challenged to generate their own adjectives to place along the gradient. This would be an advanced option.
- Preprinted words can be read aloud to students as needed.
- Varied instructional groupings.

Evidence of Student Learning/Informal Classroom-Based Assessment:

- Whole-group participation
- Discussion about text
- Completed semantic gradient template
- Small group participation
- Completed exit ticket

Directions:

1. Select a set of opposite pairs (e.g., hot/cold, fast/slow, short/tall).

2. Generate 3–5 synonyms for each word.

3. Organize the first set of synonyms from most to least extreme.

4. Organize the second set of synonyms from most to least extreme.

5. Finally, arrange both sets of synonyms from most to least extreme along the gradient.

6. Discuss with your small group.

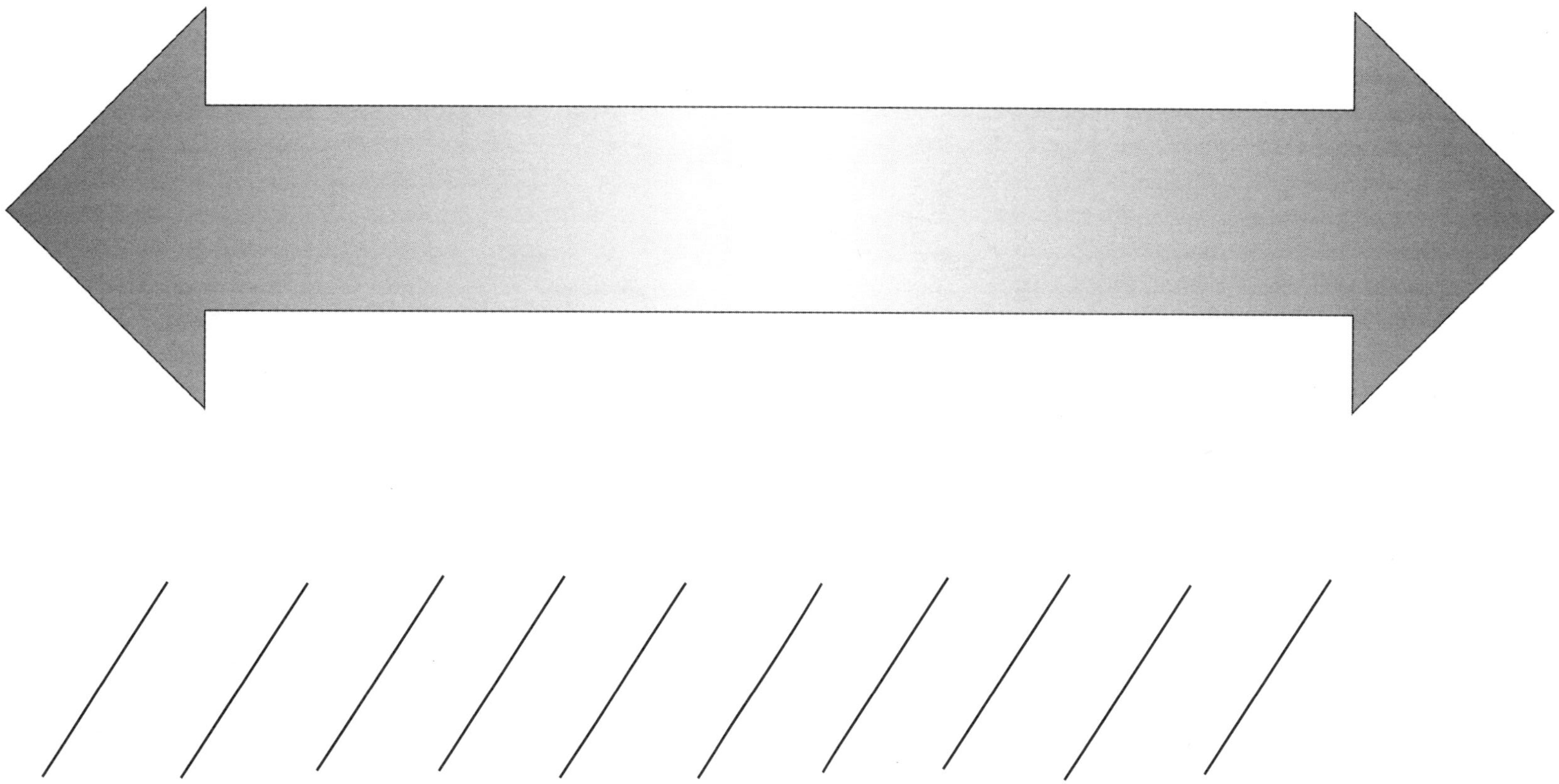

Figure 3.4. Semantic gradient template.

The Reading Comprehension Blueprint Activity Book: A Practice & Planning Guide for Teachers by Nancy Lewis Hennessy and Julia A. Salamone
Copyright © 2024 by Paul H. Brookes Publishing Co., Inc. All rights reserved.

27

Teacher Reflection in Lesson Implementation:

_____

_____

_____

_____

_____

Try This!   Now that you've seen a semantic gradient lesson in action, it's your turn to try it! Using the template in Figure 3.4, select a pair of opposite words and brainstorm five synonyms for each one. Organize each set of synonyms from most to least extreme and then place both sets in order of intensity along the gradient.

After completing this activity, reflect: Why did you place certain words in certain locations? What is your rationale? What does this exercise show you about shades of meaning and precise word choice?

_____

_____

_____

_____

Lesson 4 provides an example of an important independent word learning strategy, specifically the use of context clues, that can be used to infer word meaning.

LESSON 4

Context Clues   (textbook pgs. 78–79)

Teaching students to use context clues is an effective independent word strategy, which can be applied when students are reading on their own. However, context use must be explicitly taught so that readers understand why and when to use context, the various types of context clues encountered, and how to use these clues to support their understanding. There are five common types of context clues: definition, antonym (contrast), synonym (replacement), example, and general. The model Lesson 4 features direct instruction in the use of antonyms and synonyms, but explicit instruction must be provided in each type of clue for students to understand and use them independently. This lesson features text from the memoir _Persepolis_ by Marjane Satrapi. This text continues to build on the theme of identity, specifically how authors develop character identity when they write.

Name: Who Am I?   **Grade:** Eighth

Preparation for Instruction

Enduring Understandings:
- Individual identities are complex and show themselves in many ways.
- Everyone has multiple identities.
- Societal views can influence individual identity.
- Our identities have similarities and differences.
- It's important to see my identities as well as the identities of others reflected in the world around me.

Related Essential Questions:
- What defines our identity?
- How is identity shaped?
- Can we have more than one identity?
- Do we keep the same identity throughout our lives?
- How do authors develop a character's identity?

Content Objectives:
- Students will be able to examine the topic of identity in a variety of stories.

Literacy Objectives:
- Students will be able to
  - Understand there are many variations of the narrative genre
  - Recognize, from reading and writing, the nature of memoir
  - Analyze the impact of an author's literary choices in a memoir

Resources/Materials:
- Context clue chart (printed as a handout for students; see Figure 3.5, which is also available as a blank, downloadable worksheet on the Brookes Download Hub; see front matter for instructions to access the downloads that accompany this book)
- Passages from *Persepolis* by Marjane Satrapi to highlight the use of synonym and antonym context clues.

Sequence of Learning Events

Purpose: Students will learn how to apply antonym and synonym context clues while reading.

Review/Prerequisite Skills: To participate in this lesson, students should have the following prerequisite skills:
- Familiarity with the text *Persepolis* by Marjane Satrapi
- Participation in discussions about unfamiliar words
- Connecting prior understandings to unfamiliar words
- Awareness of the context clues strategy

Teacher and Student Instructional Activities:

Lesson opening:

1. Explain to students that they will be exploring two types of context clues: antonyms and synonyms.
2. Remind students that context clues are hints that authors give us to help us infer the meaning of unknown words.

Teacher modeling:

3. Tell students that sometimes authors use synonyms and antonyms to help us determine the meaning of unknown words.
4. Distribute/display the types of context clues handout for students to review. Direct their attention to the synonyms. Illustrate how in this example the author provides a simple, restated definition of the word *biome*. In this passage, the author simplifies the term *biome* using the words "large geographical regions."
5. Explain that they can use this strategy when reading independently. Display an example from *Persepolis* by Marjane Satrapi. A good one to highlight synonym use is *avant-garde* on page 6:

    "I really didn't know what to think about the veil, deep down I was very religious but as a family we were very modern and avant-garde" (Satrapi, p. 6).

6. Work through this example with students. Underline the parts of the sentence that tell us what *avant-garde* means (modern).
7. Have students refer to their handout and review the next type of context clues, antonyms. Illustrate how in this example, the author defines the word by providing an example of what it is NOT. In this passage, the author contrasts biotic organisms with non-living things.

8. Once again, we can use this strategy to determine the definition of unknown words when reading independently. Display an example from *Persepolis* by Marjane Satrapi. A good one to highlight antonym use is *chador* on page 75:

   "Look at her! Last year she was wearing a miniskirt, showing off her thighs to the whole neighborhood. And now madame is wearing a chador. It suits her better, I guess" (Satrapi, p. 75).

9. Work through this example with students. Underline the parts of the sentence that tell us what a chador is ("Last year she was wearing a miniskirt, showing off her thighs to the whole neighborhood"). We can infer that a chador is the opposite of a mini skirt, and is a garment worn by Muslim women covering their bodies.

Student-guided practice:

10. Display another example from *Persepolis* by Marjane Satrapi. A good one is the word *flagellate* on pg. 96:

    "Hitting yourself is one of the country's rituals. During certain religious ceremonies, some people flagellated themselves brutally" (Satrapi, p. 96).

11. Have students identify which words in the sentence provide a synonym for flagellated (hitting yourself). Students can underline the parts of the sentence that provide clues and then craft a simple definition (e.g., hitting oneself for religious reasons).

Independent Practice:

12. Provide students with examples of context use from the text. Good examples include:
    a. *decadent* (page 73)
    b. *frivolities* (page 28)
    c. *proletariat* (page 62)
    d. *secular* (page 98)

13. As students work to identify the examples of context clues given, the teacher can circulate and support. Students can then share and compare their responses once the activity is complete.

14. The teacher can facilitate discussion by asking the following:
    a. What type of context clue do you think this is?
    b. What evidence did you find to determine the meaning of the unknown word?
    c. Do you have enough information to define the term?

Differentiation/Inclusive Instructional Practices

- Display context clues chart as a poster for students to use when reading independently.
- The mnemonic IDEAS—Inference, Definition (or restatement), Examples, Antonyms and Synonyms—is a great way to help learners remember the various types of context clues they will encounter in a text.
- Use highlighting and coding to help students identify context clues.

Evidence of Student Learning/Informal Classroom-Based Assessment:

- Whole-group participation
- Text discussion
- Completed context clues activity

Teacher Reflection in Lesson Implementation

_____

_____

_____

_____

1. "'Gatsby?' demanded Daisy. 'What Gatsby?'"

   "Before I could reply that he was my neighbor, dinner was announced; wedging his tense arm imperatively under mine, Tom Buchanan compelled me from the room as though he were moving a checker to another square" (*The Great Gatsby*, Fitzgerald, 1925, Chapter 1).

   Word(s): _____

   This is effective for teaching context because . . . _____

   _____

   _____

2. "Ona was blue-eyed and fair, while Jurgis had great black eyes with beetling brows, and thick black hair that curled in waves about his ears—in short, they were one of those incongruous and impossible married couples with which Mother Nature so often wills to confound all prophets, before and after" (*The Jungle*, Sinclair, 1906, p. 3).

   Word(s): _____

   This is effective for teaching context because . . . _____

   _____

   _____

3. "If she had appeared to be catching a train, he might have inferred that he had come on her in the act of transition between one and another of the country-houses which disputed her presence after the close of the Newport season; but her desultory air perplexed him. She stood apart from the crowd, letting it drift by her to the platform or the street, and wearing an air of irresolution which might, as he surmised, be the mask of a very definite purpose" (*House of Mirth*, Wharton, 1905/2012, p. 1).

   Word(s): _____

   This is effective for teaching context because . . . _____

   _____

   _____

4. "'No, Fernand, you will not thus give way to evil thoughts. Unable to have me for your wife, you will content yourself with having me for your friend and sister; and besides,' she added, her eyes troubled and moistened with tears, 'wait, wait, Fernand; you said just now that the sea was treacherous, and he has been gone four months, and during these four months there have been some terrible storms'" (*Count of Monte Cristo*, Dumas, 1888/1997, p. 16).

   Word(s): _____

   This is effective for teaching context because . . . _____

   _____

   _____

5. "Mary . . . in consequence of being the only plain one in the family, worked hard for knowledge and accomplishments, and was always impatient for display . . . had neither genius nor taste, and though vanity had given her application, it had given her likewise a pedantic air and conceited manner, which would have injured a higher degree of excellence than she had reached" (*Pride and Prejudice*, Austen, 1813/2003, p. 16).

Word(s): _____

This is effective for teaching context because . . . _____

_____

Potential Responses:

1. "Gatsby?" demanded Daisy. "What Gatsby?"

   Before I could reply that he was my neighbor, dinner was announced; wedging his tense arm <u>imperatively</u> under mine, Tom Buchanan compelled me from the room as though he were moving a checker to another square. (*The Great Gatsby*, Fitzgerald, 1925, p. chapter 1)

   The author provides examples to cue the reader to the word's meaning. For example, before he could reply, Tom Buchanan forced him from the room by "wedging his tense arm imperatively" under the narrators. We can infer that imperatively means urgently.

2. Ona was blue-eyed and fair, while Jurgis had great black eyes with beetling brows, and thick black hair that curled in waves about his ears—in short, they were one of those <u>incongruous</u> and impossible married couples with which Mother Nature so often wills to confound all prophets, before and after (*The Jungle*, Sinclair, 1906, p. 3)

   The author here also uses examples to highlight the meaning of incongruous. Ona is described as "blue-eyed and fair" while Jurgis has "great black eyes" and "thick black hair." Thus, their appearances are incongruous or not in harmony.

3. If she had appeared to be catching a train, he might have inferred that he had come on her in the act of transition between one and another of the country-houses which disputed her presence after the close of the Newport season; but her <u>desultory</u> air perplexed him. She stood apart from the crowd, letting it drift by her to the platform or the street, and wearing an air of irresolution which might, as he surmised, be the mask of a very definite purpose (*House of Mirth*, Wharton, 1905/2012, p. 1).

   The author describes her desultory behavior as an "air," which is a quality or manner. This includes standing apart from the crowd, letting it drift past her, and wearing a look of "irresolution" or uncertainty as a "mask" that hid a distinct purpose. Thus, the character is possibly putting on a front, which helps us infer that desultory means lacking purpose or enthusiasm.

4. "No, Fernand, you will not thus give way to evil thoughts. Unable to have me for your wife, you will content yourself with having me for your friend and sister; and besides," she added, her eyes troubled and moistened with tears, "wait, wait, Fernand; you said just now that the sea was <u>treacherous</u>, and he has been gone four months, and during these four months there have been some terrible storms." (*Count of Monte Cristo*, Dumas, 1888/1997, p. 16).

   The main character, Mercédès, describes the sea as treacherous, and asks after her fiance, Edmond, who has been at sea for four months. There have been terrible storms during Edmond's time at sea, making his voyage dangerous due to the unpredictable, or treacherous, nature of the storms.

5. Mary . . . in consequence of being the only plain one in the family, worked hard for knowledge and accomplishments, and was always impatient for display . . . had neither genius nor taste, and though vanity had given her application, it had given her likewise a <u>pedantic</u> air and conceited manner, which would have injured a higher degree of excellence than she had reached (*Pride and Prejudice*, Austen, 1813/2003, p. 16).

   Straightaway the author states that Mary is not a genius and had to work hard for her "knowledge and accomplishments." Consequently, Mary was overly eager (impatient) "for display" and went so far to embarrass herself by sharing her knowledge of pianoforte when she and her family visited Netherfield.

The chart in Figure 3.5 can also be used as a handout to support teaching context clues in your own classroom!

Type of context clue	Explanation	Example
Definition	The word is directly defined in the sentence in which it appears.	**Ecosystems**, or <u>the communities where the organisms interact with their physical environment as a unit</u>, are amazingly complex.
Antonym (contrast)	The word is defined by telling what it is NOT. Can use conjunctions/signal words: *but*, *although*, *however*, and so on.	While ecosystems include **biotic** organisms, they also feature <u>nonliving</u> things like air, water, and soil.
Synonym (restatement)	The word is defined twice: once with a difficult word that is then restated in a simpler way.	There are a number of different **biomes** on Earth. These <u>large geographical regions</u> have a certain climate with specific plants and animals adapted to living there.
Example	The word's meaning is illustrated by an example. Often uses the phrases *for example*, *for instance*, *such as*, etc.	Ecosystems include **abiotic** components such as <u>rocks, temperature, and humidity.</u>
General	The word's meaning is illustrated by several words or statements.	**Biodiversity** is critically important for human well-being and is something people should strive to <u>protect</u>. In fact, the more <u>variety</u> of <u>animals, plants, fungi, bacteria,</u> and so forth <u>within an ecosystem</u>, the stronger it will be since this <u>variation</u> helps it adjust to small changes.

Figure 3.5. Types of context clues.

Intentional Vocabulary Instructional Activities

Assessment Activity

ACTIVITY 1: Word Knowledge Surveys   (textbook pgs. 83–84)

Word Knowledge Surveys are an excellent way of assessing student word knowledge before and after reading. These informal self-reporting measures help to activate students' background knowledge as well as provide educators with insight into which terms students know well and those they don't. This information can then be used to drive instruction and maximize instructional time. These activities can be adapted to include student-friendly language in order to be accessible to learners of all ages.

Word	Page	**Never met** (have not seen or heard before)	**Met** (seen or heard occasionally but do not really know)	**Friends** (hang out together, know some things)	**BFFs** (best friends forever; know everything)

The Great Gatsby: Word Knowledge Survey

Please rate your knowledge of the following words from chapter one in The Great Gatsby.

* Required

bantering *

○ Never Met (have not seen or heard before)

○ Met (seen or heard occasionally but do not really know)

○ Friends (hang out together, know some things)

○ BFFs (best friends forever; know everything and can confidently use in my speaking or writing)

complacency *

○ Never Met (have not seen or heard before)

○ Met (seen or heard occasionally but do not really know)

○ Friends (hang out together, know some things)

○ BFFs (best friends forever; know everything and can confidently use in my speaking or writing)

Created using Google Forms

With older learners, this activity can be converted into a survey or mini quiz via Google Forms. Student responses can then be reviewed by the teacher to look for trends in student word knowledge.

Try This! Now it's your turn to try out a word knowledge survey on your own. The words in Figure 3.6 are related to astronomy and cosmology. Which of these words do you consider a BFF and could use in your speaking or writing? Which have you seen or heard, but couldn't define? And which are completely new to you? Rate your understanding; then, based on your ratings, which of these words do you feel confident using, and which would you need to build a deeper understanding of?

Word	Never met (have not seen or heard before)	Met (seen or heard occasionally but do not really know)	Friends (hang out together, know some things)	BFF (best friends forever; know everything)
albedo				
atmosphere				
constellation				
ice giant				
nebula				
orbit				
pulsar				

Figure 3.6. Word knowledge survey.

Word Choice Activity

ACTIVITY 2: Word Choice   (textbook pgs. 63–65)

Direct vocabulary instruction begins with word choice. However, this can sometimes overwhelm educators, as there are so many words to choose from. To help alleviate this concern, there are several approaches to selecting words that educators can look to, including using previously published lists, working with tiers of words, and selecting words based on usefulness. In addition, educators must consider which words lend themselves to point-of-contact teaching and opportunities for instruction in independent word learning strategies. Thus, while preparing a text for instruction, it is critical that educators consider which words lend themselves to point-of-contact teaching, where a synonym or brief explanation can be provided as well as opportunities for practice and use of independent word learning strategies like context or morphology use.

Try This! The terms in Figure 3.7 are from the first grade read-aloud *Rosie Revere, Engineer* by Andrea Beaty. For this activity, sort the provided words into the instructional approach you believe to be the most appropriate. Explain why you chose your corresponding category, as well.

Rosie Revere, Engineer		
Word	**Instructional approach** (*Intentional instruction, Incidental-on-Purpose Instruction, Intentional independent word learning strategies instruction*)	**Why?**
approached		
chalk up		

chuckle		
dismayed		
doohickie		
dynamo		
eaves		
engineer		
flop		
gadget		
inventions		
perplexed		
prototype		

Figure 3.7. Word choice for vocabulary instruction activity: *Rosie Revere, Engineer*.

Tips for Success!

The question of how we choose words for instruction is critical and should be considered carefully. The word choice criteria of *usefulness, understanding*, and *growth*, coupled with knowledge of their students' needs, can help educators make informed decisions about which words to teach. The following prompts provide the attuned educator with a series of questions to ask themselves when engaged in reflecting upon a word's usefulness. Their use can be included in the planning process and are an excellent way for teachers to fully think about their word selection.

- *Usefulness and importance:*
  - Does the word provide accessibility to the text?
  - Is it a general-purpose word that will be encountered in other academic texts?
  - Does the word have enduring importance?
- *Understanding:*
  - Is the word critical to understanding varied levels of the text?
- *Growth:*
  - Does the word support growing/generating learning of other words?
    - Morphological family
    - Semantic relatives
    - Multiple meanings

Definition-Building Activity

ACTIVITY 3: Word Meaning Maps (textbook pgs. 66–67)

Word meaning maps are one strategy to support both teacher preparation and student learning. Once an educator has determined words for instruction, these organizers can be utilized to craft student-friendly definitions aligned to various parts of speech, including nouns, verbs, and adjectives. These visual tools also assist students in developing their own understanding by having them reflect on questions connected to the terms presented. For example, a word meaning map for a noun asks students to reflect on who or what a word describes as well as what category it falls under and which features it has. However, word meaning maps for a verb would prompt students to reflect on what type of action the word describes. In addition to the questions, these maps include examples and should feature context starting with the word's use in the text as well as student connections, related scenarios, and associations with other words. The templates in Figures 3.8, 3.9, and 3.10 can be utilized to construct definitional information and build student knowledge of the targeted terminology.

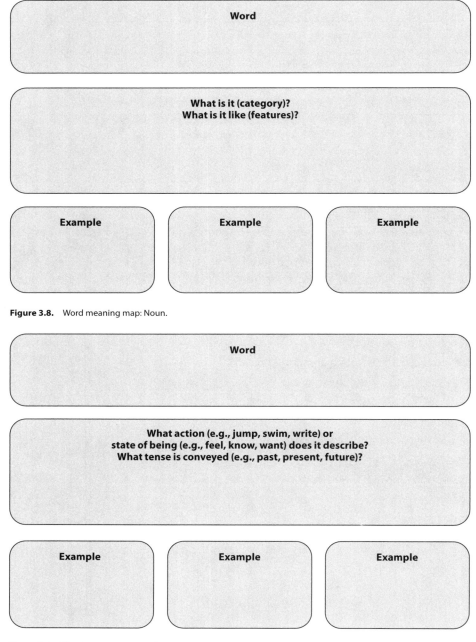

Figure 3.8. Word meaning map: Noun.

Figure 3.9. Word meaning map: Verb.

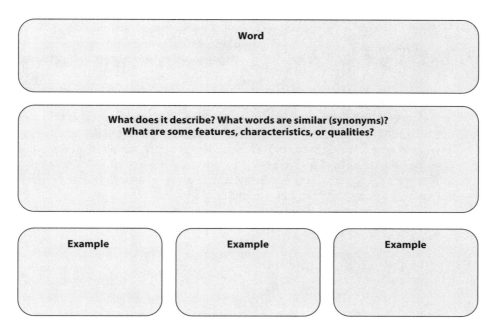

Figure 3.10. Word meaning map: Adjective.

Try This! The vocabulary term *inscrutable* is one of the major themes in the young adult novel *When the Emperor Was Divine* by Julie Otsuka. This powerful story is the account of a Japanese American family reclassified as the enemy and sent to an internment camp after the bombing of Pearl Harbor. For this activity, complete the word map for the adjective *inscrutable.* As highlighted in Figure 3.11, we have provided an example from the text and answered one of the corresponding questions. This adaptation can be used to support learners of varying abilities as well as those who come from culturally and linguistically diverse backgrounds. As you complete the activity, reflect: Did this activity expand upon your knowledge of the given word? Why or why not? How could you incorporate this into your own classroom practices?

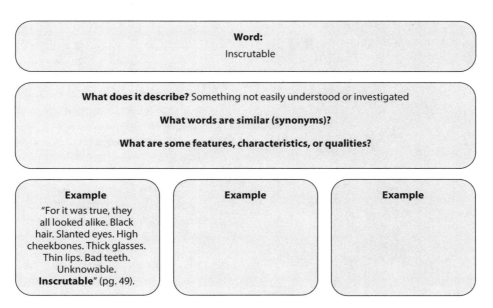

Figure 3.11. Word meaning map: Inscrutable.

ACTIVITY 4: Semantic Mapping   (textbook pgs. 69–70)

One effective way to help students build connections to words and deepen their understanding is semantic mapping. These organizers are an effective visual tool that helps students identify synonyms, antonyms, additional meanings, and examples. By determining these connections, students' understanding and recall of targeted terms is reinforced and their word knowledge is extended. The template in Figure 3.12 is an adapted four-square template. This organizer asks students to provide a student-friendly definition (*In Your Words*) examples (*Just the Facts*), a visual representation (*Paint a Picture*), and synonyms and antonyms (*Could Be Related But*). Organizers like this should be modeled by the teacher initially, with the goal of a gradual release of responsibility moving students towards independent completion. Additionally, educators can provide connections to cognates for students learning English as a second language. This allows English language learners (ELLs) to capitalize on their native language knowledge when learning new terminology in English (Cárdenas-Hagan, 2020).

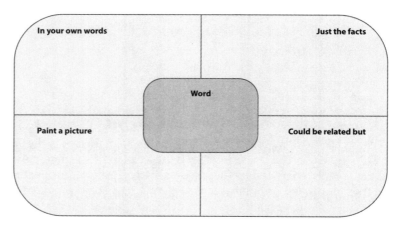

Figure 3.12.   Four-square template.

Try This!   Complete the adapted four-square template for the word *independence* that follows. Consider the following questions: Can you use other activities we've discussed in this chapter (e.g., word maps) to create a definition in your own words? What examples and nonexamples does it connect to? Can you think of cognates across languages that connect to the word? Once you have completed the template, write a sentence that demonstrates your understanding of the word. Was this process easier or harder after completing the web?

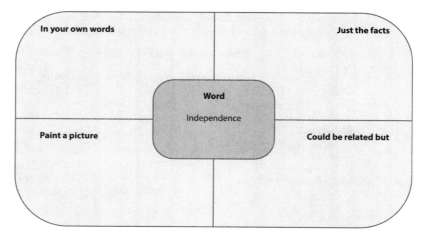

My sentence: _____

_____

Another excellent strategy to help students build connections is concept mapping. A concept map, like the example shown Figure 3.13, is a visual organizer that allows students to brainstorm concepts and ideas connected to a given word.

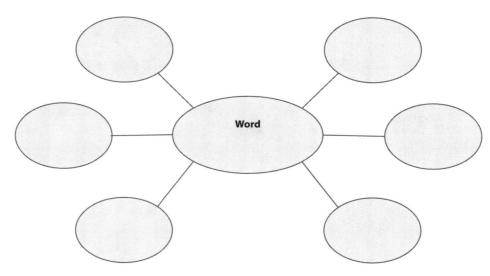

Figure 3.13.   Concept map.

After an initial brainstorming session, teachers can add an additional scaffold by having students categorize the information into corresponding groupings (see Figure 3.14). This way, learners can clearly see how concepts are connected. Activities like concept mapping can also serve as a pre- and post-assessment measure as they provide the educator with insight into students' background knowledge with a word or concept. Additionally, visuals can be added to make this activity more accessible for all ages, abilities, and cultural and linguistic backgrounds.

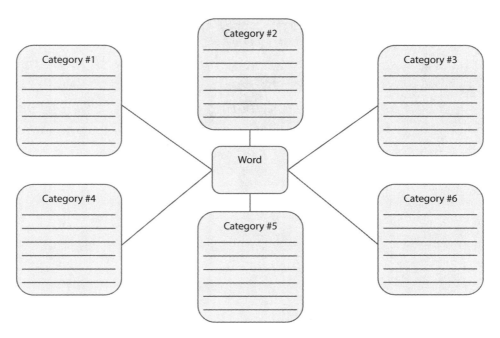

Figure 3.14.   Categories concept map.

Try This! For this next activity, complete the concept map for the word *genetics*. After you've brainstormed, read the corresponding passage. Revisit your web. Are there new words to add? How can you categorize the information you wrote down?

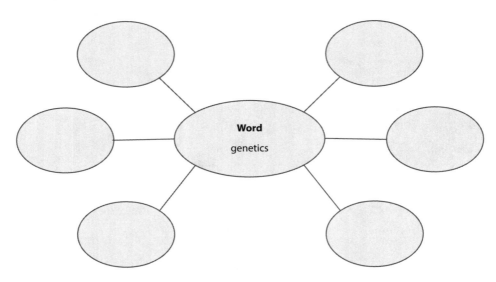

Genetics is the study of genes and heredity. It examines how living beings, including humans, inherit traits from their parents. The most basic physical unit of heredity is called a **gene**. A person has approximately 25,000 genes that determine how one looks and grows, as well as how one's body functions. These units of genetic information can control eye color and height as well as predispositions for certain diseases like high blood pressure, diabetes, or even cancer. Genes are made up of **deoxyribonucleic acid**, also known as DNA. Each cell in your body, except red blood cells, contain **DNA**. Most of the time, DNA is coiled up into an X shape we call a **chromosome**, which is located within the nucleus of each cell. Human beings have 23 pairs of chromosomes, with each parent contributing one chromosome per pair. This means that half of your chromosomes come from your mother and the other half from your father, for a total of 46 chromosomes.

Semantic feature analysis is a great way for students to examine the features of interconnected words, to see how they are similar and different. With this strategy, students are provided with a list of interrelated terms and use a grid graphic organizer to see how terms are related (see Figure 3.15). A checkmark highlights the term has the listed feature, an X signifies that it does not, and a question mark communicates that the learner does not know. After completing the chart, students can analyze their answers to see what they've determined.

Term	Feature 1	Feature 2	Feature 3	Feature 4	Feature 5	Feature 6	Feature 7	Feature 8

Figure 3.15. Semantic feature analysis chart.

Try This! The following semantic feature analysis chart features a series of geometry terms. Using the features provided, complete the grid by using a checkmark to highlight if a given word is representative of the feature, an X to signify that it does not, and a question mark if you're unsure. Compare your answers with the ones provided to the answer key. How did your answers match up? What similarities and differences did you notice and how can strategies like this one be used to deepen students' understanding of related terms and concepts?

	Quadrilateral	Two Dimensional	Has two pairs of parallel sides	Has four equal sides	Has four right angles	Has two pairs of equal-length sides adjacent to each other	Has one pair of parallel sides	Is a closed figure
Square								
Rectangle								
Rhombus								
Kite								
Parallelogram								
Trapezoid								

Potential Response								
	Quadrilateral	Two Dimensional	Has two pairs of parallel sides	Has four equal sides	Has four right angles	Has two pairs of equal-length sides adjacent to each other	Has one pair of parallel sides	Is a closed figure
Square	X	X		X	X			X
Rectangle	X	X			X			X
Rhombus	X	X	X					X
Kite	X	X				X		X
Parallelogram	X	X	X					X
Trapezoid	X	X					X	X

Representation/Visual Activity

ACTIVITY 7: Pictures & Drawings   (textbook pgs. 72–73)

Visual representations are another effective way to help students assign meaning and deepen their understanding of words. Visuals can be used to support students' definitional understanding as they provide a concrete representation of what the word means, which in turn reinforces understanding and retention. In addition, student-generated representations are an excellent way to help students show what they know while once again promoting student recognition and memory of the targeted word. This is particularly effective when working on passages that feature descriptive language, and students can create illustrations based on text passages that include targeted terms.

Try This!   On page 23 of the *Great Gatsby*, F. Scott Fitzgerald describes the *desolate* landscape of "valley of ashes." Read the passage provided and sketch what this landscape looks like.

"About half way between West Egg and New York the motor road hastily joins the railroad and runs beside it for a quarter of a mile, so as to shrink away from a certain desolate area of land. This is the valley of ashes—a fantastic farm where ashes grow like wheat into ridges and hills and grotesque gardens; where ashes take the forms of houses and chimneys and rising smoke and, finally, with a transcendent effort, of men who move dimly and already crumbling through powdery air."

From Fitzgerald, F. S. (1925). *The Great Gatsby*. New York: C. Scribner's Sons.

Now reflect: How does this description affirm the term *desolate*, a place empty of people and in a bleak and empty state?

_____

_____

_____

_____

Speaking and Writing Activities

ACTIVITY 8: Questions, Examples, & Relationships   (textbook pgs. 71–72)

The gold standard for vocabulary knowledge is use in one's speaking and writing. Thus, the utilization of oral prompts is critical to help students practice use of newly taught words in a meaningful way. The following chart features vocabulary from the picture book *Grandfather Gandhi* by Arun Gandhi and Bethany Hegedus. In this beautifully illustrated picture book, we learn the story of 12-year-old Arun Gandhi who moves from his home in South Africa to live in his grandfather's service village. It is here that Arun learns to channel his anger and frustration under the loving wisdom of his bapu, Mahatma Gandhi. Notice how the prompts challenge students to interact with the targeted words through examples, questions, and connections. This deeper engagement will help students to apply this vocabulary orally, which will in turn support their ability to apply them in writing later on.

Examples	Arun describes his grandfather as "sitting serenely on the floor." If I say an action that can be completed serenely, say "serenely." -sleeping -screaming -meditating -banging Grandfather tells Arun that anger can be transformed. If the following activity shows someone or something being transformed, stand up. -caterpillar's metamorphosis to a butterfly -the student got an "A" in semester one and an "A" in semester two -an ice cube melts into a puddle of water -the temperature was 73 degrees for three days in a row
Questions, reasons	Why would someone feel fidgety? What traits would you consider someone of good character to possess?
Connections	If someone embodies good character, can they still face injustices?
Relationships	How are the words channeled and transformed related?
Describe a time when	*Describe a time when . . .* you hung back.
Applause, applause	*Clap how much you would like to be:* -considered someone of great character -sleeping serenely after a long day's work

Try This!   The featured vocabulary is from *Sweep* by Louise Grieg. Like the read-aloud *Grandfather Gandhi*, this picture book also teaches students how to deal with big emotions such as anger. Using the terminology in the word box, craft your own questions, examples, and relationships to help learners build deeper knowledge of word meanings. After completing this activity reflect: How did this activity go? Was it easy? Challenging? How does it apply to your own practices?

Sweep					
mood	stormed	raging		pace	swept
whirlwind	determined		refused	vanished	

Examples	
Questions, reasons	
Connections	

Relationships	
Describe a time when	
Applause, applause	

Source: Edwards, Font, Baumann, & Boland (2012).

ACTIVITY 9: Sentence Stems and Purposeful Paragraphs — (textbook pgs. 71–72)

Once students are able to use targeted words in their speaking, use in writing is the next logical step. One great way to scaffold this activity is through the use of sentence stems. Sentence stems are an instructional scaffold that allow students to respond in complete sentences by giving them a sentence stem or part to start with. For example, when learning about Earth's ecosystems, seventh grade students were given the following sentence stems to help them construct definitions of important terminology:

- An organism is a . . .
- A biome is . . . They are categorized as _____, on land, or _____, on water. There are five major types: aquatic, forest, grassland, desert, and tundra.
- An adaptation is an adjustment that . . .

After learning the new words and studying about ecosystems in class, students are then asked to apply what they know in the form of a purposeful paragraph. In this activity, students must use taught vocabulary to answer a writing prompt tied to class content. In the following example, a word box is provided to scaffold the activity and help students recall taught vocabulary. Activities like this one can also serve assessment purposes as the teacher can determine whether students can truly apply the words to their writing or if their usage demonstrates a surface or superficial understanding.

Imagine you are an alien scout who has come from a distant planet to find a new place to live. You get to choose any of the five Earth biomes in which to live. Write a report to your superiors recommending your choice. In this report, describe the biome you chose, share why you made this choice, and describe the adaptations you have that will help you to live successfully in this biome.

You must use at least five words from the Word Bank:

Word Bank
organism   biome   aquatic   terrestrial   forest   grassland
desert   tundra   adaptation   weather   temperature   climate

Try This!   Purposeful paragraphs are centered on thematic or topical vocabulary. When words are taught in this manner, it provides learners with an anchor to attach meaning. As a result, students can then apply their mental efforts to written compositions as opposed to the recall of words (Jennings & Haynes, 2018). This strategy is applicable to all students but is especially beneficial for students with language-based learning disabilities as well as those from culturally and linguistically diverse backgrounds.

Now it's your turn to try it. Your assignment is to write a paragraph about your favorite season: winter, spring, summer, or fall. You must use at least five of the words in the following bank. After you have completed this activity reflect: How did it feel writing about a topic tied to thematic vocabulary? Was it easier? Harder? Explain. Where do you see activities like purposeful paragraphs fitting into your classroom?

Word Bank			
Winter	Spring	Summer	Fall
cold	warm	hot	cool
icy	rain	sunshine	leaves fall
snow	blooming	heat wave	colors change

Word Bank			
Winter	Spring	Summer	Fall
icicles	flower blossoms	ice cream	harvest
holiday(s)	holiday(s)	holiday(s)	holiday(s)
skiing	gardening	vacation	school
scarf	umbrella	swimming	raking
snow boots	rain boots	sunglasses	jackets
sledding	allergies	sunscreen	pumpkins
snowflakes	rainbows	swimming pool	wind

_____

_____

_____

_____

Independent Word Learning Activity

ACTIVITY 10: Tools for Morphology (textbook pg. 79)

Using morphology and morphemic analysis to determine the meaning of unknown words is an incredibly powerful independent word learning strategy that can serve students across a variety of disciplines. Learners are explicitly taught to use common prefixes, bases, and suffixes to determine the meaning of new and unfamiliar words. Students can be taught to examine and deconstruct words by identifying prefixes, suffixes, and bases (sometimes referred to as roots).

Like context clues, morphemes should be explicitly and systematically taught and include an instructional sequence that is logical and is based on the emergence and frequency of morphemes in spoken and written language. This includes starting with morphemes from Anglo-Saxon origin and moving on to the more sophisticated Latin and Greek layers. Latin and Greek morphemes are especially critical for middle and secondary learners, as these bases are connected to specific disciplines like science, math, and history. Educators can look to resources like _Unlocking Literacy_ by Marcia K. Henry and _Vocabulary Through Morphemes_ by Susan Ebbers to help them determine which morphemes to teach.

One great activity to help students work with morphemes is the creation of morpheme matrices. This strategy is a visual way for learners to see the connections between prefixes, bases, and suffixes. Figure 3.16 is a layout for a morpheme matrix.

Common Prefixes	Base	Common inflectional suffixes
	Free or Bound?	
Less Common Prefixes		Common derivational suffixes

Figure 3.16. Morpheme matrix. (From Cárdenas-Hagan, E. [2017]. _Working with English language learners: Teacher manual [2nd ed.]._ Brownsville, TX: Valley Speech Language and Learning Center; adapted by permission.)

Morpheme matrices allow students to see how prefixes, bases, and suffixes can be combined to create a variety of new words. Having knowledge of the individual word parts helps students understand how different combinations impact meaning and uses.

Students can then be taught to use their knowledge of morphology when reading independently. The following routine can be used to help students determine the meaning of an unknown word and can be provided as a handout and/or recreated as an anchor chart for use in the classroom.

unfinished

1. Identify and underline the root. Ask yourself, what does it mean? *To complete*

2. Circle the prefix. Ask yourself, what does it mean? *un- means not*

3. Circle the suffix. Ask yourself, what does it mean? *-ed functions as a past participle (this is derived from a verb, functions as an adjective)*

4. Put it all together. *Unfinished = not complete*

Source: Edwards, Font, Baumann, & Boland (2012).

Try This! Now it's your turn to try out morpheme matrices on your own. Using the matrix for the bound base *ject,* take a moment to brainstorm as many new words as you can. Then challenge yourself to use your words in sentences. What did you notice about the process? How could you incorporate morpheme matrices into your own classroom practices?

Common Prefixes pro- ob- sub- in-	Root ject *"to throw"*	Common inflectional suffixes -s -ed -ing
	Free or Bound? bound	
Less Common Prefixes e-		**Common derivational suffixes** -tion -or

My new words:

1. _____   2. _____

3. _____   4. _____

5. _____   6. _____

7. _____   8. _____

9. _____   10. _____

My sentences:

1. _____

2. _____

3. _____

Potential Responses:

project, projects, projected, projecting, projection, projector
object, objects, objected, objecting, objection, objector
subject, subjects, subjected, subjecting, subjection
inject, injects, injected, injecting, injection
eject, ejects, ejected, ejecting

***Sentences will vary

Connections to English Language Learners

There are many languages in which words share etymological origins, so capitalizing on morphemic analysis is a great way to assist ELLs with building vocabulary and spelling. However, the informed educator must have knowledge of students' first language in order to provide explicit instruction and modeling in how English morphology differs. This includes:

- *Affix instruction:* In English, bound morphemes construct words when prefixes and suffixes are added to the beginning or ending. However, many other languages feature infixes, which are placed in the middle of the word (Hickey & Lewis, 2013). For example, Bontoc is a Philippine language that features infixes. To change the adjective "strong" (fikas) to "becomes strong" (fumikas), an infix is added to the middle of the word. This rarely happens in English, so it is imperative that teachers know which languages feature this morphological process so they can anticipate student challenges in this area.

- *Derivational morphemes:* Teachers can also capitalize on similarities between a student's first language (L1) and second language (L2) to facilitate student understanding. For example, many English suffixes have equivalents in Spanish. The Spanish suffix *-mente* is equivalent to the English suffix *-ly* (Hickey & Lewis, 2013). Thus, words like *simplemente* would have the English equivalent of *simply*. This cross linguistic comparison can support English learners in their acquisition of vocabulary.

- *Cognates and false cognates*: Instruction in cognates, or words across languages that share similar spellings, morphology, and word origins, can be incredibly beneficial for English learners (Cárdenas-Hagan, 2020). This is especially true for speakers of Romance languages, including Spanish, French, Portuguese, Italian, Romanian, and Catalan, who come to the classroom with " . . . implicit knowledge about Latin-based morphemes because their Tier 1 vocabulary words share morphological roots with many of the Tier 2 and Tier 3 words of English" (Hickey & Lewis, 2013, p. 76). For example, the English word *galaxy* and the Spanish equivalent *galaxia* share the old Latin base *galaxias*. Thus, these words are cognates and can be used to help students see similarities between their native language and English (Hickey & Lewis, 2013, p. 76). Table 3.1, created by Dr. Elsa Cárdenas-Hagan, features English-Spanish cognates in mathematics, science, and social studies (2020). Resources like this can be used to help students transfer vocabulary knowledge across languages. Educators should also be aware of false cognates, which are words with similar spellings, but do not have the same meanings (Cárdenas-Hagan, 2020). For example, in Spanish *ropa* means "clothes," not "rope," or in French *assister* means "attend" and not "assist." Thus, drawing attention to false cognates will help students avoid misunderstandings in communication.

Table 3.1. Subject specific cognates: English and Spanish

Subject area	English term	Spanish term
Mathematics	Calendar	El calendario
	Angle	El ángulo
	Area	El area
	Divided by	Dividido por
	Equal groups	Los grupos iguales
	Exponent	El exponente
	Gallon	El galón
	Hexagon	El hexagon
	Triangle	El triángolo
Science	Classify	Classificar
	Cycle	El ciclo
	Diagram	El diagramma
	Elements	Los elementos
	Electricity	La electricidad
	Galaxy	La galaxia
	Identify	Identificar
Social studies	Map	El maps
	Society	La sociedad
	Independence	La independencia
	Community	La comunidad
	Exploration	La exploración
	Immigration	La immigración
	Liberty	La libertad
	Vote	El voto
	Geography	La geografía
	Region	La región

From Cárdenas-Hagen, E. (2020). *Literacy foundations for English learners: A comprehensive guide to evidence-based instruction.* Baltimore: Paul H. Brookes Publishing Co.

Word Consciousness Activity

ACTIVITY 11: Building Word Consciousness: Instead of This . . . Consider This   (textbook pgs. 80–81)

Word consciousness instruction is embedded throughout the four-part framework for vocabulary instruction. Word consciousness is developed through direct and indirect activities and involves fostering an awareness of words and an interest in how they work. Helping students become word conscious is a crucial endeavor for teachers across grade levels and subject areas, but especially those working with students whose prior vocabulary exposure may be limited. Think about the words you use when speaking to students in your setting. Do you use simple vocabulary or refer to the same words again and again? Are there terms you can use in your speaking that will support student vocabulary growth? The following table features words and phrases commonly encountered in a classroom. Notice how these everyday utterances have been changed up to foster student word consciousness.

Examples	
Instead of this:	*Consider this:*
classroom	cadre of learners, academic community, learning laboratory
directions	instructions, guidelines, recommendations, requirements
raise your hand	elevate your arm, put up your palm, uplift your digits
look at	examine, inspect, scan, survey, scrutinize
please	kindly, see fit to, have a mind
thank you	much obliged, with deepest gratitude, acknowledge
questions	queries, wonders, inquiries
walk	amble, strut, stroll, saunter, stride
homework/classwork	activity, lesson, assignment, practice, exercise

Try This! In this next exercise, brainstorm other ways to say these commonly used classroom words and phrases. What other words and phrases would you add?

line up	
quiz	
write	
good job	
because	
but	
so	

The Diverse Learner: Learning Challenges & Differences

Vocabulary Support for Students with Learning Disabilities

Research continues to highlight the importance of including the following in classroom instruction to support the success of all students as well as those with learning challenges:

- Teach vocabulary intentionally

- Teach independent word learning strategies (e.g., morphological analysis)

- Focus on developing semantic networks

- Increase opportunities to use new words in discussion and writing

- provide a motivating and language-rich learning environment

(Elleman et al., 2019; Farstrup & Samuels, 2008; O'Connor, 2007).

We know that individuals with learning disabilities, such as dyslexia, often have language processing deficits that not only influence the development of word recognition skills but also affect language comprehension, including the acquisition and access to word meanings. These students require increased intensity of instruction, practice, and application of new word meanings and word learning strategies. Additionally, given that wide (extensive) reading is a major source of vocabulary growth once students become independent readers, it is critical to provide access for those who are still struggling with word recognition so they can read by "ear." Several resources exist for accessing audio books including Learning Ally (learningally.org/), Audible (audible.com/), and Bookshare (bookshare.org/).

Vocabulary Support for English Language Learners

Meaningful instruction for ELLs focuses on what they know by building connections to the language skills they have acquired in their native language. Features of effective interventions for these students include purposeful and explicit instruction in the use of morphemes, cognates, and bilingual glossaries, as well as teaching basic word meanings when necessary, teaching multiple-meaning words, and

Tips for Success!

Don't forget the diverse learner!

It is critical that all teachers of reading consider opportunities for differentiation and inclusive practices while planning instruction. Note the examples in the lesson plans already provided.

The following sections on diverse learners provide some additional guidelines specific to those students with specific learning challenges.

having extended discussion that is supported by repetition and rehearsal (Cárdenas-Hagan, 2015).

The *IES Practice Guide for Teaching Academic Content and Literacy to English Learners in Elementary and Middle School* (Baker et al, 2014, p. 6) further provides practitioners with recommendations based on the science of reading. Specific to word meaning, the guide recommends the following:

- Teach a set of academic vocabulary words intensively across several days using a variety of instructional activities.

- Choose a brief, engaging piece of informational text that includes academic vocabulary as a platform for intensive academic vocabulary instruction.

- Choose a small set of academic vocabulary for in-depth instruction.

- Teach academic vocabulary in depth using multiple modalities (writing, speaking, listening).

- Teach word learning strategies to help students independently figure out the meaning of words.

The teacher script in Figure 3.17, created by Dr. Elsa Cárdenas-Hagan, is an example of individual vocabulary instruction for ELLs. This example combines language components ". . . including reviewing the sounds of vocabulary words, the meaning and word parts within words, the spelling of the word, and the grammatical function and various uses of the word" (Cárdenas-Hagan, 2020, p. 196). Additionally, this script prompted cross-linguistic transfer by making connections between the student's native language and English, which ultimately supports ELLs in their ability to use the targeted word in speaking and writing.

Teacher Script Template for Individual Vocabulary Instruction

To teach the first word from a particular vocabulary lesson, apply the following script.
We have had several discussions related to the topic of _____.
Today we will explore words related to the topic of _____.
This will help you understand and use words when you speak and when you write.
The word is _____. It means _____.
In your native language, the word is _____.
Say the word in your native language.
Say the word in English.
How many sounds do you hear in this English word?
How many sounds do you hear in this word from your native language?
Do the words have the same number of syllables?
How many letters are used in English for this word?
How many letters are used in Spanish for this word?
What is the same? What is different between these words?
The part of speech is a _____ for this word.
Let's look at a visual that represents these words and discuss any other meanings.
Can we act out the word?
Let's use the word in a sentence in English.
Let's use the word in a sentence in your native language.
Good job. Now we will add this word to our word bank or word wall for use in the future.
We will have many opportunities to practice using our new vocabulary words.

Repeat procedure for remaining words.

Figure 3.17. Teacher script template for individual vocabulary instruction. (From Cárdenas-Hagan, E. [2017]. Working with English language learners: Teacher manual (2nd ed.). Brownsville, TX: Valley Speech Language and Learning Center; adapted by permission.)

Putting It All Together: Vocabulary Instruction

An Instructional Tool Set for Vocabulary

The Comprehensive Instructional Framework (Figure 3.3) identified varied approaches to teaching word meaning and highlights important aspects of instruction.

Intentional instruction	Incidental on purpose instruction	Intentional independent word learning strategies instruction
✔ **Word Choice** ✔ **Simple Instructional Routine:** Definitional & Contextual Information ✔ **Complex Instructional Routine:** Processing & Practice Activities	Structured Point of Contact Teaching Structured Teacher-Student Talk Structured Shared Reading Structured Independent Reading	Using the Dictionary Using Context Clues Using Morphemic Analysis
Word consciousness	**Word consciousness** *Purposeful Activities*	**Word consciousness**

© 2018 Nancy Hennessy

Figure 3.3. A comprehensive instructional framework for vocabulary.

The Tool Set (see Table 3.2) provides an overview of the instructional activities and strategies that are the focus of intentional instruction in this framework. The first two columns include activities that focus on word choice and creating definitions and include many already described in this chapter as well as additional suggestions. The

Table 3.2. Instructional Tool Set

Word Choice	Definition	Connect	Represent	Use
How might we choose words for instruction?	In what ways, might we define words?	In what ways can we build connection to words related in meaning?	In what ways might we represent meaning visually?	In what ways might we use words orally and in writing?
Guidelines Example: • Usefulness • Growth • Understanding	Word maps Example: • Word • Category • Features • Examples	Semantic maps Example:	Pictures or Drawings Example:	Writing Examples: • Sentence Stems/ Generation • Purposeful Paragraphs • Academic Vocabulary Logs
Vocabulary Lists Examples: • Academic Vocabulary Lists • (Coxhead, 2000) • *Words Worth Teaching* • (Biemiller, 2010) • *Middle School Vocabulary Lists* • (Coxhead & Green, 2015) • Tiers One–Three • (Beck, Mc Keown & Kucan, 2002)	Four Square Example: • In Your Words • Just the Facts • Paint a Picture • Related but . . .	Semantic Gradients: Example: • Scaling (e.g., good-bad)	Vocabulary Videos Example: https://www.vocabulary .com/help/videos/	Speaking Examples: • Questions, Connections to text *Why would . . .* *When have . . .* *Would you want to be . . .*
	Dimensions of Word Knowledge Example: • Word • Phonology • Orthography • Meaning	Attributes • sight • sound • smells • places	Word walls Examples: • Parts of speech • Morphological families • Shared word walls (e.g., Padlet)	Instructional Approaches Examples: • Academic Conversations • Socratic Circles

remaining columns highlight activities necessary for processing and practice of word meaning. These include building semantic representations, creating representations of meaning, and/or using words orally or in writing. Similarly, some of these are also described earlier in the text but others are also recommended.

While this instructional resource is supportive of informed instruction, it does not necessarily include all the tools available to educators. It recognizes that you, as a practitioner, may have access to and/or use other evidence-based activities for these critical tasks.

Try This! Take a moment to review the Tool Set (see Figure 3.2). Reflect on the activities described in the chapter and those that you implement in your practice. Then, consider what evidence-based activities you might add to each of the columns.

Voices From the Field

The more we can connect direct and explicit connections for students, the stronger their ownership of words will be.

—A Blueprint Book Study Participant

Reflect & Connect

In what ways will these lessons and activities influence your instruction?

Listening Link

Science of Reading: The Podcast

S3-09 Deconstructing the Rope: Vocabulary with Nancy Hennessy

https://www.buzzsprout.com/612361/8449280-s3-09-deconstructing-the-rope-vocabulary-with-nancy-hennessy

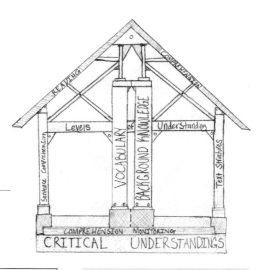

4

Implementing the Blueprint

Sentence Comprehension

The focus of this chapter is the contribution of syntax and sentence comprehension including the what, why, and an introduction to the how of instruction as it relates to the Reading Comprehension Blueprint.

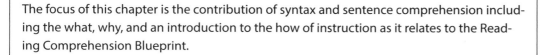

CHECK IN: Connect to current knowledge and practices!

Surface and script what comes to mind in the map (Figure 4.1) when you think about the what, why, and how of sentence comprehension.

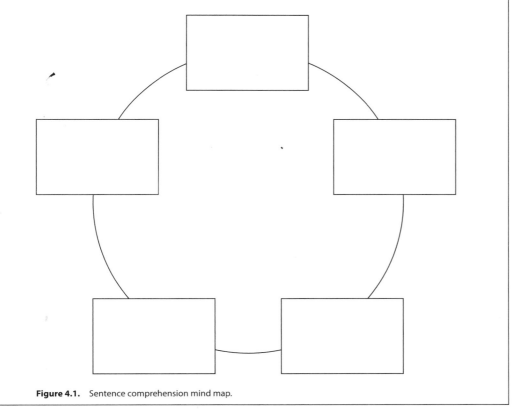

Figure 4.1. Sentence comprehension mind map.

> *"The sentence lies at the heart of communicating thought and meaning, whether you are the writer or the reader. The rules of our language, syntax and grammar, allow for the creation of an infinite number of sentences that serve as the 'worker bees of text'."*
>
> Scott, 2004, p. 340

What: Definition & Description

The focus in this section is the role of syntax and sentence comprehension. Understanding sentence comprehension calls for an explanation of the connection between semantics (word meaning) and syntax. Syntax can be described as word order or the internal structure of a sentence. It provides the architecture for expressing the meaning of words, phrases, clauses, and their relationships. Our spoken or written words carry *meaning*, while syntax provides the *structure* for organizing and communicating ideas. As stated in Poulsen and Gravgaard (2016, p. 325), "Syntax explicitly conveys information about how the word meanings should be integrated into a proposition (a unit of meaning) so that the reader does not have to infer who did what to whom."

Syntax lives within the sentence. So, how should we define the sentence? It is often defined grammatically. For example, the Oxford Dictionaries define the sentence as:

> A set of words that is complete in itself, typically containing a subject and predicate, conveying a statement, question, exclamation, or command, and consisting of a main clause and sometimes one or more subordinate clauses (https://www.oxforddictionaries.com).

However, our focus is sentence comprehension. This requires thinking about the sentence as a vehicle for conveying ideas. The parts of speech, phrases, and clauses are the building blocks of a sentence and carry the meaning (see Figure 4.2).

Sentence comprehension requires not only understanding these building blocks as grammatical forms but also their function, that is, how they contribute to meaning. While each block represents a grammatical category that includes a label and description, their primary function or job is to contribute to and communicate the meaning of different types of sentences and ultimately, the text.

Consider different parts of speech as seen in Table 4.1. Each part has the job of answering questions in a sentence in order to convey meaning.

These guiding questions are the bridge to understanding how the building blocks (words, phrases, and clauses) convey who or what did what to whom when, where, how, and why.

Lexicon Check: Form Versus Function

The grammatical form describes what the building blocks are while their function tells us what they do.

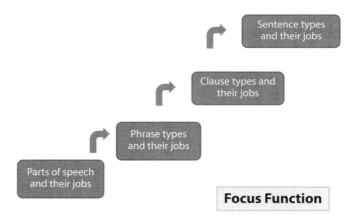

Figure 4.2. The building blocks of meaning.

Table 4.1. The form and function of parts of speech

Form: Parts of Speech	Function: Meaning
Noun-subject	Who or what?
Verb-predicate	Doing or did?
Adjective-modifies the noun	Which one, what kind, how many?
Adverb-modifies the verb	Where, when, how, why?

Why: The Science

We know that when skilled readers come to a text, they recognize and retrieve the meaning of individual words and also "work out the syntactic structure and sense of the sentence" (Cain & Oakhill, 2007, p. xii). Studies over the years have shown a clear relationship between syntactic or grammatical sophistication and reading comprehension; that is, as students learn to employ more complex sentences in their oral and written language, their ability to make sense of what they read increases, too (Shanahan, 2013). The literature tells us that students' performance on language tasks at the sentence level is related to text comprehension (Adlof & Catts, 2015; Brimo, Apel, & Fountain, 2015). While most students acquire this knowledge, it potentially remains problematic for others including those with language problems (Leonard, 2014) or those acquiring a second language.

How: The Design of Instruction

Introduction

"The ability to understand sentences contributes to students' reading comprehension. However, many reading programs tend to underemphasize explicit instruction aimed at enhancing students' knowledge of sentence structures."

Zipoli, 2017, p. 1

 Tips for Success!

It is important to remember that sentences found in academic texts can be challenging and complex based on construction. These potential troublemaker sentences may interfere with understanding. They are often longer, contain multiple ideas, varied types of clauses, separation of the who and do, and written in passive voice (see Figure 4.3). Knowing the function of the building blocks can support the parsing of these sentences and the identification of the key ideas expressed in the sentence.

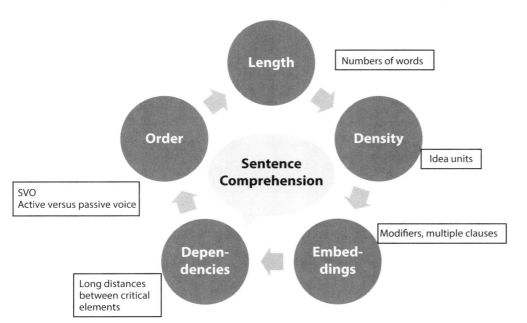

Figure 4.3. Potential troublemakers. (*Source:* Scott & Balthazar, 2013.)

The ability to understand and express meaning in sentences grows over time with instruction and experience. An effective instructional approach builds on the connection between oral and written language and reflects both direct and indirect approaches to working with the building blocks of sentences, the sentence itself, and the connections between sentences. The focus is understanding how the ideas are expressed in each sentence and how these are integrated within the text. While knowing the syntactic forms and labels (e.g., parts of speech, phrases, clauses) is necessary for the construction of sentences, understanding their function or how they convey meaning within the sentence is essential for both expressing and understanding meaning. Planning focused lessons that reflect this approach and connect to critical understandings is essential for developing sentence comprehension.

A knowledge of general guidelines, coupled with critical questions and the recommendations found in the Sentence Comprehension Framework, provides the educator with direction for the design and delivery of effective instruction.

Consider the following guidelines and the potential implications for current instructional practices (Zipoli, 2017, pp. 221–222). Note the emphasis on connecting oral with written language experiences and reading comprehension with written expression.

- Many diverse learners benefit from receiving instruction in both the oral and written modalities.

  These include ELLs and students with reading or language difficulties.

- Many students benefit from being taught about sentence structure by strategically integrating reading and writing.

  Writing and comprehension instruction are related, and instruction needs to reflect that relationship.

- Teaching is more effective when explicit instruction on sentence structures is combined with opportunities to practice skills during activities embedded within the general education curriculum.

The questions featured in the Blueprint (see Figure 4.4) provide additional direction and are designed to support educators as they plan for the design and delivery of instruction.

Instructional activities for syntax and sentence comprehension include both intentional-on-purpose or direct instructional opportunities and indirect or incidental-on-purpose methods. Although these approaches differ, both play an

Blueprint for Comprehension Instruction
TEXT READING
Sentence Comprehension
Are there parts of speech, phrases, clauses, and/or sentence structures that may be difficult for your students? How and when will you directly teach sentence comprehension? How and when will you teach students to work with these structures? How will you facilitate the integration of ideas (e.g., the use of cohesive ideas and connectives)? How and when will you teach students to work with these?

Figure 4.4. The Blueprint Questions: Sentence Comprehension. (*Source:* Hennessy, 2020.)

Table 4.2. Instructional tool set for sentence comprehension

Intentional-on-Purpose Instructional Focus	Intentional-on-Purpose Activities	Incidental-on-Purpose Focus	Incidental-on-Purpose Activities
Building Blocks of Sentences		**Building Blocks of Sentences**	**Reading Experiences**
• Parts of Speech & their Jobs	Questioning/Parsing		• Shared
• Phrases & their Jobs	Structured Organizers		• Group
• Clauses & their Jobs	Sorts (pictures, words)		• Independent
	Visual Representations		• Fluency Connection
The Sentence		**The Sentence**	**Oral Experiences**
• The Sentence & their Jobs	Questioning		• Oral Response
• The Problem Sentence	Structured Sentence Organizers		• Student/Teacher Talk
	Sentence Frames		**Writing Experiences**
	Diagramming		• Sentence Instruction
	Anagrams (word cards)		• Written Responses
	Oral & Written		
	Sentence Building: Combining & Expansion		
Cohesive Devices		**Writing Connections**	
• The Role of Cohesive Ties	Questioning		• Written Responses
• The Role of Connectives	Coding		

Tips for Success!

In the following sections, you will be initially introduced to model lesson plans and activities for intentional instruction. These are followed by examples for developing sentence comprehension incidentally but on purpose. Consider how you might use/adapt these examples for your practice.

important role in the development of syntactic awareness and sentence comprehension. The Blueprint questions, coupled with a knowledge of the building blocks for sentences, serve as a useful reminder for the importance of using a structured sequential approach to instruction. The contents of this instructional organizer (see Table 4.2) provide direction for focus and activities that align with an informed approach.

The following section begins with a discussion of lesson planning and intentional-on-purpose sentence comprehension activities and then explores incidental-on-purpose instruction. Both these approaches should be considered as educators preview and prepare the text and are critical components of informed sentence comprehension instruction.

Intentional Instruction: Lesson Plans & Activities

Model Lesson Plans

The lesson plans in this section focus on the development of sentence comprehension. As we have discussed previously, the unit organizer serves as the foundation for the design of individual lessons, as this provides the big picture roadmap of what will be learned. The following lessons are connected to the identity unit plans shown previously and provide models for developing students' sentence comprehension and syntax. As you read through these plans, notice how each lesson connects to its unit's enduring understandings and essential questions to address the overarching goals of the unit, while mapping out specific objectives, activities, and assessments to grow students' understanding of sentence structure and syntax.

Lessons 1 and 2 provide intentional instruction examples focused on understanding how words individually and in combination convey meaning using questioning/parsing, sorts, and anagrams.

Sentence Parsing

Sentence parsing is an effective way to help students identify and understand the function of words, phrases, and clauses by deconstructing sentences. The guiding questions identified earlier (Table 4.1) provide the necessary vehicle for analyzing the roles of words and phrases in the given sentences. The students would be taught to parse less sophisticated structures first, moving on to more complicated ones. Once students have practiced and mastered this activity, sentence parsing serves as an excellent warmup or exit ticket for any class. This lesson highlights how parsing is introduced to students through direct, explicit instruction. The sentences are aligned to the eighth-grade unit, *Who Am I?*, which explores themes of identity and belonging and features sentences from the short story "The Jacket" by Gary Soto. The text was prepared in advance for instruction and the sentences featured were preselected.

Name: Sentence Parsing with "The Jacket"

Grade: Eighth

Preparation for Instruction

Enduring Understandings:
- Individual identities are complex and show themselves in many ways.
- Everyone has multiple identities.
- Societal views can influence individual identity.

Related Essential Questions:
- What defines our identity?
- How is it shaped?
- Do we keep the same identity throughout our lives?
- How do authors develop a character's identity?

Content Objectives:
- Students will be able to
  - Reflect on the various ways certain social contexts impact our identities
  - Examine the topic of identity in a variety of stories

Literacy Objectives:
- Students will be able to identify and understand the function of words, phrases, and clauses and how they work together to create sentences

Resources/Materials:
- Sentences from the short story "The Jacket" by Gary Soto
- Structured sentence organizer (individual copies for students and one for display purposes. See Figure 4.5, which is also available as a blank, downloadable worksheet on the Brookes Download Hub; see front matter for instructions to access the downloads that accompany this book.)

Sequence of Learning Events

Purpose: Students will learn about the function of various words, phrases, and clauses by parsing sentences from the short story "The Jacket" by Gary Soto.

Review/Prerequisite Skills: To participate in this lesson, students should have the following prerequisite skills:
- Understanding of the parts of speech in sentence construction
- Understanding of phrases and clauses in sentence construction
- Understanding of word order within sentences

Teacher and Student Instructional Activities:

Lesson opening:

1. Explain to students that today we will learn about an activity known as sentence parsing. Sentence parsing is a really helpful way to improve our understanding of tricky sentences because we are able to determine the function of the words, phrases, and clauses within sentences.

Teacher modeling:

2. Explain to students that we can break apart, or parse, sentences by using question words and a structured sentence organizer.

3. Display the following organizer for students. This can be recreated on chart paper or via a document camera or slideshow. Then review the question words with students.

Which one, what kind, how many?	Who or what?	Is/was doing or happening?	To what, whom?	When, where, why, how?

4. Next, display the sentence *"The next day when I got home from school, I discovered draped on my bedpost a jacket the color of day-old guacamole"* (Soto, pg. 1). Remind students that this is from the short story "The Jacket" by Gary Soto.

5. Model for students how to break apart the sentence to answer the corresponding question words. For example:
   a. Who is this sentence about? (the author Gary Soto who uses the pronoun *I*)
   b. What is he doing? *discovered*
   c. What did he discover? *a jacket*
   d. Where was the jacket? *draped on my bedpost*
   e. When did he discover it? *The next day when I got home from school*
   f. Which jacket? the one *the color of day-old guacamole.*

6. This can be sorted under the proper question in the structured sentence organizer, shown as follows.

Which one, what kind, how many?	Who or what?	Is/was doing or happening?	To what, whom?	When, where, why, how?
~the color of day-old guacamole	~I (Gary Soto)	~discovered	~a jacket	~The next day when I got home from school **(when)** ~draped on my bedpost **(where)**

Student-Guided Practice:

7. Display the next sentence for students to see: *"From my bed, I stared at the jacket (Soto, pg. 1)*

8. Use guiding questions to help students break apart the sentence to answer the question words. For instance:
   a. Who is this sentence about? (the author Gary Soto who uses the pronoun *I*)
   b. What is he doing? *stared*
   c. What did he stare at? *at the jacket*
   d. Where did he stare at the jacket? *from my bed*

9. Once again, the following structured sentence organizer* can be used as a scaffold to support students' thinking.

Which one, what kind, how many?	Who or what?	Is/was doing or happening?	To what, whom?	When, where, why, how?
X	~I (Gary Soto)	~stared	~at the jacket	~from my bed

* In this example make sure to point out to students that not every box in the frame is filled in, and that's normal! It just depends on the parts of the sentence and which question they answer.

Independent practice:

10. Provide students with the following sentence, *"The next day I wore it to sixth grade and got a D on a math quiz"* (Soto, pg. 2).
11. Students can deconstruct this sentence independently as the closing activity.
12. The teacher can circulate the room and support students as they work on completing the activity.
13. Once complete, the teacher can have students share out and compare their response to the one that follows.

Which one, what kind, how many?	Who or what?	Is/was doing or happening?	To what, whom?	When, where, why, how?
~math (quiz) ~sixth (grade)	~I (Gary Soto)	~wore ~got	~it ~a D on a math quiz	~The next day ~to sixth grade

Differentiation/Inclusive Instructional Practices:

- Students can respond orally instead of in writing.
- Students can work in partnerships to complete the final activity.
- Words, phrases, and clauses can be prewritten on word cards for students to use as a sort instead of writing.

Evidence of Student Learning/Informal Classroom-Based Assessment:

- Student participation in the lesson
- Completed sentence parsing activity
- Teacher questioning

Teacher Reflection in Lesson Implementation

_____

_____

_____

_____

_____

_____

Try This!   Now it's your turn to try! Using the structured sentence organizer provided, parse the sentence that follows according to the question words it answers. Once you've finished, reflect: what did you think of this activity? What challenges might your students encounter when engaging in activities like this one?

Gary Soto shares his childhood experiences growing up in 1950s California.

Which one, what kind, how many?	Who or what?	Is/was doing or happening?	To what, whom?	When, where, why, how?

Answer key:

Which one, what kind, how many?	Who or what?	Is/was doing or happening?	To what, whom?	When, where, why, how?
~ his childhood **(which experiences)**	~ Gary Soto	~ shares	~ his childhood experiences growing up	~ in 1950s **(when)** ~ California **(where)**

Sentence Anagrams

Sentence anagrams are an effective instructional activity that help students build syntactic awareness and reading comprehension but are also fun and foster cooperation. Sentences are pre-written on word cards and can be taken directly from key moments in the text, or teacher-created to focus on specific facts or summary statements connected to important moments. Students are then tasked to put the sentences back together. As with sentence parsing, students should practice unscrambling less sophisticated structures first, moving on to more complex ones. The sentences in the lesson that follows are from the text *Frederick* by Leo Leoni and are connected to the unit *All About Me!*

Name: *All About Me!*

Grade: First

Preparation for Instruction

Enduring Understandings:

- I am part of a family and a classroom community.
- My family is unique.
- All of the people in my class are unique and have their own interests and can do different things.

Related Essential Questions:

- What is a community?
- What makes my family unique?
- What makes my classmates unique?

Content Objectives:

- Students will be able to:
  - Recognize that everyone has similarities and differences.
  - Describe a community.

Literacy Objectives:

- Students will be able to:
  - Identify and discuss story elements (characters, setting, events, conclusion.)
  - Think about, discuss, and unscramble sentences connected to the text *Frederick* by Leo Leoni.

Resources/Materials:

- Sets of individual word cards (based on sentences from *Frederick* by Leo Leoni)

These can be preprinted on index cards or post-it notes; additionally, technology can be leveraged. Jamboard, an extension for Google Chrome, is an interactive whiteboard that allows students to work collaboratively on anagrams in a digital environment.

Sequence of Learning Events

Purpose: Students will learn to understand sentence structure by thinking about, discussing, and ultimately unscrambling sentences connected to the text *Frederick* by Leo Leoni.

Review/Prerequisite Skills: To participate in this lesson, students should have the following prerequisite skills:

- Understanding of the parts of speech, phrases, and clauses in constructing sentences
- Familiarity with the text *Frederick* by Leo Leoni
- Understanding of word order within sentences
- Ability to engage in flexible thinking

Teacher and Student Instructional Activities:

Lesson opening:

1. Explain to students that we will be completing a fun activity called sentence anagrams, or sentence scrambles. Tell students that in groups they will be provided with a set of "scrambled" word cards, which they will reassemble into a complete sentence. However, first you will model this activity, so students can see the process.

Teacher modeling:

2. Prior to the lesson, the teacher-created sentence *The mice gather supplies and prepare for the long winter ahead,* should be premade on individual word cards. Display the cards for students like in the following image:

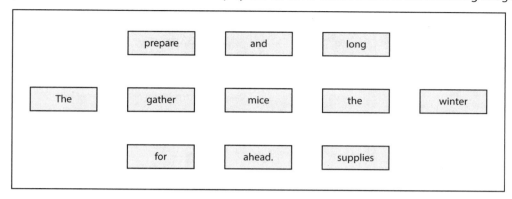

Crofutt, G. A. (1873). American Progress [painting]. Library of Congress https://www.loc.gov/pictures/item/97507547/

3. To begin, instruct students to look for capitalization and ending punctuation first. Ask them: where do these items usually go in a sentence? Move those words to their proper location.

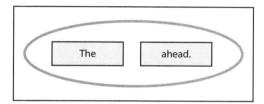

4. Next model identifying verbs. Ask students: which words connect those verbs? In this sentence "prepare" and "gather" are both verbs. "Supplies" are something one might gather, so this is grouped. Additionally, the phrase "prepare for" is commonly seen, so this is also put together.

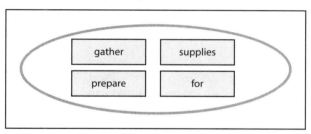

5. Then tell students they should look for the adjectives and the nouns they describe. Group these words together. In this sentence, "long winter" seems like a likely combination.

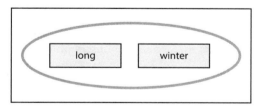

6. After that, students should ask themselves, are there any conjunctions? How can they be used to link ideas? In this sentence the conjunction "and" is present. This conjunction is used to join ideas, so it seems like the purpose of this conjunction is to join the two actions, so it is grouped like so:

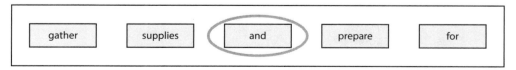

7. Then, ask students: are there any groups of words that logically go together? In this sentence "the long winter ahead" seems like a likely grouping. Also, if we ask the question *Who gathers supplies?*, the answer would be "the mice" so this is grouped together, as well.

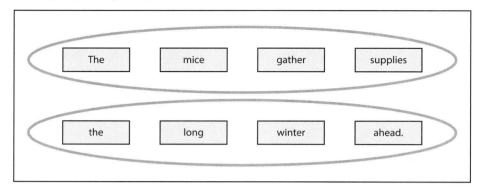

8. Finally, unscramble the sentence. Remind students that this might take some trial and error, and that's perfectly okay.

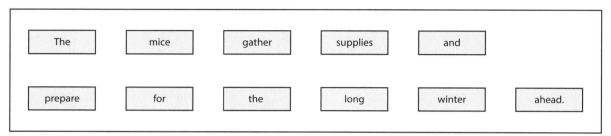

Student-guided practice:

9. Display the next scrambled sentence, *Frederick prepares in his own special way by collecting words.*

10. Go through the following steps with students, using questioning to guide their thinking:
    a. Look for capitalization and ending punctuation first. Where do these items usually go in a sentence?
    b. Identify verbs. Which words connect those verbs?
    c. Next, find the adjectives and the nouns they describe.
    d. Locate conjunctions (and any mid-sentence punctuation). How can they be used to link ideas?
    e. Look for words that go logically together and group them together.
    f. Finally, unscramble the sentence. This may take some trial and error.

Independent practice:

11. The teacher should distribute sets of word cards to small groups. Students should then work together to build sentences that tell them something about the text *Frederick* by Leo Leoni. Students can refer to the checklist (mentioned in step 10) to assist with the process.

12. The teacher circulates and supports student groups as they complete the activity.

13. Once completed, students share their unscrambled sentence(s) and discuss how they solved the arrangements.

Differentiation/Inclusive Instructional Practices:

- The steps for unscrambling sentences can be created as a checklist for students.
- Sentences can be differentiated based on length and levels of complexity.

Evidence of Student Learning/Informal Classroom-Based Assessment:

- Completed sentence anagram activity
- Participation in classroom discussion
- Teacher questioning

Teacher Reflection in Lesson Implementation:

Try This! Now let's try a sentence anagram activity on our own. Using the steps provided, unscramble the words to create a complete sentence. Once finished, compare your answer with the one provided. How did your answer match up? Was it easy? Difficult? And what challenges do you anticipate your students might have with an activity like this?

our	Unscrambling	of	supports	how
understanding	words	sentences	make	and
arrange	authors	meaning.	select	to

Remember to:

1. Look for capitalization and ending punctuation first. Where do these items usually go in a sentence?
2. Identify verbs. Which words connect those verbs?
3. Next, find the adjectives and the nouns they describe.
4. Locate conjunctions (and any mid-sentence punctuation). How can they be used to link ideas?
5. Look for words that go logically together and group them together.
6. Finally, unscramble the sentence. This may take some trial and error.

My unscrambled sentence:_____

Answer Key:

Unscrambling sentences supports our understanding of how authors select and arrange words to make meaning.

Intentional Sentence Comprehension Instructional Activities

Intentional-on-purpose or direct instruction in syntax and sentence comprehension is a critical contributor to overall comprehension of text (Hennessy, 2020). Frequently, syntax and sentence comprehension are taught in the context of writing; however, instruction embedded within reading comprehension provides a unique opportunity to highlight the various functions of the parts of speech, phrases, clauses, and sentences; the internal structure of a sentence; and how word order impacts meaning. The sentence-attuned educator provides meaningful and successful learning experiences that include instances of teacher modeling and explanation of targeted concepts as well as opportunities for group and independent practice. They also build student knowledge of syntax and sentences in a systematic way, moving from simple to complex. Thus, we will address intentional-on-purpose activities that first focus on the parts of speech, moving on to phrases and clauses, and then sentences, which together construct the text.

Before we continue with a discussion of grammar-based deconstruction activities, it is extremely important to note that research has consistently shown that teaching grammar in isolation does not work. In fact, students learn grammar and syntax best when instruction is tied to their own writing and rooted in what they are learning and reading about. This reduces the need for the rote memorization of complex grammatical terminology, which can lead to confusion and doesn't necessarily help students when it comes to their own writing. As writing expert Judith Hochman and colleagues (2017, p. 15) note, "Although it's useful for students to have a general familiarity with basic concepts such as 'noun' and 'verb,' that won't necessarily prevent them from writing 'sentences' that lack one or the other," Thus, educators can use simplified, student-friendly language to emphasize the function of grammatical terminology, while guiding students to apply these concepts to what they are reading and writing about in school.

Words Working Together: Parts of Speech & Their Jobs

The parts of speech serve as the foundational building blocks of sentences. Thus, it is critical for students to develop an understanding of how these individual words function within sentences and can be used as a meaning-making resource. This section explores activities that tap into this word-level knowledge, which serves as the cornerstone to building students' reading comprehension and writing skills.

ACTIVITY 1: Questioning (textbook pg. 102)

Questioning is a widely recognized strategy used to support students' reading comprehension (Carnine, Silbert, Kame'enui, & Traver, 2010). These guiding questions for each part of speech assist students in understanding that each has a specific function within the sentence. Basic questions, shown in Table 4.3, are foundational and, while questioning can be used as a standalone strategy, questioning is embedded throughout the sentence comprehension activities featured in this section.

Table 4.3. The form and function of parts of speech

Form: Parts of Speech	Function: Meaning
Noun-subject	Who or what?
Verb-predicate	Doing or did?
Adjective-modifies the noun	Which one, what kind, how many?
Adverb-modifies the verb	Where, when, how, why?
Preposition-	What is the relationship between the words before and after?
Conjunction-	What is connected or needs to be glued together?

Prior to reading, educators should review and select sentence(s) from the current text to practice with. For example, *Chrysanthemum* by Kevin Henkes is one read-aloud text connected to our first grade unit, *All About Me!* This text can be used to support student knowledge of the enduring understandings connected to identity as outlined in the unit plan, while simultaneously building understanding of how individual words contribute to meaning. Consider the sentence, *"On the first day of school, Chrysanthemum wore her sunniest dress and her brightest smile"* (Henkes, 2009). The sentence-attuned educator can use a structure like this to craft a series of questions that tap into the function of the parts of speech. The teacher can then model and review responses with the class. Potential questions for this sentence might include:

- Which word answers who/whom? *Chrysanthemum*
- Which word tells what she did? *wore*

- Which word(s) tell what she wore? *dress and smile*
- Which word tells what kind of dress? *sunniest*
- Which word tells what kind of smile? *brightest*

Activities like this develop initial student understanding through oral language interactions. This can be expanded upon, as we will see later, and developed into sorting activities for pairs of students or small groups.

Try This! Now it's your turn to try it! Read the sentence below and answer the series of questions that follow. Afterward, reflect: how did your responses compare with the key provided?

Chrysanthemum thought it was wildly funny and she giggled throughout the Dance of the Flowers.

(Henkes, 2009).

Which word answers who/whom?	
Which word(s) tell what she did?	
Which word(s) tell what she thought?	
Which word tells how funny it was?	
Which word(s) tell when she giggled?	

Answer Key:

Which word answers who/whom?	*Chrysanthemum*
Which word(s) tell what she did?	*thought* and *giggled*
Which word(s) tell what she thought?	*it was funny*
Which word tells how funny it was?	*wildly*
Which word(s) tell when she giggled?	*throughout the Dance of the Flowers*

ACTIVITY 2: Sorting With a Structured Sentence Organizer   (textbook pgs. 102–103)

Once students are ready to move on from oral language interactions, they can begin to combine their knowledge of the parts of speech through the use of a structured sentence organizer (Figure 4.5). The following structured sentence organizer features questions related to word functions. For instance, as discussed previously, a noun answers the question who/what while the verb refers to is/was doing.

Who/what?	Is/was doing?	Which one, what kind, how many?	Where, when, how, why?

(continued)

Figure 4.5. Structured sentence organizer.

Figure 4.5. *(continued)*

Who/what?	Is/was doing?	Which one, what kind, how many?	Where, when, how, why?

After instances of teacher modeling and practice have been provided orally, students can be given a set of cards that feature individual words from a current text along with the structured sentence organizer. Working in small groups or partnerships, students are then tasked to sort the words into the correct category. Activities such as this can be used before or after reading and can be adapted to support student understanding of phrases and clauses once students understand the function of the parts of speech. An activity that targets the function of groups of words (e.g., phrases and clauses) will be highlighted later.

Try This!   The word cards that follow are from *Six Mass Extinctions in 440 Million Years,* a ReadWorks article geared toward 9th and 10th graders. Read through the given words and sort them according to the questions they answer. Then check your understanding by reviewing the answer key provided. How did your answers compare? Did you notice any problematic or tricky words while sorting?

species	proposed	widely	bony
catastrophic	remains	identified	towards
extinction	hypothesis	developed	vanished
marine	casualties	culprit	reshaped
extremely	anatomist	factors	several

Who/what?	Is/was doing?	Which one, what kind, how many?	Where, when, how, why?

Answer Key:

Who/what?	Is/was doing?	Which one, what kind, how many?	Where, when, how, why?
species	proposed	bony	widely
*remains	*remains	catastrophic	towards
extinction	identified	*marine	extremely
hypothesis	developed	several	
casualties	vanished		
culprit	reshaped		
anatomist	*factors		
*factors			

*In this article, words like *remains* and *factors* prove to be tricky as both can be considered a noun or verb. For example, the Great Dying extinction from 252 million years ago *remains* a great mystery; however, *remains* can also refer to parts leftover or a living being's body after death. Additionally, the word *marine* can function as an adjective or a noun, as it is used to describe things that come from the ocean or sea but also refers to a specific branch of the U.S. armed forces. Thus, it is important to consider potential student responses when crafting activities such as these to troubleshoot misconceptions and provide solutions.

ACTIVITY 3: Picture-Prompted Generation (textbook pgs. 109–110)

Once students have an understanding of the parts of speech and can recognize examples in text, they can begin to create examples on their own. To scaffold this activity, the use of picture prompts is especially useful. Initially one can depict familiar images that are not connected to in class content. This allows students to learn and practice with images from everyday experiences. The following image depicts a well-known subject matter (e.g., dogs) and can be paired with the structured sentence organizer to help students expand upon information by answering targeted question words.

The teacher should first model and then guide students in careful examination of the image in order to answer the questions provided in the structured sentence organizer. Take a moment and review the completed table that follows. It highlights potential student responses. As you review and reflect, are there additional items you would add? Can you think of any problematic answers students may provide?

Who/what?	Is/was doing?	Which one, what kind, how many?	Where, when, how, why?
dogs	sleep/sleeping	two	on the bed
puppies	nap/napping	sleepy	soundly
	snooze/snoozing	fluffy	during naptime
		shaggy	

To add an additional challenge, the teacher could then ask students to orally provide a sentence using the answers they generated. For instance, *The sleepy puppies nap soundly on the bed* includes words from each column in the structured sentence organizer.

Once students have been given opportunities to practice with everyday images, those tied to content can be provided. This next image, *American Progress* by George Crofutt, is connected to an eighth-grade unit on westward expansion. This illustration depicts an allegorical representation of America leading pioneers westward by foot, wagons, and train. As they move onward, they encounter Native Americans and herds of American bison, both of which can be seen moving further west. This image can once again be paired with the structured sentence organizer to help students expand upon information through answering targeted question words. The following completed table includes potential student responses. After you review the answers provided, what other responses could you provide? What potential sentences could students generate?

Crofutt, G.A. (1873). American Progress [painting]. Library of Congress, https://www.loc.gov/pictures/item/97507547/

Who/what?	Is/was doing?	Which one, what kind, how many?	Where, when, how, why?
pioneers	ventured	male	west
settlers	moved	uncertain	by train
Native Americans	fleeing	fearful	by Oregon Trail
bison			by covered wagon
			on horseback

Try This! Now that we have explored picture-prompted generation, it's your turn to put this strategy into action. The image that follows, entitled *The First Picket Line,* was created in 1917 and is part of the expansive collection of primary source documents housed at the National Library of Congress. Examine the image carefully, and then complete the accompanying structured sentence organizer. Once you have generated answers to the questions highlighted, compose a sentence using your ideas. For an extra challenge, try to use words from each column.

Source: The first picket line - College day in the picket line. Washington D.C., 1917. Feb. [Photograph] Retrieved from the Library of Congress, https://www.loc.gov/item/97500299/.

Who/what?	Is/was doing?	Which one, what kind, how many?	Where, when, how, why?

Answer Key:

Who/what?	Is/was doing?	Which one, what kind, how many?	Where, when, how, why?
protestors	picketed	female	outside of the White House
women	protested	brave	in 1917
activists	fought	determined	in the winter
suffragettes	dissented	stalwart	for equal rights
reformers	demonstrated		for the right to vote
champions			
advocates			

Sample sentence:

In the winter of 1917, the stalwart suffragettes demonstrated for equal rights outside of the White House.

Fill-in-the-blank activities, or cloze passages, are excellent ways to check-in with student comprehension and understanding of the parts of speech. In these activities, words are omitted from a given sentence or passage and students are required to fill them in. The example that follows is connected to the novel *The House on Mango Street* by Sandra Cisneros. Students must read the given sentences and determine the best word to go in each blank. This activity taps into their knowledge not only of syntax and the parts of speech, but also of vocabulary and semantics.

Directions: Circle the word that best completes the given sentence.

1. The house on Mango Street is not the one Esperanza _____, but her
   (envisioned, ignored, lucid)

   parents tell her the house is only _____.
   (fitting, temporary, new)

2. Esperanza admires her great grandmother for her _____.
   (strength, anger, optimism)

3. Although the horse, an animal that represents strength, is seen as a sign of bad luck for women,

   Esperanza _____ this idea and believes this _____ was
   (accepts, solves, rejects)   (offer, notion, place)

   started to prevent women from being strong.

Try This!   The following fill-in-the-blank tasks are based on fourth-grade geometry content. Take a moment to review the sentences that follow and select the word that best completes each sentence. Once finished, compare your answers with the key provided. Then, reflect: how could this strategy be used as a quick check-in or informal assessment with your students?

Directions: Circle the word that best completes the given sentence.

1. The diameter is the length of the line from one side that passes _____
                                                                    (through, below, next to)
   the center directly to the opposite edge of the circle.

2. A _____ extends from a circle's center to the outside edge.
      (vertex, radius, arc)

3. The circumference, or the distance around a circle, is also known as the circle's
   _____.
   (tangent, perimeter, chord)

Answer Key:

Directions: Circle the word that best completes the given sentence.

1. The diameter is the length of the line from one side that passes _____

   (**through**, below, next to)

   the center directly to the opposite edge of the circle.

2. A _____ extends from a circle's center to the outside edge.

   (vertex, **radius**, arc)

3. The circumference, or the distance around a circle, is also known as the circle's

   _____.

   (tangent, **perimeter**, chord)

ACTIVITY 5: List Making
(textbook pg. 112)

Making lists is another excellent way to support students in generating their own examples that answer the question words and target the parts of speech. Let's return to the book *Chrysanthemum* by Kevin Henkes. Prior to reading the book, students could be instructed to be on the lookout for words that give us clues about what kind of character Chrysanthemum is. Then words can be collected throughout the read-aloud and added to a semantic web, as shown in Figure 4.6.

Once students have practiced this as a whole group, they can begin list-making activities on their own. The next example shows a list-making activity connected to a fourth-grade science unit on the formation of the solar system. After reading about this phenomenon in class, students were tasked to list objects in the solar system and words that describe them.

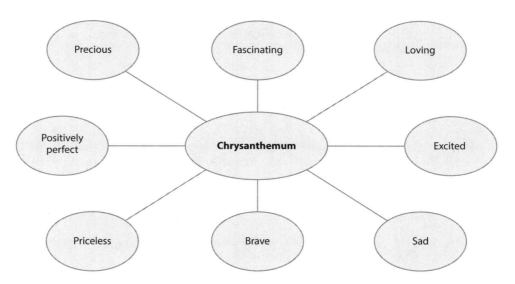

Figure 4.6. Sample semantic web analysis of *Chrysanthemum*.

Which one, what kind, how many?	Who/what?
dusty	nebula(s)
rocky	planet(s)
gas, ice	giant(s)
hydrogen	atom(s)
massive	asteroid(s)
icy	comet(s)

The last example highlights a list-making activity, but at the high school level, where students are reading *The Great Gatsby* by F. Scott Fitzgerald. Once again, students have been tasked to list words that describe characters in the novel, which serves to assess not only their knowledge of adjectives, but their understanding of character as well.

Nick Carraway: honest, tolerant, nonjudgmental, naive	*Jay Gatsby:* aloof, enigmatic, fatally idealistic/optimistic, childish, self-made, dishonest
Daisy Buchanan: cynical, needy, sardonic, selfish, shallow, hurtful	*Tom Buchanan:* arrogant, hypocritical, aggressive, super wealthy, amoral, unlikeable

Activities like list making can also be utilized as prewriting activities to help students brainstorm ideas prior to writing a longer piece. For example, the *Great Gatsby* activity sample could be used to help students brainstorm and compose an essay that compares two story characters. However, construction of background knowledge is critical, and students must have this fundamental knowledge in order to generate ideas.

Try This! Now it's your turn to practice! Using the following category-specific prompts, generate your own list. Remember, activities like this one can be used before writing as a warmup and are a great way to help students collect ideas. Once you complete this activity, reflect: how might this activity be useful for your classroom and students?

What actions can you do in the wintertime?	What places can you visit in the summertime?

Describe the weather in the fall.	What do plants and animals do in the spring?

Answer Key:

What actions can you do in the wintertime?	What places can you visit in the summertime?
ice skating	beach
sledding	pool
tubing	camp
skiing	amusement park
snowboarding	
Describe the weather in the fall.	**What do plants and animals do in the spring?**
cool	awaken
blustery	bloom
crisp	blossom
nippy	emerge
colorful	flourish
rainy	grow

How Words Work Together: Phrases and Clauses & Their Jobs

The various parts of speech alone do not make a sentence and must be combined to create phrases and clauses in order to construct varied sentence types. Building an awareness of the common phrase types, as well as the function of independent and dependent clauses, help students understand each structure's role in making meaning. Students should build an understanding that phrases are groups or clusters of words that work together, but these phrases do not include BOTH a *who* or *what* (subject) and an *is/was doing* (predicate), and therefore do not make a sentence.

Clauses, however, are groups or clusters of words that work together and include a subject and predicate. There are two types of clauses: independent and dependent. Independent clauses are those that can stand on their own and constitute a simple sentence, while dependent clauses are those that cannot stand alone and typically begin with a subordinating conjunction (e.g., although, before, when) or relative pronoun (e.g., that, which, who). As we mentioned in the beginning of this chapter, too much emphasis on rote memorization of grammatical terminology or labeling is not the goal here. Instead, students need to develop an understanding of how these structures can be combined to create varied sentence types. In this section, we will explore activities that help students develop an understanding of the job of phrases and clauses, and how each uniquely contributes to sentence construction.

ACTIVITY 6: Questioning   (textbook pgs. 102, 105–106)

We will start with questioning as it is a highly effective strategy for supporting reading comprehension for all students. However, we will focus this strategy on phrases and clauses. Once again, prior to reading, educators should review and select phrases and clauses from a current text to practice with. Let's return to the article *Six Mass Extinctions in 440 Million Years,* a ReadWorks article geared for 9th and 10th graders. Consider the sentence, *"Towards the end of the Devonian period around 370 million years ago, a pair of major events known as the Kellwasser Event and the Hangenberg Event combined to cause an enormous loss in biodiversity"* (ReadWorks, 2018). The sentence-attuned educator can use a sentence like this one to craft a series of questions that tap into the function of the phrases and clauses it contains. Potential questions for this sentence might include:

- Who or What? *a pair of major events*
- Is or was doing? *combined to cause an enormous loss in biodiversity*
- Where? *toward the end of the Devonian period*
- When? *around 370 million years ago*
- Which events? *the Kellwasser Event and the Hangenberg Event*

Remember, it is critical to provide instances of teacher modeling, and students should have a solid understanding of the parts of speech before moving on to activities that feature phrases and clauses. As before, students should have the opportunity to practice these activities orally and in writing. This includes middle and high school students who benefit from hearing and reading about these structures in order to differentiate and work with both.

Try This!   Now we will practice the questioning strategy while working with phrases and clauses. The following sentence is also from the ReadWorks article *Six Mass Extinctions in 440 Million Years*. Read the sentence and then complete the table. Once you've finished, compare your answers with the key that follows.

"The earliest known mass extinction, the Ordovician Extinction, took place at a time when most of the life on Earth lived in its seas" (ReadWorks, 2018).

Who or what?	
Is or was doing?	
When?	
Which kind of extinction was it?	

Answer Key:

Who or what?	*the Ordovician Extinction*
Is or was doing?	*took place*
When?	*at a time when most of the life on Earth lived in its seas*
Which kind of extinction was it?	*the earliest known mass extinction*

ACTIVITY 7: Sorting Phrases and Clauses   (textbook pgs. 105–106)

Instructional activities that ask students to sort phrases and clauses help them determine how these different structures contribute to meaning. The first example shows a common phrase type sort based on the text *The House on Mango Street*. Students were provided with the phrase cards and then tasked to sort the phrases by type: noun, verb, adjectical, adverbial, and prepositional.

Noun phrase	Verb phrase	Adjectival phrase	Adverbial phrase	Prepositional phrase
the syllables	baptize myself	sad and red and crumbly	before that	by the window

To scaffold this activity further, the phrase headings can be paired with the question words they answer. For example, noun phrases answer the question who or what, while verb phrases answer the question is or was doing.

The next example highlights a sort of dependent and independent clauses from an 11th-grade ReadWorks text about the New Deal. Students were tasked to sort the various clauses and explain their answers afterward.

Dependent clause	Independent clause
• before the end of Roosevelt's first term • although for some he is the brilliant tactician • while a fuller perspective reveals how bounded these changes were	• the Supreme Court struck down critical parts of his keystone AAA and NRA agencies • others view him as a devious and unprincipled compromiser • the swift pace and broad scale of the reforms conveyed a resolute engagement with the people's troubles

Activities like this also help students to see how these clauses work together to create complex syntactic structures. For example, the dependent clause *"before the end of Roosevelt's first term"* goes with the independent clause *"the Supreme Court struck down critical parts of his keystone AAA and NRA agencies."* Once the sort is complete, as an additional challenge, students can be tasked to match up the structures to form complex sentences.

 Try This! Now we will practice a clause sort of our own. Read the phrases and clauses from the ReadWorks article in the box then sort them into the table. Once you've sorted the sentence parts, match up the independent and dependent clauses. Then rewrite the complete sentence using correct capitalization and ending punctuation on the lines provided.

1. when he ran for vice president on the Democratic ticket
2. after winning his historic reelection
3. he moved decisively to equip the British forces
4. foreign affairs took over by the late thirties
5. the reform tide had passed
6. if domestic policy and the Depression set the agenda for Roosevelt's first two terms

Dependent clause	Independent clause

Answer Key:

1. <u>When he ran for vice president on the Democratic ticket,</u> <u>the reform tide had passed.</u>
            (dependent clause)   (independent clause)

2. <u>After winning his historic reelection,</u> <u>he moved decisively to equip the British forces.</u>
           (dependent clause)   (independent clause)

3. <u>If domestic policy and the Depression set the agenda for Roosevelt's first two terms,</u>
                                     (dependent clause)

   <u>foreign affairs took over by the late thirties.</u>
               (independent clause)

The Sentence & Its Job

Understanding of sentence structure is key to making meaning. Students need to develop an understanding of the four sentence types (declarative, interrogative, imperative, exclamatory) and the various sentence constructions (simple, compound, complex, compound-complex) that authors use. Once again, emphasis should not be on memorization and naming, but on function. For example, when considering the four sentence types, students need to understand that there are sentences that provide statements (declarative), questions (interrogative), commands (imperative), and exclamations or show excitement (exclamatory).

Authors use various sentence constructions to help them express ideas. This includes simple, compound, complex, and compound-complex sentences. Again, emphasis should be placed on function over label. A simple sentence is one independent clause and expresses one idea unit. Compound sentences represent two independent clauses, or two related idea units, joined by a coordinating conjunction. A complex sentence includes at least one dependent clause and an independent clause. It consists of two idea units with one subordinate to the other. Finally, a compound-complex sentence consists of two independent clauses and one dependent clause. Figure 4.7 highlights examples of each of these sentence types taken from the novel *The Great Gatsby* by F. Scott Fitzgerald. A basic understanding of sentence types and structures is essential to help students navigate the demands of academic text and create written compositions that are interesting and varied. This section explores activities that help students understand these various structures and how they contribute to reading comprehension.

Sentence Type	Definition	Example
Simple	Consists of one independent clause that expresses a single idea unit.	*The name sounded faintly familiar* (pg. 93). *I stayed late that night* (pg. 109).
Compound	Consists of two independent clauses, or two related idea units, joined by a coordinating conjunction.	*My family all died and I came into a good deal of money* (pg. 65). *I had nothing to do in the hall, so I went into the room* (pg. 86).
Complex	Consists of at least one dependent clause and an independent clause. It features two idea units with one subordinate to the other.	*As my taxi groaned away I saw Gatsby walking toward me across the lawn* (pg. 81). *I sat on the front steps with them while they waited for their car* (pg. 107).
Compound-Complex	Consists of two independent clauses and one dependent clause.	*He told me all this very much later, but I've put it down here with the idea of exploding those first wild rumors about his antecedents, which weren't even faintly true* (pg. 101).

Figure 4.7. Sentence types and examples from *The Great Gatsby*. (*Source:* Fitzgerald, 1925.)

Both sentence combining and sentence expansion, which we examine later, are typically discussed in the realm of writing instruction. While this is a wonderful activity to support students' writing, sentence combining and expansion can support students' reading comprehension as well. With sentence combining, students are asked to combine two or more kernel sentences using varied syntactic patterns, which are based on a logical sequence. For this activity, teachers provide focused questions and kernel sentences from the texts students are reading in class. For example, the table that follows features a sentence combining sequence and examples from the text *Frederick* by Leo Leoni.

Targeted pattern	Question and kernel sentences	Combined response
Adjectives and adverbs	*How would you describe Frederick?* • Frederick spends his days collecting sun rays, colors, and words. • He is a daydreamy mouse.	Daydreamy Frederick spends his days collecting sun rays, colors, and words.
Compound subjects and objects	*How do the other mice feel about Frederick?* • The mice think Frederick is lazy. • They think he's a dreamer.	The mice think Frederick's laziness and dreams are frustrating.
Compound sentences using coordinating conjunctions	*What did Frederick contribute to his community?* • Frederick contributed poetry. • He brought great joy to his community.	Frederick contributed poetry and he brought great joy to his community.
Possessive nouns	*How do the other mice contribute to their community?* • The mice make a contribution by preparing for the winter. • They do this by gathering nuts, corn, grain, and wheat.	The mice's contribution is preparing for the winter by gathering nuts, corn, grain, and wheat.
Adverbial clauses using subordinating conjunctions	*Why did the other mice change their minds about Frederick?* • Frederick tells the mice to visualize the colors of spring. • They understand how his poetry helps to nourish their minds and hearts.	As Frederick tells the mice to visualize the colors of spring, they understand how his poetry helps to nourish their minds and hearts.
Relative clause	*What makes a community?* • A community is a group of people living and working together. • It is constructed by combining different people's unique talents and gifts.	A community, which is a group of people living and working together, is constructed by combining different people's unique talents and gifts.

 Try This! The following sentences are connected to a middle school science text on the water cycle. Combine the pair of kernel sentences shown. Use the word in parenthesis to help you!

1. The water cycle is the constant movement of water throughout the Earth.

   The water cycle is storage of water throughout the Earth. **(and)**

   _____

   _____

   _____

2. The amount of water on the planet and in its atmosphere remains the same.

It moves around constantly in three states. **(although)**

_____

_____

_____

_____

_____

Challenge!

Now try combining three kernel sentences without the added scaffold. What did you notice about combining sentences this time?

3. Condensation is crucial to the water cycle.

Condensation is responsible for the formation of clouds.

Clouds allow water to return to Earth as precipitation.

_____

_____

_____

_____

_____

Answer key:

Possible answers include:

1. The water cycle is the constant movement and storage of water throughout the Earth.
2. Although the amount of water on the planet and in its atmosphere remains the same, it moves around constantly in three states.
3. Condensation is crucial to the water cycle because it is responsible for the formation of clouds that allow water to return to Earth as precipitation.

Sentence Expansion   (textbook pgs. 107–108)

Sentence expansion is another excellent way to support student comprehension and writing skills. With this strategy, students are asked to elaborate upon a kernel sentence using a series of question words (*what, when, where, how, why*). When designing sentence expansion activities, teachers select key idea units from the text and provide the question words to prompt student thinking. This activity can initially be introduced as an oral exercise and then written responses. The following activity is from a second-grade unit on weather. To scaffold the activity further, an image was provided to help the students elaborate upon the given kernel sentence.

Directions: Using the image and question words, expand upon the kernel sentence below.

Kernel sentence: Lightning flashes.

How?: brightly

Where?: in the night sky

Expanded sentence: Lightning flashes brightly in the night sky.

As students master this activity, picture supports can be eliminated, and students can work on expanding sentences using the question words only. The example that follows is taken from *The House on Mango Street* by Sandra Cisneros. Notice how this example highlights a comprehension check of what students have previously read.

Directions: Expand the following sentence using the question words below.

Kernel sentence: The water pipes broke.

Where?: at the flat on Loomis

Why?: because they were too old

Expanded sentence: At the flat on Loomis, the water pipes broke because they were too old.

Try This! Using the following image and question words, expand upon the kernel sentence. As you work on this activity, consider what you must know in advance to complete it (hint: think background knowledge). Once it is completed, take a moment to reflect: how could you use sentence expansion activities, like the ones shown here, in your own classroom practices?

Daniels, J.T. (1903). The Wright Brothers. [Photograph]. Imperial War Museum. https://www.iwm.org.uk/collections/item/object/205026482

Directions: Using the image and question words, expand upon the kernel sentence below.

Kernel sentence: They flew.

Who?:

(did) What?:

When?:

Where?:

Expanded sentence:

Answer key:

Kernel sentence: They flew.

Who?: Wright brothers

(did) What?: made history; flew the first flight

When?: December 17, 1903

Where?: Kitty Hawk, North Carolina

Expanded sentence: On December 17th, 1903, the Wright brothers made history and flew the first flight in Kitty Hawk, North Carolina.

Use of visual representations is another way to support students' comprehension during and after reading. Young learners can benefit from using pictures to clarify problematic sentence structures. Passive sentence construction, where the subject is being acted upon instead of doing the action, can be especially tricky for many students. For example, consider the passive sentence *My Halloween candy was eaten by the dog*. This is less straightforward than the active construction *The dog ate my Halloween candy*, where the dog (the subject) is doing the action. Having students visualize and draw passive structures can help them to clarify the meaning of this tricky sentence structure.

Another useful strategy is sentence diagramming. With sentence diagramming, students produce a pictorial representation of a sentence's grammatical structure. To begin sentence diagramming, the subject (who or what) and the predicate (is or was doing) are placed on a straight line. A vertical line is used to separate the two, like so:

subject/predicate   Nenny/laughs.

As the sentence expands, angled lines can be added to connect modifiers to related words.

---
subject/predicate   Nenny/laughs.
        /   /
                       dreamy (which Nenny?)

subject/predicate   Nenny/laughs.
                               /
                       like broken glass (how does she laugh?)

Sentence diagramming also lends itself beautifully to the incorporation of technology. Kami, an online annotation and markup tool for Google Chrome, is a wonderful extension to drive engagement and can be used to foster collaboration with sentence diagramming.

 Try This! Consider the sentence, *Different occupations are held by people in a community*. This sentence, which connects to the topic of community in the *All About Me!* unit, features passive sentence construction. Visualize and sketch out the meaning of this problematic sentence construction in the space provided. How did sketching out the sentence help you to clarify meaning?

Different occupations are held by people in a community.

_____

_____

_____

The Role of Cohesive Ties and Connectives

It is also important to discuss the role of cohesive ties and connectives in sentence comprehension. These important devices bridge ideas within and between sentences. This not only requires an understanding of syntax and sentence structure, but also includes the ability to make inferences. The reader must use cohesive devices or connectives at the sentence level to infer meaning between different sentence parts, as well as recognize how conjunctions signal relationships between clauses. Thus, we discuss cohesive ties and connectives in depth when we review Local Coherence Inference later.

Incidental-On-Purpose (Indirect) Instructional Activities

Incidental-on-purpose or indirect learning opportunities in sentence comprehension also play an important role in the development of students' syntactic awareness. Creation of these activities involves preparation and planning on the part of the educator. When previewing and preparing a text, educators should be on the lookout for opportunities to highlight or discuss targeted syntactic patterns as well as problematic structures that may be tricky for students to navigate. In this next section, we discuss the role of read-alouds or shared readings as well as make connections to fluency used in group and independent readings.

Read-Alouds or Shared Reading   (textbook pgs. 111–112)

Read-alouds or shared reading opportunities provide a natural place to incorporate discussion and questioning of complex syntactic structures. Although vocabulary and instruction on word meaning is typically introduced at this time, it also provides a natural opportunity to discuss the various sentence structures students will encounter in the text. Once again, the previewing of targeted texts is critical because it allows educators to identify and prepare opportunities to think aloud and pose questions that support students' understanding of difficult sentences.

Consider the following sentence, taken from the text *The Day You Begin* by Jaqueline Woodson. This is a wonderful read-aloud for students in early elementary grades and features Woodson's lyrical text, which is beautiful but tricky to navigate. The chosen sentence, shown here, includes dependent and relative clauses, subordinating and coordinating conjunctions, and a common classroom rule breaker: it starts with "And."

An educator might choose to highlight the dependent and relative clauses and have a discussion about the features that make them so (e.g., include a subject and predicate, but are not a complete thought; begin with a subordinating conjunction and a relative pronoun).

> *"And as you stand in front of that room,* you can only remember how the heat waved as it lifted off the curb, and your days spent at home caring for your little sister, *who made you laugh and hugged you hard at naptime.*
>
> –Jacqueline Woodson, 2018, pg. 12

Or the educator could use the conjunction as another talking point. Here, the independent clause and the dependent clause that follows it are joined by the coordinating conjunction "and."

> *"And as you stand in front of that room,* <u>you can only remember how the heat waved as it lifted off the curb,</u> and <u>your days spent at home caring for your little sister,</u> who made you laugh and hugged you hard at naptime.
>
> –Jacqueline Woodson, 2018, pg. 12

Finally, this sentence highlights a common classroom rule breaker as it starts with "And." This provides an excellent conversation starter where the rationale for this rule could be explained. For example, teachers often instruct in writing to never start a sentence with conjunctions, such as the word "and." There is some thought that this practice arose due to student overuse of words like "and" or "but," and instead of limiting their usage, students were told to eliminate them altogether. However, when used in moderation, this can be an excellent way to express voice and vary sentence structures.

Try This! Find a read-aloud or shared reading text that you are using (or will use) with your students. Take a moment to review the text for challenging and/or problematic sentence structures. Then using the space provided, reflect: What sentence did you choose and why?

My sentence: _____

_____

_____

_____

Teaching ideas: _____

_____

_____

_____

Group or Independent Reading: The Fluency Connection (textbook pg. 112)

Use of incidental-on-purpose reading experiences also provide an excellent means for teaching prosody. In addition to reading accuracy and automaticity, prosody is a factor that contributes to fluency and is necessary for comprehension. Prosody is the use of tone, pitch, and expression and includes phrasing. Phrasing is used by the proficient reader to mirror spoken language and convey meaning.

As educators, we can emphasize reading with prosody by providing instances of teacher modeling and think-aloud. This allows students to clearly see how written cues impact prosody. For example, a proficient reader understands that a comma often coincides with places where we pause in speech. The sentence-attuned educator can draw attention to this while reading aloud by asking students to identify and note the function of prosody in this instance. For example, "What did you notice I did when I came to the comma? How does this help us understand what we are reading?"

Scooping sentences is one effective practice to assist students with the development of prosody. With scooping, the reader underlines syntactic units to create a visual representation of how to parse a sentence. When modeling this skill, the teacher can preview and select sentences to highlight how this strategy supports both reading with prosody and comprehension.

Let's revisit *The Day You Begin* by Jaqueline Woodson. Notice how the example shown here is "scooped" into syntactic units to assist reading with prosody. This allows students to clearly see which groups of words go together and should initially be accompanied by teacher modeled think-aloud so the rationale is clearly explained. For example, when working with the passage above, the sentence-attuned

> "And as you stand in front of that room, you can only remember how the heat waved as it lifted off the curb, and your days spent at home caring for your little sister, who made you laugh and hugged you hard at naptime."
>
> —Jacqueline Woodson, pg. 12

educator could explain that each of the "scoops" represents an idea unit, or that many of the pauses take place after a comma. Remember: you are the best reader in the room, so definitely capitalize on this advantage to make reading with prosody transparent for students!

✧ ✧ Try This!   The sentence that follows is from the classic text *The Great Gatsby* by F. Scott Fitzgerald. Take a moment to read through the sentence and then "scoop" or parse the sentence into syntactic units. Afterward reflect: why did you choose to scoop the sentence in this way? If possible, compare your scooped sentence with a colleague's. Are there similarities? Differences?

"His head leaned back so far that it rested against the face of a defunct mantelpiece clock, and from this position his distraught eyes stared down at Daisy, who was sitting, frightened but graceful, on the edge of a stiff chair" (Fitzgerald, p. 86).

Rationale: _____

_____

_____

Oral Language Experiences: Opportunities for Teacher and Student Talk   (textbook pg. 112)

Teacher talk is a powerful tool to elevate students' vocabulary and sentence use. Although everyday spoken language is less formal, the sentence attuned educator can model the use of complete sentences and incorporate more complex sentence structures into their daily speaking. One effective tool to help students infuse academic language into our oral interactions is sentence stems. Sentence stems, or starters, provide learners with a frame to express their thoughts in speaking or writing. This tool is incredibly useful for learners of all abilities, but especially those with language-based learning differences and non-native English speakers. These learners may struggle to express their ideas in classroom conversations because they are not confident in their ability to respond. Thus, sentence stems provide a scaffold to provide learners with the support necessary to practice the task with the goal of a gradual release of the tool as students grow in confidence.

Sentence starters can be used across subject areas and are easily adapted to any discussion or task. The following table shows a variety of sentence starters that align to various disciplines. They can be adapted for a variety of ages and grade levels.

Math	Science
• _____ has _____ sides/angles. • My first step to solve the problem is . . . • I can check my answer by . . . • _____ is a tool to measure _____. • Variables are used to represent . . .	• My data shows . . . • I can predict _____ because . . . • My hypothesis was correct because . . . • I observed . . . • The cause of _____ is _____. • The effect of _____ is _____.
History/Social Studies	Language Arts
• The _____ . . . led to . . . _____, which led to . . . . • _____ had a significant influence on . . . • Based on the time this was written, I believe . . . . • This evidence shows that . . . , • Living in this time period, people would have experienced	• I predict _____ will happen because . . . . • There are several clues that let us know how _____ felt. One is . . . . • On page _____, it says . . . . • Based on _____, I can infer that . . . . • The key information is . . . . • I think this represents . . . .

When crafting sentence starters, educators should first consider the task and its purpose, specifically: what do you want students to be able to communicate? Next, any relevant vocabulary should be considered. For example, if a history teacher provides the sentence stem, *This primary source document is important to the suffrage movement because . . .*, the educator would want to make sure the terms *primary source document* and *suffrage movement* are familiar to students. Finally, if a sentence starter features a blank to be completed by students, it is important to anticipate potential student responses. Ideally, students should be familiar with the content to be discussed; however, anticipating allows educators to prepare for potential misunderstandings and support students more fully in the lesson.

Try This! Create a list of sentence starters that are appropriate to the discussion or task you are providing the students. Remember to consider the purpose of your task or discussion, relevant vocabulary, and the anticipated student language that will replace the blanks. Keep in mind that activities like sentence starters can be adapted to any subject, age, or grade level.

Task:
Relevant vocabulary:
Potential sentence starters:

Assessment (textbook pgs. 114–115)

Classroom-based assessments allow educators to focus their attention on meeting the learning needs of the class by determining what students know and what is still unclear. Students' real-time reading performance provides an excellent opportunity to informally assess their sentence comprehension and glean this information (Scott & Balthazar, 2013). Educators can use a variety of oral response methods including teacher-crafted text questions and student-generated questions to demonstrate their understanding of or difficulties with targeted sentences. Student responses are particularly helpful as they can provide insight into misunderstandings or gaps in knowledge for the individual or small group of learners.

Students' written work can also provide insight into their sentence skills. For instance, a writing sample can show if a student lacks syntactic variety, writes in fragments, or features limited word choice. Additionally, in a written response students are expected to follow the conventions of punctuation, capitalization, and grammar. This formative information can once again be collected during the learning process and should be followed by opportunities for students to practice and implement feedback. Many of the activities featured in this chapter for processing and working with sentences can also be utilized for assessing student knowledge and skill. They must be differentiated based on student skill level and needs and the nature of the text, but can provide a quick snapshot of student strengths and needs when working at the sentence level.

Try This! Think about the various activities for processing and working with sentences in this chapter. Which of these activities could you envision utilizing as an informal assessment in your classroom?

_____

_____

_____

_____

_____

The Diverse Learner: Learning Challenges & Differences

It is critical that all teachers of reading consider opportunities for differentiation and inclusive practices while planning instruction. Note the examples in the lesson plans already provided.

Support for Students With Learning Disabilities

Here are some additional considerations specific to those students with specific learning challenges.

Students who struggle with reading comprehension may have problems with syntactic awareness and sentence understanding (Nation, 2005). Difficulties with syntax and grammar are often found in individuals with specific language difficulties (Balthazar & Scott, 2018). These students require more explicit instruction based on their demonstration of understanding at the sentence level both orally and in writing. The speech-language pathologist in your setting is an important resource for instructional planning for students with co-occurring language problems.

Support for English Language Learners

Language variations can influence the student's ability to work with both the straightforward and more complex sentences found in academic texts. It is important to be aware of links between oral language ability and spoken language variation for students who speak a second language or a dialect. For example, the use of African American English impacts the syntax of American English (consider the habitual use of "be" in sentences—"he be getting food"). While other languages may have similar syntactic structures, there are also differences (e.g., adjectives often follow the noun in Spanish). Teaching the structure of English sentences and explicitly infusing opportunities for oral/written language skills practice are important.

Putting It All Together: Sentence Comprehension

Take a moment to review and connect again with the contents of the tool set (see Table 4.4). Then, consider what evidence-based activities you might add to each of the columns.

Table 4.4. An instructional tool set for sentence comprehension

Intentional-on-Purpose Instructional Focus	Intentional-on-Purpose Activities	Incidental-on-Purpose Focus	Incidental-on-Purpose Activities
Building Blocks of Sentences • Parts of Speech & their Jobs • Phrases & their Jobs • Clauses & their Jobs	Questioning/Parsing Structured Organizers Sorts (pictures, words) Visual Representations	**Building Blocks of Sentences**	**Reading Experiences** • Shared • Group • Independent • Fluency Connection
The Sentence • The Sentence & their Jobs • The Problem Sentence	Questioning Structured Sentence Organizers Sentence Frames Diagramming Anagrams (word cards) Oral & Written Sentence Building: Combining & Expansion	**The Sentence**	**Oral Experiences** • Oral Response • Student/Teacher Talk **Writing Experiences** • Sentence Instruction • Written Responses
Cohesive Devices • The Role of Cohesive Ties • The Role of Connectives	Questioning Coding	**Writing Connections**	• Written Responses

© 2022 Nancy Hennessy

Voices From the Field

For me, syntax and sentence comprehension was eye-opening. I'm going to spend more time on this.

—A Blueprint Book Study Participant:

Reflect & Connect!

In what ways will these lessons and activities influence your instruction?

Viewing Link

CORE Resources: Seriously, Syntax Matters: Critical Connections to Comprehension (Webinar)
https://www.corelearn.com/resource-posts/syntax-webinar/

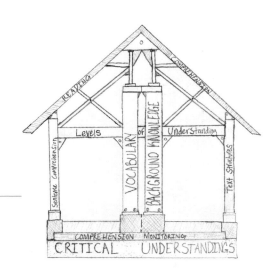

5

Implementing the Blueprint

Text Structures

The focus of this chapter is the contribution of text structure knowledge, including the what, why, and how of instruction, providing multiple instructional examples based on the Reading Comprehension Blueprint framework. Check in and surface current connections to this topic.

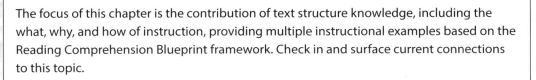

CHECK IN: Connect to current knowledge and practices!

Surface and script what comes to mind in the map (see Figure 5.1) when you think about the what, why, and how of text structures.

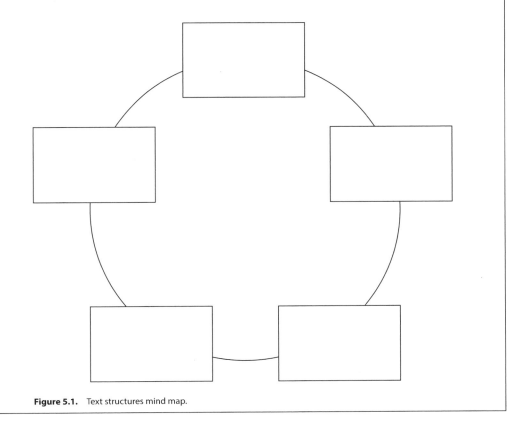

Figure 5.1. Text structures mind map.

Readers who are familiar with the particular structure of the text have several advantages: they know what to expect from different parts of the text, where to search for particular types of information and how the different parts of the text are linked together.

Oakhill et al., 2015, p. 82

What: Definition & Description

The focus in this section is literacy knowledge, specifically genre or text types and their structure, as a critical contributor to skilled reading (Scarborough, 2001). Both fiction and nonfiction genres are represented in text by two broad categories of text structures—narrative and informational (expository). Text structure is the way an author organizes information to achieve a purpose. Knowledge of these different structures is considered a specific type of prior or background knowledge that skilled readers use in constructing meaning (Williams, 2017).

Narrative texts are typically more familiar to many students because of their early exposure to narration through watching television programs and movies and listening to children's literature and the conversations surrounding them (Williams & Pao, 2011). Narrative texts portray a story or sequence of related events—fictional or sometimes nonfictional. Their primary purpose is to entertain while providing an account of a problem or conflict with a series of events leading to a resolution. These events are sequenced temporally or causally and occur in specific settings described by the narrator; events are also described through the portrayal of the characters and their interactions with one another. The primary elements of a story are represented through story grammar, a set of rules that serve to organize the important elements of a story into a logical structure (Dymock, 2005). This provides the schema necessary for the reader to work through the text (e.g., setting, characters, problem, initiating event, responses, climax, resolution).

Informational or expository text requires students to move beyond the familiar story structure and work with less familiar and more complex structures. By the time students reach fourth grade, much of the content they encounter in the classroom is presented in the form of expository text.

The specialized vocabulary, density of details, unfamiliarity of content, and less explicit organization of this text type often present challenges for the reader (Mesmer et al., 2012). The primary purpose of informational or expository text is to inform or instruct by describing, persuading, explaining, or reporting. This text type "conveys information about the natural or social world" (Duke & Bennett-Armistead, 2003, p. 17). The main informational text types usually include:

- Compare and contrast (comparison)

- Problem and solution

- Cause and effect (causation)

- Sequence (chronology)

- Description (categorization, generalization) (Meyer, 1985)

Argumentation (pro and con) has surfaced in the research literature (Newell et al., 2011) and as a writing expectation for students (National Governors Association Center for Best Practices & Council of Chief State School Officers, 2010). The first Common Core Anchor Standard for Writing (K–12) focuses on this type of writing: "CCSS.ELA-LITERACY.CCRA.W: Write opinions/arguments to support claims in an analysis of substantive topics or texts using valid reasoning and relevant and sufficient evidence" (2010, p. 41).

While similar to informational writing, the purpose for argumentative writing is different in that it asks the writer to represent different points of view often, with the intention of changing one's opinion or beliefs.

Why: The Science

Text structures provide a mental map of the conceptual territory represented in both narrative and informational text. Knowledge of these structures is a specialized type of background knowledge that facilitates the reader's ability to understand the information presented in the text. As the reader accesses the meaning of the words and sentences found within the text, they are also grappling with making sense of the connected sentences and paragraphs and underlying meanings that convey essential understandings of the text. Skilled readers automatically access the text structure knowledge that supports working with the organization of the text. This ability to recognize and use the structural features of text is a critical text processing skill. It allows the reader to anticipate how information will be presented and to search for, remember, organize, and process information more strategically and efficiently. For example, a student who is reading a narrative text knows it will include characters, initiating events, a problem or conflict, and so forth. This awareness helps the student identify critical ideas and their relationships to overall meaning. Similarly, a reader's knowledge of informational or expository text structure helps them organize information and complex patterns found in content area texts (Pyle et al., 2017). The reader's prior knowledge of structures and text signals supports their understanding of relationships expressed in the text, and "in this way, the reader is guided to identify the macrostructure of the text and to organize it into a coherent mental representation" (Williams, 2018, p. 1925).

The Institute of Education Sciences (IES) practice guide on improving reading comprehension recommended that educators "teach each student to identify and use the text's organizational structure to comprehend, learn, and remember content" (Shanahan et al., 2010, p. 17). This is based on evidence that students in the early grades who are taught to understand text structure demonstrate larger gains in reading comprehension than those who are not (Reutzel et al., 2005, Williams, 2017).

> *"Readers who can identify the structure of a text are better able to locate the information they need for successful comprehension."*
>
> (Williams, 2017, p. 1)

How: The Design of Instruction

Introduction

Many of us have taught students who struggle to comprehend complex texts. Sometimes these students struggle to prioritize or locate information, and others may have difficulty distinguishing between relevant and irrelevant details. While children are typically exposed to text structures informally through early experiences, it is important that they are directly taught the patterns found within narrative and informational text. As students move through the grades, knowledge of text structure and its corresponding signal words provides students with knowledge of these critical patterns and structures. This not only allows them to focus on key information in the text, but also to locate and retain major themes and ideas. As teachers we need to ensure that our instruction is explicit, intensive, and persistent so we can help students become aware of text organization, a skill that will support them as they read widely across disciplines and classes.

Instruction should initially focus on the basics of text structure including purpose, structure, and features, as well as related signal words as represented in Figures 5.2 and 5.3.

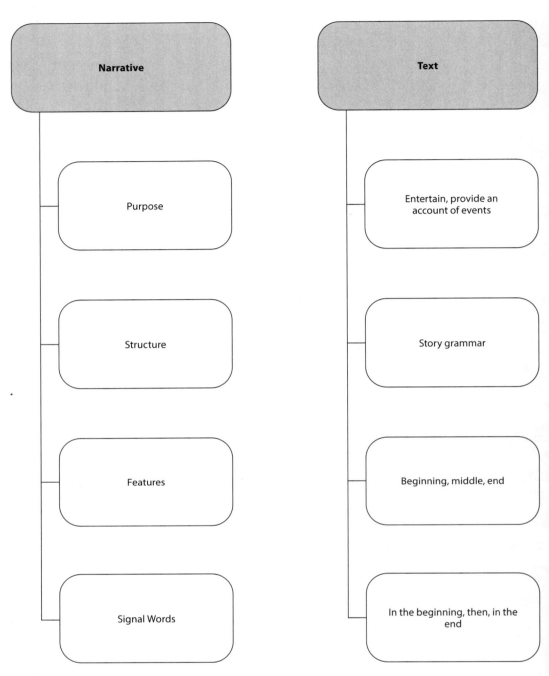

Figure 5.2. Instructional focus for narrative text.

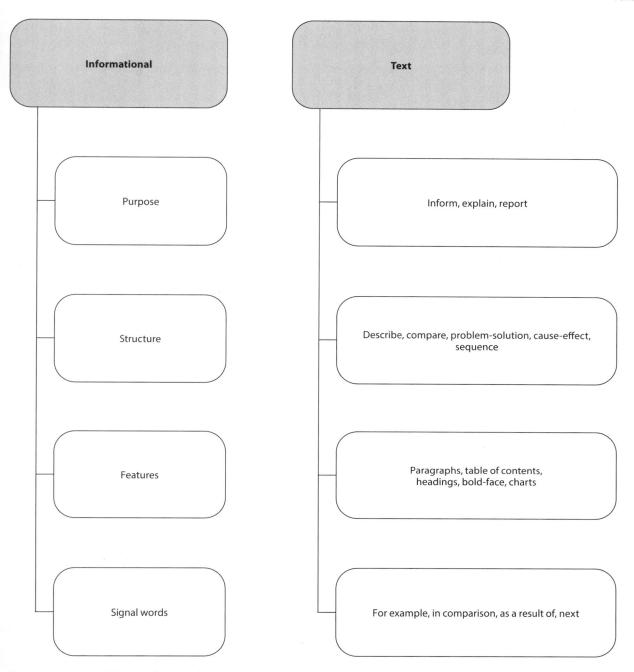

Figure 5.3. Instructional focus for informational text.

General Guidelines

The literature has surfaced general practices that guide explicit instruction and support understanding of how varied structures convey meaning. These include:

- *Use of exemplar texts*—initially choosing texts that clearly contain the features of each text type and, when necessary, adapting texts to student skill level, then moving to more complex texts

- *Use of visual representations*—using visual cues and graphic organizers to scaffold organization of information found in narrative or informational texts

Tips for Success!

As you review the following section, take note of how text structure instruction is intertwined with and involves other language comprehension skills (e.g., vocabulary knowledge and sentence comprehension). While strategies and activities are typically specific to an instructional target, there are approaches that are effective in accomplishing goals related to other contributors to comprehension. Those that include questioning strategies are a good example.

- *Use of text structure strategies*—applying strategies that highlight varied patterns used in narrative or informational text to communicate purpose

- *Attention to signal devices*—understanding how words and phrases cue relationships between ideas and how text features support understanding of the organization of text

- *Planning for effective teacher and student questioning*—incorporating focused questioning before, during, and after instruction to surface, build, and apply knowledge of text structures; teaching students to monitor their own comprehension using these questions

These provide direction for implementing specific strategies and activities designed to support the acquisition and application of text structure knowledge.

(Hennessy, 2020, p. 125)

The Blueprint

Instruction should begin in kindergarten using picture books and read-alouds to build foundational knowledge. As students move through the grades, they will need to become familiar with varied formats for each text type and the characteristics of more complex readings encountered in both English Language Arts (ELA) and other disciplinary settings. The Blueprint surfaces questions that the educator should consider as they prepare instruction (see Figure 5.4).

Blueprint for Comprehension Instruction
TEXT READING
Knowledge
Text Structure
How is the text organized? How and when will you directly teach the purpose, features, and signal words of different genres? How will you teach students to use the structure to understand purpose? To organize and express their understanding?

Figure 5.4. Blueprint questions: Text structure. (*Source:* Hennessy, 2020.)

Intentional Instruction: Lesson Plans & Activities

In this section, we discuss how to create learning activities that focus on effective explicit approaches that follow these guidelines and include direct explanation and instances of teacher modeling, student practice, and opportunities for application with text. We begin with examples of model lesson plans and then move on to instructional activities for first narrative and then informational text structures. Remember that each lesson connects back to its unit's enduring understandings and essential questions to address the overarching goals of student learning, while mapping out specific objectives, activities, and assessments to grow students' understanding of literacy knowledge.

Model Lesson Plans

Comparison of Character Conflict (textbook pgs. 126, 133)

In this first lesson, students will explore two elements of narrative text, character, and conflict. This begins with a review of the four primary types of conflict in literature, followed by an analysis of conflict present in the short stories "The Jacket" by Gary Soto and "Fish Cheeks" by Amy Tan. Notice the use of exemplar texts emphasized in this lesson, as both short stories emphasize character conflict and lessons learned. This lesson is also chunked into two parts: the first part focusing on analysis of conflict in the stories individually, while the second part compares and contrasts the characters' experiences with conflict.

Name: Character Conflict Comparison   **Grade:** Eighth

Preparation for Instruction

Enduring Understandings:

- Individual identities are complex and show themselves in many ways.
- Everyone has multiple identities.
- Societal views can influence individual identity.
- Our identities have similarities and differences.

Essential Questions:

- How do authors develop a character's identity?

Content Objectives:

- Students will be able to:
  o Reflect on the various ways certain social contexts impact our identities.
  o Examine the topic of identity in a variety of stories.

Literacy Objectives:

- Students will be able to:
  o Analyze influences on characters, such as internal and external conflict and motivation, and the way those influences affect the plot.
  o Compare characters and self to create connections and demonstrate understanding of the character within a story.

Resources/Materials:

- "The Jacket" by Gary Soto
- "Fish Cheeks" by Amy Tan
- Conflict chart (for modeling and students)
- Compare and contrast chart (for modeling and students)

Sequence of Events

Purpose: To compare and contrast character conflict in two short stories

Review/prerequisite skills: To participate in this lesson students should have the following prerequisite skills:

- Knowledge of compare/contrast text type
- Knowledge of conflict in literature (character vs. character, character vs. self, character vs. nature, character vs. society)

Teacher and Student Instructional Activities

Lesson opening:

1. Explain to students that today will be analyzing the conflict faced by characters in two short stories: "The Jacket" by Gary Soto and "Fish Cheeks" by Amy Tan
2. Review the term *conflict* with students (a struggle between two people or opposing forces) and the various subtypes:
   a. External conflict: a character struggles with an external force, which could be another character, society, or nature.
   b. Internal conflict: a character's struggle within their own mind. It might be a struggle between opposing needs, wants, or emotions.
3. Have students summarize/recap the short stories "The Jacket" and "Fish Cheeks."

Teacher modeling (Part 1):

4. Display the conflict chart for students. Using teacher think aloud, model completion of one type of conflict from "Fish Cheeks" shown in the following chart.

Type of conflict	Characters involved	What is the conflict?	How is the conflict solved?
Character vs. character	Amy and her mother	Amy's mother invites her crush, Robert, and his family over for a traditional Chinese dinner.	Amy's mother supports her desire to be American by gifting her a miniskirt, but reinforces that she should be proud of her Chinese heritage, too.
Character versus self	Amy	Amy finds her Chinese culture and customs embarrassing. She doesn't want to be different.	Years later Amy comes to understand the purpose of her mother's menu choices and the value of her lesson.

Student-guided practice (Part 1):

5. Walk students through the completion of a type of conflict in the story. Use student feedback to complete this portion of the chart. Teacher questioning can be used here. For example:
   a. Who can tell me another example of conflict in the story?
   b. Is the conflict internal or external? How do you know?
   c. Which character(s) does the conflict impact?
   d. What happens?
   e. How is the conflict resolved?

Independent practice (Part 1):

6. Distribute the character conflict chart to students. Students should complete this organizer for the short story "The Jacket" individually or in small groups. A completed example is shown here. Once complete, students can share their responses with the whole class.

Type of conflict	Characters involved	What is the conflict?	How is the conflict solved?
Character vs. society	Gary and mom, family	Gary wants a black studded biker jacket. Instead, his mother, who works hard to make ends meet, buys him an ugly guacamole-colored, vinyl jacket, which is what his family can afford.	Eventually, Gary embraces the jacket and appreciates what he has.
Character vs. self	Gary	Gary feels the jacket has a negative impact on his life and luck in sixth grade. He lets this impact his behavior.	In the end, Gary takes ownership of his actions and choices, instead of laying blame on the jacket.

Teacher modeling (Part 2):

7. Once the character charts have been completed, reconvene as a whole group.
8. Explain to students that the class will now compare and contrast the conflicts faced by the main characters of each short story.
9. Display the compare and contrast chart for students. Model identifying one similarity between the short stories (shown in the following figure).

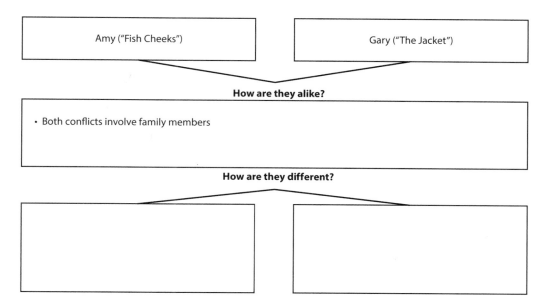

Student-guided practice (Part 2):

10. Instruct students to identify one difference between the stories (see the following example). The teacher can refer students back to the character conflict chart for assistance. Teacher guiding questions can be used to support student thinking. For example:

    a. What is unique about Amy's conflict? How is it different from Gary's?

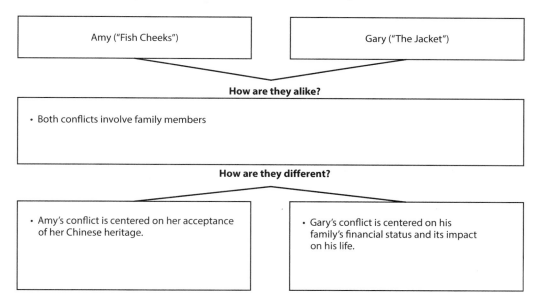

Independent practice (Part 2):

11. Distribute the compare and contrast chart to students. Students can work independently or in small groups to complete the compare and contrast chart. A completed chart is shown here for your reference.

Amy ("Fish Cheeks")	Gary ("The Jacket")

How are they alike?

- Both conflicts involve family members.
- Both characters are teenagers.
- Both Amy and Gary face instances of embarrassment.

How are they different?

• Amy's conflict is centered on her acceptance of her Chinese heritage. • Amy is embarrassed about her family's lack of American manners.	• Gary's conflict is centered on his family's financial status and its impact on his life. • Gary's embarrassment relates to the negative attention he receives because of the jacket.

12. Once complete, students can share their findings with the whole group.
13. If time permits, students can complete an individual written response comparing and contrasting the instances of conflict faced by each character.

Differentiation/Inclusive Instructional Practices:

- To promote student recall, the teacher can display anchor charts that feature the four primary types of conflict: character vs. character, character vs. self, character vs. nature, character vs. society.
- To assist students with discussion and writing, learners can be provided with compare and contrast sentence frames.
- Flexible grouping is used throughout the lesson.

Evidence of Student Learning/Informal Classroom-Based Assessment:

- Completed character chart
- Completed compare and contrast chart
- Participation in whole group lesson
- Discussion
- Compare and contrast written response (if added)

Teacher Reflection in Implementation:

Reflect & Connect!

In what ways is this lesson plan reflective of effective practices for narrative text highlighted in the guidelines and literature?

Informational Text Structure & Purpose: Using the Text Structure Strategy to Identify Informational Text Structures

(textbook pg. 138)

In this lesson, first grade students are learning to use the text structure strategy to identify descriptive text structure. Notice how the lesson and informational passage used aligns to the unit *All About Me!* Although this unit primarily focuses on narrative text, even our youngest learners need exposure to and practice with informational text, which can start in kindergarten. Again, this lesson is chunked into two parts: The first involves a close reading of the text, while the second involves construction of a written response.

Name: What Is a Community? (*All About Me!*) **Grade:** First

Preparation for Instruction

Enduring Understandings:
• I am part of a family and a classroom community.

Essential Questions:
• What is a community?

Content Objectives:
• Students will be able to:
  ○ Describe a community

Literacy Objectives:
• Students will be able to:
  ○ Use a text structure strategy to identify the text structure of an informational text
  ○ Identify the author's purpose after reading

Resources/Materials:
• What is a community? information passage
• Description sentence frames (see Figure 5.18, which is also available as a blank, downloadable worksheet on the Brookes Download Hub; see front matter for instructions to access the downloads that accompany this book)

Sequence of Events

Purpose: Students will use a text structure strategy to identify the text structure of an informational text.

Review/Prerequisite Skills: To participate in this lesson, students should have the following prerequisite skills/ knowledge:

• Authors and texts have specific purposes.
• Texts have a main idea that an author wants to express.

- Knowledge of the signal words aligned to descriptive text.
- Ability to understand descriptive text at the sentence level.

Teacher and Student Instructional Activities:

Lesson opening:

1. Explain to students that today we will be learning a strategy to work with informational text.
2. Remind students that authors write informational text to inform, explain, or report. Our passage today will explain, or describe, what a community is.

PART 1

Teacher modeling:

3. Display the passage *What is a community?* for students.

> *What is a community? A community is a group of people living and working together. A community can include big groups of people or small ones. People in a community share a common location, like a county, town, or neighborhood. They may also share common interests and perspectives. This might include a shared culture, like celebrations, language, or traditions, or shared interests like hobbies. Finally, people in a community work together toward a common goal. For example, one goal of a school community is to collaborate and learn together.*

4. Read the paragraph one time for students to get the general gist.
5. During the second read, explain to students that they will be on the lookout for any signal words that can help alert them to the text structure of this passage.
6. Do this with the first four sentences. Language that signals the reader to text type is:
   a. "A _____ is a . . ." (This sentence structure is typically used to describe something in informational text.)
   b. Examples of what a community might look like: big or small groups of people; might be in a county, town, or neighborhood.

Student-guided practice:

7. Instruct students to review the next two sentences with teacher guidance to identify the signal words and cues that show descriptive text. Examples include:
   a. Use of the signal word *also*
   b. Examples of what shared interests and perspectives might look like: celebrations, traditions, language

Independent practice:

8. Finally, students should work as partners to determine which signals and cues are provided in the last two sentences. A completely marked-up passage is provided.
9. Once finished, have students reconvene as a whole group and share their findings.

> *What is a community? <u>A community is a</u> group of people living and working together. A community can include <u>big groups of people or small ones.</u> People in a community share a <u>common location</u>, like a <u>county, town, neighborhood</u>, or <u>school</u>. They may also share <u>common interests and perspectives</u>. This might include a shared <u>culture</u>, like <u>celebrations, language,</u> or <u>traditions</u>, or shared <u>interests like hobbies</u>. Finally, people in a community <u>work together</u> toward a common goal. <u>For example,</u> one goal of a school community is to collaborate and learn together.*

PART 2

Teacher modeling:

10. Display the sentence frame: A _____ is a _____.
11. Remind students that we have found evidence that the author's purpose for this passage is to describe a community. We are going to use the sentence frame above to sum up the text into its main idea.
12. Model completion of the sentence frame for students. A completed example could be:
    a. A community is a place where people share common interests and perspectives and work together toward a mutual goal.

Student-guided practice:

13. Tell students that they are now going to find some details to support this.
14. Display the sentence frame: One detail that supports this is _____.
15. Guide student responses in completing this frame. A completed example could be:
    a. One detail that supports this is people in a community can have a common culture and participate in shared celebrations, languages, and traditions.

Independent practice:

16. Finally, students can work as partners or in small groups to complete one more detail sentence frame.
17. As students work together, the teacher can circulate in the room and support partners or groupings as needed.
18. Once finished, students can come back to the whole group to share their ideas.

Differentiation/Inclusive Instructional Practices:

- Have students work at the sentence level if they are struggling to identify descriptive text structure at the passage level.
- Provide additional instruction in descriptive signal words.
- Use a descriptive web to display information in a visual manner.

Evidence of Student Learning/Informal Classroom-Based Assessment:

- Participation in whole-group lesson
- Participation in partnerships or small groups
- Classroom discussion
- Completed sentence frames

Teacher Reflection in Implementation:

Reflect & Connect!

In what ways is this lesson plan reflective of effective practices for informational text highlighted in the guidelines and literature?

Intentional Instructional Activities for Narrative Text Structure

Activities for Story Structure and Elements

(textbook pgs. 125–128)

Instruction centered on narrative text structure is a natural starting point in the classroom as many youngsters are familiar with narration through early exposure to read-alouds, television programs, and movies, as well as conversations held with and around them at home. However, it is important to note that early experiences vary and that not all children have the same exposure to narrative story structures. Narrative story structure, or story grammar, is a feature unique to narrative text and includes the elements of *setting, characters, problem or conflict, sequence of events, outcome or resolution,* and *theme*. These elements are often differentiated depending on the age and developmental readiness of the learner. For instance, first grade students reading the book *Last Stop on Market Street* by Matt de la Peña would be tasked to keep track of basic elements of story grammar, highlighted in the following chart.

Story element	Description	Examples in the text
Character(s):	Who is this story about?	CJ, Nana, passengers on the bus
Setting	Where and when does this story take place?	The bus, the neighborhood
Problem or purpose	What is the main character's problem or what do they want to achieve?	CJ wonders why he and his Nana have to take the bus every Sunday to the soup kitchen, instead of driving in a car like his friend.
Sequence of events	How does the character try to solve their problem or achieve their goal?	CJ gives up his seat to a blind man, watches butterflies in a jar held by a woman, sees a tattooed man on his mobile phone, and asks a musician to play his guitar.
Outcome	What happens at the end of the story? How does the character end up?	Nana helps CJ notice the beauty of their weekly routine as they travel through their neighborhood.
Themes	What lesson(s) did the character learn?	Finding the beauty in everything and everyone; appreciating differences and what we have

One particularly useful strategy is the C-SPACE mnemonic developed by Steve Graham and Karen Harris. Designed to enhance students' self-regulated strategy development (SRSD; see Chapter 7 for more on SRSD), C-SPACE is a writing strategy that highlights the elements of a good story including *Character, Setting, Purpose* or *Problem, Actions, Conclusion* and *Emotions*. While designed for story writing, this strategy is an excellent introduction to foundational story elements used by authors. Furthermore, the SRSD model has had many powerful impacts for students with learning disabilities including knowledge of grammar as well as generalization across settings, and overall maintenance of the skill over time (Graham & Harris, 2003).

Tips for Success!

Considerations for Students From Culturally and Linguistically Diverse Backgrounds

The narrative stories taught in school are commonly based on European storytelling traditions. Although many children will come to school with an understanding of this narrative structure, we cannot assume that all learners possess this knowledge. This is especially true of students from diverse linguistic and cultural backgrounds who may utilize storytelling traditions that differ from narratives based on European story structure. Thus, educators must explicitly teach narrative story structure and allow students to dictate or write stories that come from their own culture (McCabe, 1997). By doing so we validate the voices of the students we teach, while motivating and engaging learners from all backgrounds.

Table 5.1. Freytag Pyramid story structure

Stage	Description
Exposition	The story's introduction. Here the main characters, setting, and source of the conflict are explained.
Rising action	The series of events leading up to the climax. These events are used to build story tension.
Climax	Where the "turn in the story" takes place. Story conflict peaks and character outcomes are decided.
Falling action	Where the outcome of the climax is explored. Can be tricky to write since the main conflicts begin to be wrapped up and themes are explored while moving the story towards resolution.
Resolution	The end of the story. You learn what happens to the characters after the conflict is resolved.

As students progress through the grades, additional elements can be explored. For example, students in middle and high school may be familiar with the Freytag Pyramid devised by 19th-century playwright Gustav Freytag. Using this model, story structure is broken into five stages including *exposition, rising action, climax, falling action,* and *resolution*. Notice how the stages, highlighted in Table 5.1, build upon and deepen the foundational terminology used to introduce students to narrative story structure.

These terms represent a story arc as shown in Figure 5.5. In this example, middle school students used the Freytag Pyramid to map out and analyze the short story "Fish Cheeks" by Amy Tan.

Pairing the elements of story structure with visuals is an effective way to help students clearly picture a narrative's organization, while also assisting with student retell. As students progress through the grades, additional advanced elements such as theme, symbolism, foreshadowing, and figurative language use can be included; however, like the basic elements, these advanced components will need to be directly taught.

Author Amy Tan uses many advanced literary elements to enhance her short story "Fish Cheeks," as shown in Table 5.2. This deeper analysis allows students to understand that the choices authors make are intentional, including the use of specific words, ideas, and structures. For example, author Tan intentionally chose fish cheeks to represent pride of one's culture and heritage, while her gifted miniskirt represents the desire to be American. This symbolism reinforces the central theme: *to be proud of who you are* and *that identity is multifaceted*.

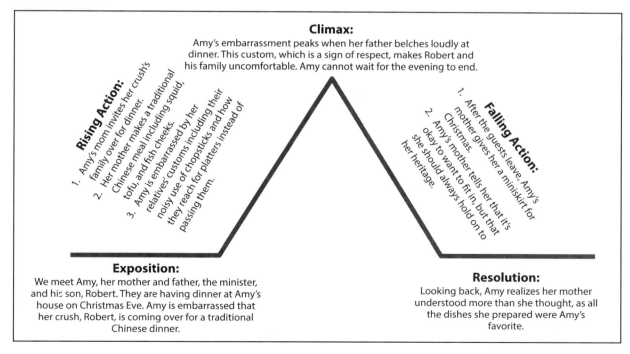

Figure 5.5. Sample Freytag Pyramid mapping and analyzing the short story "Fish Cheeks" by Amy Tan. (*Source:* Tan, 1987.)

Table 5.2. Literary elements from Amy Tan's "Fish Cheeks"

Literary element	Description	Evidence in the text
Theme	The story's lesson	To be proud of who you are.
Point of view	The narrator of the story	Use of the word "I" shows first-person point of view, so Amy is telling the story.
Symbolism	Symbols used to represent important ideas and relationships	Fish cheeks are a symbol of Chinese culture, while the miniskirt is a symbol of American culture.
Foreshadowing	Advanced hints	At the beginning of the story, Amy worries that her family will embarrass her.
Figurative language	Use of metaphor, simile, alliteration, hyperbole, personification, etc.	"He was not Chinese, but as white as Mary in the manger." (simile) "A plate of squid, their backs crisscrossed with knife markings so they resembled bicycle tires." (metaphor)
Imagery	Descriptive language used to appeal to the five senses	"She was pulling black veins out of fleshy prawns." "appalling mounds of raw food" "slimy cod with bulging eyes"

Source: Tan, 1987.

Try This! Using a well-known childhood story, map out its story elements in the following table. Stories could include *The Three Little Pigs*, *Little Red Riding Hood*, *Jack and the Beanstalk*, and so forth. Once you've recorded the basic story elements, reflect: does this story include any of the advanced elements discussed in this lesson? If so, which ones did your story include?

My Story: _____

Story element	Description	Examples in the text
Character(s):	Who is this story about?	
Setting	Where and when does this story take place?	
Problem or purpose	What is the main character's problem or what do they want to achieve?	
Sequence of events	How does the character try to solve their problem or achieve their goal?	
Outcome	What happens at the end of the story? How does the character end up?	
Themes	What lesson(s) did the character learn?	

Potential Response:

My Story: Goldilocks & the Three Bears

Story element	Description	Examples in the text
Character(s):	Who is this story about?	Goldilocks, Papa Bear, Mama Bear, and Baby Bear
Setting	Where and when does this story take place?	The three bears' house in the woods
Problem or purpose	What is the main character's problem or what do they want to achieve?	Goldilocks went into the bears' house and used their belongings without permission.
Sequence of events	How does the character try to solve their problem or achieve their goal?	Goldilocks ate their porridge, sat in their chairs (breaking Baby Bear's chair), and slept in their beds.
Outcome	What happens at the end of the story? How does the character end up?	At the end of the story, the Bear family discovers Goldilocks asleep in Baby Bear's bed. She awakens, jumps out of bed, and runs away.
Themes	What lesson(s) did the character learn?	The lesson of the story is to respect others' property and that your actions have an impact on others.

As we've seen, visual representations are essential when introducing students to the elements of narrative text. However, visuals can also be used to help students internalize, practice, and process understanding of this text type. Graphic organizers are one useful tool that can be leveraged to improve students' comprehension of narrative story structure and inform their writing as well. One such organizer is a story map.

Story maps provide students with a framework to keep track of narrative story elements. Some maps include basic elements like beginning, middle, and end as highlighted in Figure 5.6. In this example, writing is used to recall what happened at the start, middle, and end of the book *Frederick* by Leo Leoni; however, depending upon their ability, students could use drawings and pictures to capture their thinking, as well.

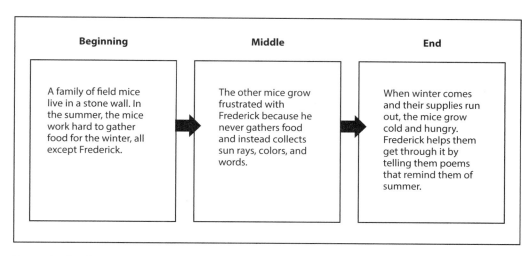

Figure 5.6.   Sample story map for Leo Leoni's *Frederick*. (*Source:* Lionni, 1967.)

The second story map, shown in Figure 5.7, highlights the same story, *Frederick*, but includes more sophisticated elements such as plot and theme. As we've seen previously, an advanced option, such as the Freytag Pyramid, is a great graphic organizer to utilize with students in middle and high school. Thus, students of varying ages and abilities can be offered different ways to organize and express their understanding of story structure and elements in a visual manner.

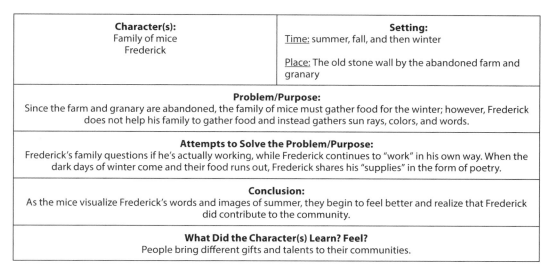

Figure 5.7.   Advanced story map of Leo Leoni's *Frederick*. (*Source:* Lionni, 1967.)

Another useful visual tool to pair with narrative text is the use of *story frames*. Story frames support students' understanding of how story content fits into narrative structure by providing them with a frame to follow. Take a look at the basic story frame in Figure 5.8, which can be used to help students express their thoughts in speaking and writing.

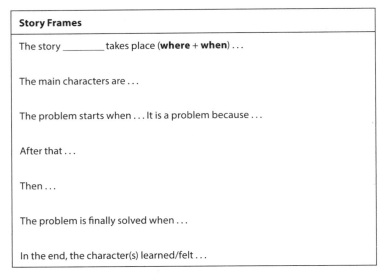

Story Frames
The story _____ takes place (**where + when**) . . .
The main characters are . . .
The problem starts when . . . It is a problem because . . .
After that . . .
Then . . .
The problem is finally solved when . . .
In the end, the character(s) learned/felt . . .

Figure 5.8.   Basic story frame template.

Story frames are a wonderful support for students of all abilities, but especially those with language-based learning disabilities and ELLs, since this tool can be used to reinforce academic language and sentence structure, as well. This format can also be adapted for older students by adding in advanced elements like conflict and theme as shown in the example in Figure 5.9 for the short story "Fish Cheeks."

Story frame for "Fish Cheeks" by Amy Tan
The story **"Fish Cheeks"** *takes place* **on Christmas Eve at Amy's parents' house.**
The main characters are **Amy, her mother and father, the minister, and his son, Robert.**
The conflict starts when **Robert, Amy's crush, is invited over for a traditional Chinese meal.** *This conflict is an example of* **person versus self** *because* **Amy feels embarrassed about her heritage and traditions.**
At dinner . . . **Amy is embarrassed by her relatives' customs including their noisy use of chopsticks and how they reach for platters instead of passing them.**
Then . . . **Amy's embarrassment peaks when her father belches loudly at dinner. This custom, which is a sign of respect, makes Robert and his family uncomfortable.**
Afterward . . . **Amy's mother gives her a miniskirt for Christmas. Amy's mother tells her that it's okay to want to fit in, but that she should always hold on to her heritage.**
In the end, **Amy** *learned* **her mother understood more than she thought she did, as all the dishes she prepared were Amy's favorites.**

Figure 5.9.   Sample story frame for "Fish Cheeks" by Amy Tan. (*Source:* Tan, 2003.)

Finally, *character mapping* is another great way to help students organize and understand story characters in a visual way. Characters are an incredibly important story element, as they serve as the driving force for story action. Characters also adapt and change throughout a text, so character mapping can not only serve as an important tool to describe story characters, but also allows learners to analyze their actions and behaviors over time. The first example (see Figure 5.10) shows a basic character map for the story *Frederick*. Here students are tasked with describing Frederick, his actions, thoughts and feelings, and words.

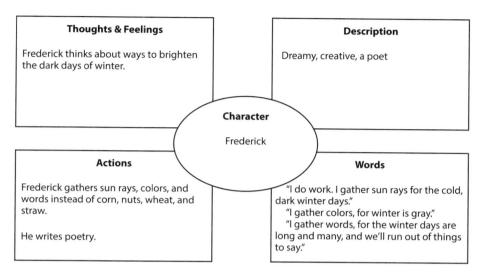

Figure 5.10. Basic character map for Leo Leoni's *Frederick*. (*Source:* Lionni, 1967.)

Like story maps, character maps can be adapted to include more advanced elements. For instance, older learners can be tasked with tracking character traits to watch for growth and change over time. This is highlighted in the map in Figure 5.11, which shows how Amy changes as a result of story events in "Fish Cheeks."

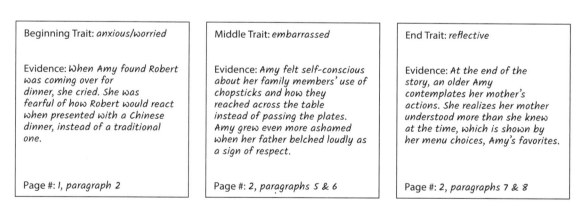

Figure 5.11. Advanced character map for Amy Tan's "Fish Cheeks".

Try This!   Now it's your turn to try! Using a character from the well-known childhood story used previously, complete the following character chart. Once finished, reflect: how can you incorporate the use of visual representations into your work with students?

My Story: _____

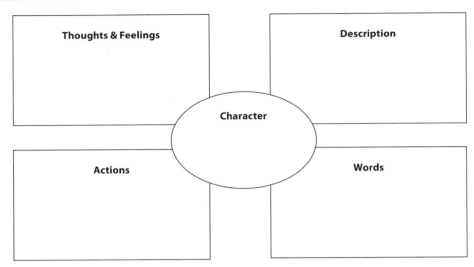

Potential Response:

My Story: Goldilocks & the Three Bears

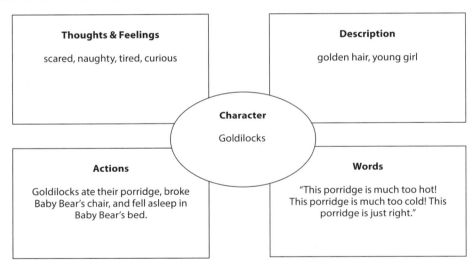

Working With Signal Words for Narrative Text   (textbook pgs. 129–130)

Narrative text structure also provides students with the opportunity to practice signal words. Narrative signal words typically align to the beginning–middle–end structure, which signals the reader to the passage of time. Consider the traditional opening of many fairy tales, "Once upon a time . . ." or "A long time ago . . .," both of which are used to cue the reader to when the story takes place. However, these important words and phrases can be seen throughout literature, with authors such as F. Scott Fitzgerald using them as shown in the following sentence from *The Great Gatsby*: "An hour *later* the front door opened nervously, and Gatsby, in a white flannel suit, silver shirt, and gold-colored tie, hurried in" (Fitzgerald, pg. 65).

Teachers can draw attention to signal words by highlighting their use during class read-alouds and while students work with narrative texts. Additional activities, such as the sorting task shown in Figure 5.12, can help students develop an understanding of where these important words show up within a story.

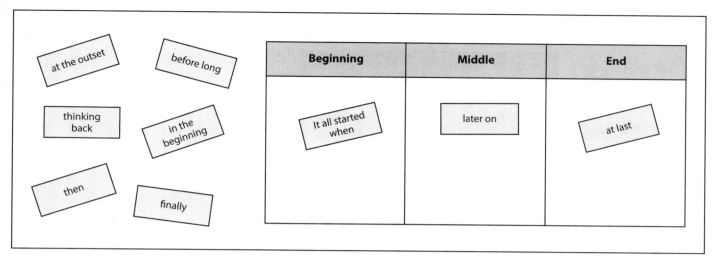

Figure 5.12. Sample sorting task.

Once students have built an awareness of narrative transition words, they can begin to apply these words to their own speaking and writing. The chart shown in Figure 5.13 features a series of sentence starters that include signal words aligned to the structure of narrative text. Initially, these starters can be used to aid students in retelling key parts of the text, and later utilized as a concrete support for writing their own stories. For example, our model unit, *Who Am I?*, includes a literacy goal that students will compose a personal narrative that develops a real experience or event in their lives. After using this chart to practice their retells, students could use it as a resource to assist them in crafting their own narratives.

Story Element	Sentence Starters	Example
Exposition (Beginning)	In the beginning . . . It all started when . . . At the outset . . . Initially . . .	<u>It all started</u> when Amy's parents invited her crush, Robert, and his family over for a traditional Chinese dinner on Christmas Eve.
Rising Action (Kick-Off Event)	Meanwhile . . . During . . . Next . . . Throughout . . .	<u>During</u> the meal, Amy was embarrassed by her family members' loud use of chopsticks.
Climax (Middle)	All of a sudden . . . As soon as . . . Immediately . . . All at once . . .	<u>All of a sudden</u>, Amy's father belched loudly at dinner as a sign of respect, causing her embarrassment to grow even more.
Falling Action (Wrap up)	Eventually . . . Some time after . . . Later on . . . Then . . .	<u>Some time after</u> the guests departed, Amy's mother gifted her with a miniskirt, a symbol of Amy's desire to be American; however, she told Amy that she must always be proud of her heritage.
Resolution (Conclusion)	In the end . . . Thinking back . . . From that day on . . . Finally . . .	<u>Thinking back</u> on that day, Amy realized that her mother understood more than she thought as the dinner featured all of Amy's favorite foods.

Figure 5.13. Sentence starters with signal words for narrative texts.

Try This! Using your well-known childhood story from earlier, complete the following table. After you've finished, consider the following questions: How did an activity like this one assist you with your comprehension of your chosen tale? How can you use a strategy like this to support BOTH students' comprehension of narrative texts and their writing?

My Story: _____

Story element	Sentence starters	Example
Exposition (beginning)	In the beginning . . . It all started when . . . At the outset . . . Initially . . .	
Rising Action (kick-off event)	Meanwhile . . . During . . . Next . . . Throughout . . .	
Climax (middle)	All of a sudden . . . As soon as . . . Immediately . . . All at once . . .	
Falling action (wrap up)	Eventually . . . Some time after . . . Later on . . . Then . . .	
Resolution (conclusion)	In the end . . . Thinking back . . . From that day on . . . Finally . . .	

Potential response:

My Story: Goldilocks & The Three Bears

Story element	Sentence starters	Example
Exposition (beginning)	In the beginning . . . It all started when . . . At the outset . . . Initially . . .	It all started when Goldilocks went into the Bears' house when they were not home.
Rising Action (kick-off event)	Meanwhile . . . During . . . Next . . . Throughout . . .	During her exploration of their house, she ate their porridge and tried sitting in each of their chairs.
Climax (middle)	All of a sudden . . . As soon as . . . Immediately . . . All at once . . .	As soon as she sat in Baby Bear's chair, it broke, so she decided to take a nap in his bed instead.
Falling action (wrap up)	Eventually . . . Some time after . . . Later on . . . Then . . .	Later on that day, the Bear family came home. They discovered their porridge eaten, their chairs sat in and broken, and a little girl sleeping in one of their beds!
Resolution (conclusion)	In the end . . . Thinking back . . . From that day on . . . Finally . . .	In the end, Goldilocks awoke from her slumber and upon seeing Mama, Papa, and Baby Bear, ran away!

As we have discussed previously, questioning is an incredibly powerful tool, especially when combined with other strategies such as graphic organizers. Questioning can also stand alone and be used as a comprehension check or to help guide student retells or summaries. Table 5.3 highlights questions aligned to various story elements at both the basic and advanced levels. These questions can be adapted to the text itself and can be asked before, during, or after reading.

Teacher-directed questioning helps students to engage actively with text and can reinforce their participation. Effective questioning can also help students work with the text at multiple levels. At the most basic level, teacher questioning helps students to recall or explain story events. However, more sophisticated questions help students make connections across texts or ideas and even appraise character actions. Informed educators design effective questions by previewing the text and reflecting on the following steps:

1. Consider the focus of the read-aloud/story/chapter: what are your goals for student understanding? How can you align your questions to the ideas you want students to walk away with?

2. What levels of questioning are you targeting? Are you tapping into more basic levels (identify, describe, explain), more advanced thinking (analyze, justify, compare/contrast), or a combination of both?

3. Which questioning strategies have you used? For example, did you include both closed- and open-ended questions? Closed-ended questions can provide a quick check-in on student understanding of information that can be located easily within the story, while open-ended questions provide opportunities for discussion and debate.

4. Finally, have you thought about potential student responses? This allows you to anticipate student difficulties and misunderstandings and apply support as needed.

Table 5.3.   Story element questions

Elements	Basic questions	Advanced questions
Setting	Where did the story take place? When did it happen? Does the setting change?	What might the setting foreshadow? How does the setting contribute to mood? What language does the author use to describe the setting? Does the setting affect the conflict?
Character	Who is the story about? What is _____ like? What is _____'s physical appearance? Personality traits? What are _____'s values and motives?	Who is the protagonist? Who is the antagonist? How does the antagonist get in the way of what the protagonist needs or wants? How does the external world affect the character's internal world? How do the characters' internal emotions affect their understanding of the external world?
Problem or purpose	What is the main character's problem? What does the character need or want? What "kicks off" or starts this problem?	What type of conflict does the main character face? Describe the conflict. How does the conflict affect the context? What does the conflict reveal about the character's values and motives?
Sequence of events	What did _____ do about _____? What will _____ do now? What would you do now?	What motifs are represented throughout the text?
Outcome	How did _____ solve the problem? How did _____ achieve the goal?	What events led to the outcome? How did the process influence the outcome? Who wins? Who loses? Explain. What has changed since the beginning of the story? Explain.
Theme	What is the story's major point or big idea? What is the story's moral or lesson? What did _____ learn in the end?	What story actions contribute to theme? Explain the main themes present in the text.
Symbolism	Identify an example of symbolism in the story. What does this symbol represent?	What is the symbol's significance to the main characters? Why do you think the author chose to use this symbol?
Point of view	Who is the narrator in the story? What narrative point of view is used in the story (i.e., first-person, second-person, third-person limited, or third-person omniscient)?	How does the narrator's point of view impact the events in the narrative? Can we trust the narrator's version of events? Are they reliable? What is the tone of the narrator's point of view (i.e., is it humorous, disengaged, hopeful)? Why do you think the author chose to write the story from this point of view?

Table 5.4. Question-Answer-Relationship Question Stems

In the book		In my head	
Right There:	*Think & Search:*	*Author & Me:*	*On My Own:*
The answer is found in the text in one place.	The reader must search for the answer in different parts of the text. You must "think and search" to put this information together.	The answer is not in the text. The reader must combine their own knowledge with information from the text to craft a response.	The answer is not in the text. The reader must use their own experiences to craft a response.
• Who?	• Retell	• Predict what will happen next.	• How would you feel if . . . ?
• What?	• Summarize	• Why did the author . . . ?	• Based on the story/novel/ chapter title, what do you predict might happen?
• Where?	• Give examples of	• Do you agree with . . . ?	• Have you ever . . . ?
• When?	• Compare and contrast (characters, setting, etc.)	• What is the author's message?	
• How?		• What is the theme/moral/ lesson of . . . ?	
• Define			
• Name			
• List			

Source: Raphael & Au, 2005.

Student-generated questioning is also a critical part of comprehension as it teaches students to become independent and active readers. In fact, the National Reading Panel (2000), found that teaching students to generate questions while reading had the strongest scientific evidence to improve students' comprehension. Question generation allows students to engage with the text "by making queries that lead to the construction of better memory representations" (National Institute of Health, 2000, p. 87). Furthermore, student-generated questioning also increases learners' awareness of whether they understand what is being read since it allows them to clarify unclear portions of the text and/or draw attention to puzzling information.

The Question-Answer-Relationship (QAR) strategy helps students ask and answer their own questions to promote higher levels of literacy. QAR develops a common questioning language for teachers and students alike that includes four different question types, ranging in levels of complexity (Raphael & Au, 2005). This includes answers that can be found in the book (Right There and Think & Search) and in the reader's head (Author & Me and On My Own). Table 5.4 highlights these categories of questions along with potential question stems to help students generate their own queries about the narrative texts they read. Students must be provided with direct instruction of this strategy, including instances of teacher modeling and opportunities for practice, prior to writing questions on their own.

Try This!   Now it's your turn to practice using the QAR strategy. Using your well-known childhood story, craft your own QAR questions. What did you notice about this process? How did crafting your own questions support your comprehension?

My Story: _____

Question type	My example
In the Book	
Think & Search	
Author & Me	
On My Own	

Potential Responses:

My Story: Goldilocks & the Three Bears

Question type	My example
In the Book	*What color hair did Goldilocks have?*
	Whose bed was "just right"?
	What did the Bear family have for breakfast?
Think & Search	*Why was Baby Bear upset when he got home?*
	How did Goldilocks describe Mama Bear's belongings?
Author & Me	*How would you describe Goldilocks?*
	Is Goldilocks a good person? Why or why not?
	What is the lesson of Goldilocks & the Three Bears?
On My Own	*How would you feel if someone broke one of your belongings?*
	Why is it important to respect others' property?
	How can we show respect for other people's belongings?

Intentional Instructional Activities for Informational Text Structure

Working with informational text requires students to move beyond the familiar structures of narrative stories to work with more complex structures. It's not surprising that this text type is more challenging for students, as it requires them to work with multiple text structures each with their own organization and purpose. This section explores strategies for working with informational text. We discuss ways to differentiate and adapt based on student age and developmental readiness.

> ### Tips for Success!
>
> #### A Note About Argument
>
> As mentioned previously, the Common Core State Standards (CCSS) place a heavy emphasis on argument writing and deem this skill necessary for college and career readiness. In fact, knowledge of argument is described as being "important for the literate, educated person living in the diverse, information-rich environment of the twenty-first century" (National Governors Association Center for Best Practices & Council of Chief State School Officers, 2010, p. 25). Typically, however, students spend less time reading and unpacking this genre due to a focus on narrative and other informational texts in school. Thus, it is important to create opportunities where students develop the ability to understand the content and organization of this genre since understanding and expressing sound arguments is a critical skill needed for life beyond school.

The Importance of Teaching Basic Paragraph Structure   (textbook pgs. 132–133)

Understanding of basic paragraph structure serves as foundational knowledge for working with informational text structures. Typically, a basic paragraph consists of a topic sentence that expresses the main idea, detail sentences that support the topic, and a closing or concluding statement that wraps up the paragraph. Work with paragraph structures usually happens in writing; however, knowledge of basic paragraph structure is critical to comprehending informational text as well as synthesizing what has been read.

One such strategy that taps into how a paragraph conveys meaning is the RAP paraphrasing strategy (Schumaker, Denton, & Deshler, 1984). It consists of three steps:

Read a paragraph.

Ask yourself about the main idea and details in the paragraph.

Put the main idea into your own words.

Initially, these steps must be explicitly taught to students with the goal of independent application when reading on their own. The RAP strategy is beneficial to all students, but especially those with learning disabilities as the RAP approach teaches them to self-monitor their own comprehension by asking the question, *What are the main idea and details in this paragraph?* prior to paraphrasing. This scaffold helps students to detect and also remember key information in a given expository paragraph (Hagaman et al., 2012a, 2012b, as cited by Leidig et al., 2018).

Consider how the high school passage from the article "The Green Book: Traveling the Jim Crow South" could be used to apply the RAP strategy (ReadWorks, 2022).

Read	*In the 1930s, Victor Green, a Black American postal worker, lived in the New York City neighborhood of Harlem. Harlem was a Black American community, yet even in that neighborhood, there were places where Green and other Black people were not welcomed. One such place was the Cotton Club, a popular nightclub where famous Black Americans performed while people of color were not allowed in the audience. Green decided to compile a list of places in New York that were friendly to Black people who lived in and traveled to the city. In 1936, inspired by* The Jewish Vacation Guide *for Jewish travelers, Green published* The Negro Motorist Green Book. *The 15-page guide listed hotels, restaurants, clubs, drug stores, beauty salons, and other businesses in New York.*
Ask	Why Victor Green created the Green Book (to help Black people find businesses in New York that were friendly to them)
Put	Victor Green created the Green Book to help Black Americans identify places that welcomed and were friendly to Black people in 1930s New York.

Another strategy that can be used to help students summarize after reading is getting the gist (Vaughn et al., 2013; Cunningham, 1982). This strategy can be used across content areas and is a great tool to help students identify the most important content in a passage or paragraph. With the gist strategy students are instructed to:

- Read the passage or paragraph provided.
- Using what you read, answer the 5Ws (who, what, where, when, why) and 1H (how) questions.
- Restate the meaning of the paragraph or passage in 40 words or less.

Notice how the passage from "The Green Book: Traveling the Jim Crow South" has been analyzed using the gist strategy (ReadWorks, 2022).

Read the passage:
In the 1930s, Victor Green, a Black American postal worker, lived in the New York City neighborhood of Harlem. Harlem was a Black American community, yet even in that neighborhood, there were places where Green and other Black people were not welcomed. One such place was the Cotton Club, a popular nightclub where famous Black Americans performed while people of color were not allowed in the audience. Green decided to compile a list of places in New York that were friendly to Black people who lived in and traveled to the city. In 1936, inspired by The Jewish Vacation Guide *for Jewish travelers, Green published* The Negro Motorist Green Book. *The 15-page guide listed hotels, restaurants, clubs, drug stores, beauty salons, and other businesses in New York.*
Answer the 5Ws and 1H questions:
Who: Victor Green
What: published the Green Book
Where: in New York City
When: 1930s
Why: to help Black people identify places that were welcoming to Black folks
How: by compiling a list of Black-friendly businesses
Write the gist of what you have read in 40 words or less:
In the 1930s, Victor Green compiled the Green Book, a list of Black-friendly businesses in New York City, to help Black people identify places that were welcoming and safe.
30 words total

Try This! Take a moment and apply what you've learned about the gist strategy to the paragraph provided here. After you've finished, reflect: how can a strategy like this one be useful in your classroom practices?

Read the passage:
Prokaryotic cells first appeared around 3.5 to 4.5 billion years ago. These single-celled organisms feature a simple structure and lack a nucleus and membrane-bound organelles. A prokaryote's DNA is typically located in a region called the nucleoid that floats in the cell's cytoplasm. These cells are also much smaller than their eukaryotic counterparts because they have less DNA overall. Prokaryotes make up cells in the Bacteria and Archaea domains, while all other domains on Earth are made up of eukaryotic cells. However, prokaryotic organisms are abundant on Earth, and you can find them almost everywhere! In fact, they are an essential part of Earth's biome because they recycle nutrients and assist with metabolic processes.
Answer the 5Ws and 1H questions:
Who: What: Where: When: Why: How:
Write the gist of what you have read in 40 words or less:
   _____ **words total**

Potential answer:

Read the passage:
Prokaryotic cells first appeared around 3.5 to 4.5 billion years ago. These single-celled organisms feature a simple structure and lack a nucleus and membrane-bound organelles. A prokaryote's DNA is typically located in a region called the nucleoid which floats in the cell's cytoplasm. These cells are also much smaller than their eukaryotic counterparts because they have less DNA overall. Prokaryotes make up cells in the Bacteria and Archaea domains, while all other domains on Earth are made up of eukaryotic cells. However, prokaryotic organisms are abundant on Earth, and you can find them almost everywhere! In fact, they are an essential part of Earth's biome because they recycle nutrients and assist with metabolic processes.
Answer the 5Ws and 1H questions:
Who: prokaryotes   What: single-celled organism that lack a nucleus   Where: are found almost everywhere   When: first seen 3.5 to 4.5 billion years ago   Why: are an essential part of the Earth's biome   How: because they recycle nutrients and assist with metabolic processes
Write the gist of what you have read in 40 words or less:
Prokaryotes, which first appeared on Earth 3.5 to 4.5 billion years ago, are single-celled organisms that lack a nucleus. They are found almost everywhere and play an essential role in recycling nutrients and assisting with metabolic processes.   **37** **words total**

Use of Visual Representations for Informational Text (textbook pgs. 138–140)

The use of visual representations, like graphic organizers, is another powerful tool to use when working with informational text. Graphic organizers can be used before, during, and after reading and must be modeled for students, so they can learn to apply this strategy independently. Like with narrative, graphic organizers for informational text can be adapted across age and grade levels, as we will explore later in this section.

Before students read a given passage, the teacher should display the given organizer and make connections to purpose and text structure. For instance, if reading a descriptive paragraph about prokaryotic cells, teachers should explain the purpose of a descriptive organizer like the one shown in Figure 5.14.

Figure 5.14. Description web.

For instance, when using this organizer, students would list the topic, prokaryotes, in the center of the web. They then fill in the remaining bubbles with words that are attributes or features of the topic. For example, the phrase "singled-celled" could be added as a descriptive detail. Thus, when students read, they are tuned in to the text's purpose and can fill in pertinent information on their graphic organizer. This is shown in the example in Figure 5.15, which highlights the given descriptive passage and the completed description web which includes features that describe prokaryotes.

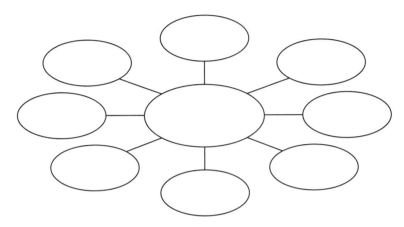

Prokaryotic cells first appeared around 3.5 to 4.5 billion years ago. These singled-celled organisms feature a simple structure and lack a nucleus and membrane-bound organelles. A prokaryote's DNA is typically located in a region called the nucleoid, which floats in the cell's cytoplasm. These cells are also much smaller than their eukaryotic counterparts because they have less DNA overall. Prokaryotes make up cells in the Bacteria and Archaea domains, while all other domains on Earth are made up of eukaryotic cells. However, prokaryotic organisms are abundant on Earth, and you can find them almost everywhere! In fact, they are an essential part of Earth's biome because they recycle nutrients and assist with metabolic processes.

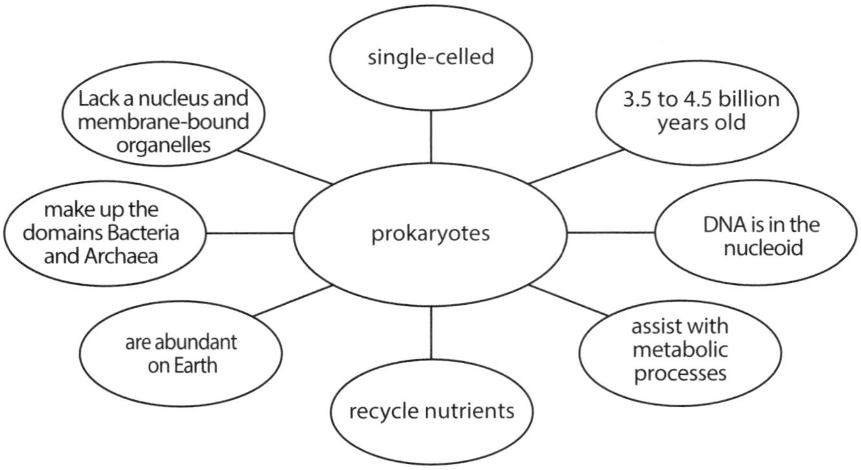

Figure 5.15. Sample completed description web.

Then, after reading, students can use the contents of their organizers to complete written summaries or drive in-class conversations.

Graphic organizers are flexible learning tools that can be adapted across grade and age levels. Consider the two graphic organizers in Figures 5.16 and 5.17. The first is a simple organizer that could be used with students in elementary school to track cause-and-effect thinking.

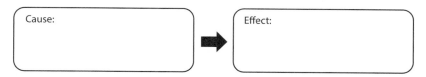

Figure 5.16. Sample cause-and-effect simple graphic organizer.

Figure 5.17 is a *fishbone diagram* that could be used with students in middle and high school. While the basic version (Figure 5.16) allows students to track a single cause-and-effect relationship, the fishbone diagram asks students to identify many potential causes for a specific event. Here, the effect in question is listed on the head or mouth of the fish, while the potential causes are listed on the ribs. Students can then list connected evidence that relates to each cause below. Once complete, the fishbone diagram provides learners with a road map for writing summaries on the given topic.

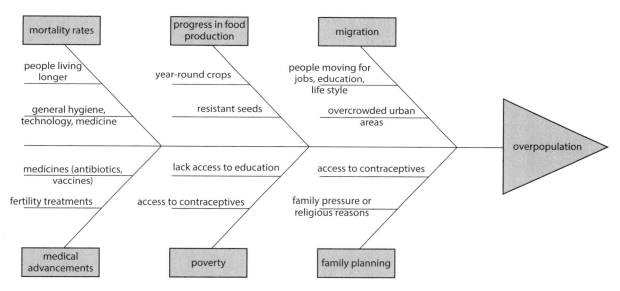

Figure 5.17. Sample cause-and-effect fishbone graphic organizer.

Try This!   Read the given passage on the causes of deforestation. As you read, fill in the fishbone organizer provided. Then write a short summary about what you learned. After you've finished, reflect: how was this process for you? Could you envision using a graphic organizer like this one to help your students deepen their understanding of cause-and-effect relationships?

> *Deforestation, or the clearing of the forest cover, has several major causes. One of the most prominent culprits of deforestation is the presence of industrial agriculture. In this situation, trees are felled to make way for the planting of crops or to provide grazing land for livestock. Today the production of beef, palm oil, and soy are included among the biggest drivers of agricultural deforestation. Another threat is timber logging for wood-based industries like paper and lumber production. In fact, the global demand for paper goods has led to the loss of over 930,000 acres of forest land annually. Mining for in-demand minerals is another major source of deforestation in tropical rainforests. Since they feature an abundance of these sought-after deposits, people clear the trees in order to extract and profit from the minerals there. Unfortunately, the construction of mines frequently goes hand in hand with other threats like the creation of roadways and infrastructures. In these instances, trees are initially cleared to create roads that offer easy access to the mines. However, when this occurs it often leads to the expansion of people into these desirable locations. Therefore, the formation of additional infrastructures like communication networks, sewage, and water supply systems is also necessary and results in the depletion of more trees. Finally, disasters like forest fires also contribute to deforestation. These occurrences, which can be caused by humans (e.g., slash and burn) or nature (e.g., lightning), are especially devastating and can result in the loss of massive amounts of forest cover.*

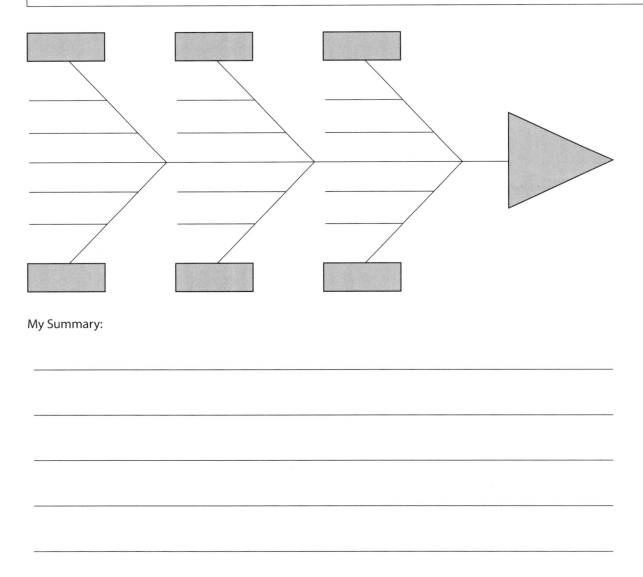

My Summary:

_____

_____

_____

_____

Potential Response:

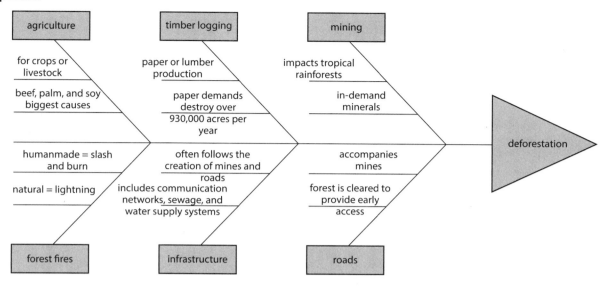

Potential summary:

> *Deforestation has several major causes including agriculture, timber logging, mining, the creation of roadways and infrastructures, and forest fires. Agricultural causes include the removal of trees for the production of crops and livestock, while timber logging is driven by global demands for paper goods. Mining has a tremendous impact on our tropical rainforests due to their abundance of in-demand minerals. Mining can also lead to the development of roadways and additional infrastructures as people require easy access to the mines. Finally, forest fires also contribute to deforestation which can stem from humanmade causes, like slash and burn practices, or natural ones, like fires started by lightning.*

Use of Signaling Devices for Informational Text: Signal Words & Text Features   (textbook pgs. 135–137)

As with narrative, informational text includes its own unique signaling devices: signal words and text features. Remember, informational text features five unique text types including *description, chronological sequence, compare and contrast, problem and solution,* and *cause and effect.* Each type of text has its own distinctive signal words as shown in Table 5.5.

Identification and coding of signal words is one strategy students can use to help determine basic text structure. However, this must be taught explicitly through modeling and instances of teacher-directed think aloud. This begins with direct explanation and discussion of the corresponding signal words. For example, an author may use the words *because, since, as a result, led to,* or *cause* when writing a paragraph that features a cause-and-effect structure. Good readers are on the lookout for these words because they help determine the text type and its purpose. The informed educator can take a passage, like the following on deforestation, and use a combination of highlighting, questioning, and discussion to help students understand that these seemingly small words help to determine this passage's purpose: the many causes of deforestation.

Deforestation, or the clearing of the forest cover, has several major <u>causes</u>. One of the most prominent culprits of deforestation is the presence of industrial agriculture. In this situation, trees are felled to make way for the planting of crops or to provide grazing land for livestock. Today the production of beef, palm oil, and soy are included among the biggest drivers of agricultural deforestation. Another threat is timber logging for wood-based industries like paper and lumber production. In fact, the global demand for paper goods

Table 5.5. Informational text signal words

Paragraph and text types	Purpose	Signal words
Description	Gives details of the attributes/features of a person, place, thing, or topic	For example, such as, consists of, attributes or characteristics (looks, sounds, feels like)
Chronological sequence	Provides the order or timing of events/steps in a process	Before, during, after, soon as, first, second, next, at that point, then, initially, afterward, finally
Compare and contrast	Indicates two or more things are alike (compare) or different (contrast)	Same, as well as, similarly, in common, different, although, however, on the other hand, in comparison, either/or
Problem and solution	Identifies what is wrong (problem) and how to fix it (solution)	Because, resolved, result, so that, consequently, answer
Cause and effect	Tells how or why an event happened (cause) and what resulted from an event (effect)	Because, since, as a result of, was caused by, led to, reason, therefore, when/then, if/then

has led to the loss of over 930,000 acres of forest land annually. Mining for in-demand minerals is another major source of deforestation in tropical rainforests. Since they feature an abundance of these sought-after deposits, people clear the trees in order to extract and profit from the minerals there. And unfortunately, the construction of mines frequently goes hand in hand with other threats like the creation of roadways and infrastructures. In these instances, trees are initially cleared to create roads that offer easy access to the mines. However, when this occurs, it often leads to the expansion of people into these desirable locations. Therefore, the formation of additional infrastructures like communication networks, sewage, and water supply systems is also necessary and results in the depletion of more trees. Finally, disasters like forest fires also contribute to deforestation. These occurrences, which can be caused by humans (e.g., slash and burn) or nature (e.g., lightning), are especially devastating and can result in the loss of massive amounts of forest cover.

It's also important to note that as students work with increasingly complex texts, they will encounter passages that include more than one text structure. For example, in an article about the industrial revolution, an author may choose to begin with a chronological sequence paragraph highlighting when the industrial revolution began and how long it lasted. This might be followed by casualty paragraphs about its potential effects (cultural change, transportation, etc.), and then end with a paragraph about problems caused by poor working conditions. Thus, students must be aware that a single article or textbook chapter may contain multiple text structures, which makes informational text more difficult to navigate.

Once students are readily able to identify these words in paragraphs and texts, they can then be challenged to apply them to their writing. Initially, this can be scaffolded at the sentence level, as in the following sample. Here students are given a cause, an effect, and a connected signal word and must create a sentence that highlights both.

> **Cause:** Tropical rainforests have an abundance of in-demand minerals.
>
> **Effect:** People clear away trees to access these valuable deposits
>
> **Signal word:** since
>
> **My sentence:** Since tropical rainforests have an abundance of in-demand minerals, people clear away trees to access these valuable deposits.

Activities like this one also tap into student knowledge of syntax, as learners are asked to combine these two sentences into one using the connected signal word. Once students have mastered the ability to use informational signal words at the sentence level, they can begin to incorporate these words into their paragraphs and essays as well. Use of sentence frames can be a helpful tool for scaffolding written responses and supporting students' academic discussions as well. Frames, like those shown in Figure 5.18, can even be posted around the classroom as a quick visual reminder to support student recall and use.

Paragraph and text types	Sentence frame
Description	_____ is a kind of _____ that . . . _____ has _____ features/characteristics/attributes. In addition, the _____. It also _____.
Chronological sequence	First . . . Then . . . Next . . . After that . . . Finally, _____. _____ begins with . . ., is followed by . . ., and ends with . . . Here is how _____ is made . . . On (date) _____ occurred by . . .
Compare and contrast	_____ and _____ both have . . . _____ has _____, while _____ has . . . _____ and _____ are different because . . . _____ and _____ are the same because . . .
Problem and solution	_____ is a problem because . . . The problem _____ is due to . . . Another potential option would be . . . One possible solution is . . .
Cause and effect	The reason why _____ happens is because . . . Some people think _____ is caused by . . . One effect of _____ is _____. The effects of _____ are significant because . . .

Figure 5.18. Sample sentence frames.

Although there is some overlap with narrative in the form of chapter titles and glossaries, text features are a primary characteristic of informational and expository text. These features include their own location and purpose and must be explicitly taught so students can use these elements as they read. A text feature scavenger hunt or search is a great way to help students identify the various features and determine the role of each.

Text Feature Scavenger Hunt		
Feature	**Location/page #**	**How can this help me in my learning?**
Title		*What is the overall topic? What might this text be about?*
Table of contents		*Where can I find information about _____?*
Chapter titles		*What is the topic for this chapter? Make a prediction about what you might learn.*
Headings/subheadings		*What are the key concepts (i.e., headings)? What are the supporting ideas (i.e., subheadings)?*
Charts, diagrams, pictures		*What charts, diagrams, or pictures did I find? How do they support my understanding of the topic?*
Sidebars/fact box		*What additional facts can I find about the topic?*
Bold print		*Which words are bolded? How do they connect to key ideas presented in the chapter?*
Index		*Does the index help me locate topics with ease?*
Glossary		*Does the glossary help me find the meanings of words with ease?*

Once students have been introduced to these various features through instances of teacher modeling and think aloud, they can use activities like this in small groups to practice and apply their knowledge collaboratively.

Try This! Read the following passage and highlight/underline the signal words that clue you in to the text structure. In the space provided, write which text structure(s) this short text features and why.

> One of the most impactful debates in 20th-century astronomy was centered on objects referred to as spiral nebulae, or spiral-shaped patches of light seen through telescopes. Two leading scholars of the time, Heber Curtis and Harlow Shapley, disputed both the scale and contents of the universe itself. Shapley believed the Milky Way was so large that it comprised the entire universe, and the spiral nebulae were smaller objects within the Milky Way. Curtis, however, believed the spiral nebulae were far outside the Milky Way and were not nebulae, but were in fact spiral galaxies all their own! Both men brought their own insight and interpretation to the data. Curtis was correct about the existence of galaxies far outside of our own, while Shapley was right about the size of the Milky Way being much larger than originally believed.
>
> It wasn't until 1925–29 when astronomer Edwin Hubble finally determined the distances of objects like the Andromeda Nebula (now called the Andromeda Galaxy), one of the most well-known spiral nebulae at the time. Hubble showed that the distances to these objects were so large, it was impossible for them to exist within the Milky Way. Consequently, today the term spiral nebulae is no longer used as we now know that these objects are in fact spiral galaxies.

I identified the following text structure(s): _____

I know this because: _____

_____

_____

Potential Response:

> One of the most impactful debates in 20th-century astronomy was centered on objects referred to as spiral nebulae, or spiral-shaped patches of light seen through telescopes. Two leading scholars of the time, Heber Curtis and Harlow Shapley, disputed both the scale and contents of the universe itself. Shapley believed the Milky Way was so large that it comprised the entire universe, and the spiral nebulae were smaller objects within the Milky Way. Curtis, <u>however</u>, believed the spiral nebulae were far outside the Milky Way and weren't nebulae, but were in fact spiral galaxies all their own! <u>Both</u> men brought their own insight and interpretation to the data. Curtis was correct about the existence of galaxies far outside of our own, <u>while</u> Shapley was right about the size of the Milky Way being much larger than originally believed.
>
> It wasn't until 1925–29 when astronomer Edwin Hubble finally determined the distances of objects like the Andromeda Nebula (now called the Andromeda Galaxy), one of the most well-known spiral nebulae at the time. Hubble showed that <u>since</u> the distances to these objects were so large, it was impossible for them to exist within the Milky Way. <u>Consequently</u>, today the term spiral nebulae is no longer used as we now know that these objects are in fact spiral galaxies.

> **I identified the following text structure(s):** compare and contrast, cause and effect
>
> **I know this because:** The author uses signal words like *however, while,* and *both* to describe the conflict between Shapley and Curtis. This lets me know we are comparing and contrasting these two men's beliefs. In the second paragraph, the author uses signal words like *since* and *consequently* to describe Hubble's discovery. This lets me know that we are learning about the results, or effects, of Hubble's findings.

As with narrative text, questioning can be used to deepen and broaden students' understanding of informational and expository texts. Table 5.6 highlights questions aligned to the five types of informational text structures at both the basic and advanced levels. Once again, these questions can be adapted to the text itself, and teachers can incorporate them before, during, or after reading.

Table 5.6. Informational text structure questions

Text structure	Basic questions	Advanced questions
Description	Who/what is being described? What is included in this description?	What are the parts or features of _____ ? How did the author describe _____ ? How else could you describe _____ ? Which of the five senses does _____ evoke?
Chronological sequence	What is happening? In what order? Does the order matter? Can it be changed?	What are the most important events/ideas/steps to remember? Why? How are these events/ideas connected? What would happen if this event/idea/step was removed? What happens right after _____ ?
Compare and contrast	What is being compared? In what ways are they alike? In what ways are they different?	What is the central focus, claim, or goal of each? What conclusions do they offer? What did you notice as true about _____ and _____ ? What elements are unique to _____ ? Why? Which of these do you identify with and why? Who is providing the information? How might it differ if shared from a different account?
Problem and solution	What is the problem? Why is it a problem? What is being done? Does the possible solution work?	Can you think of a similar problem to _____ ? Can you think of a better way to _____ ? Is there a better solution to _____ ? What solutions would you suggest for _____ ?
Cause and effect	What happened? Why did it happen? What caused it to happen? What is affected?	When _____ occurred, what was the outcome? How did _____ lead to _____ ? How would you analyze the impact of _____ ?

The QAR strategy, which we explored in the narrative section, can also be utilized with informational and expository texts to help students ask and answer their own questions. Table 5.7 features the four different question types, *In the Book, Think & Search, Author & Me,* and *On My Own,* and includes example questions aligned to various content area topics. And as with narrative, students must be provided with direct instruction of this strategy prior to writing questions on their own.

Table 5.7. Four question types for informational texts and sample questions

Question type	Example
In the Book: The answer is found in the text in one place.	• Who ruled England during the Black Death? • What is an equilateral triangle? • Which animals lay eggs? • Where did George Washington cross the Delaware River? • When does a lunar eclipse occur? • How many chemical elements are in water?
Think & Search: The reader must "think and search" the text to put information together.	• Explain the political differences between Thomas Jefferson and Alexander Hamilton. • List two statistics that support the decline in death rate over the last century. • Compare and contrast an element and a compound.
Author & Me: The reader must combine their own knowledge with information from the text to craft a response.	• Why do you think the U.S. Forest Service chose to present the information on deforestation in table form? • How was the passage of childhood during the Industrial Revolution different from life today? • Discuss a time when you planned a healthy meal and compare it to the guidelines illustrated by MyPlate.
On My Own: The reader must use their own experiences to craft a response.	• In your opinion, which is better: impressionism or realism? • What would you do if you found an injured animal? • What strategy did you use to solve the problem?

Try This! Now it's your turn to practice using the QAR strategy with informational text. Using the passage about the "Great Debate," write your own comprehension questions. Once you finish, reflect: what did you notice about this process? Was crafting questions aligned to informational text more challenging? Why or why not?

> *One of the most impactful debates in 20th-century astronomy was centered on objects referred to as* spiral nebulae, *or spiral-shaped patches of light seen through telescopes. Two leading scholars of the time, Heber Curtis and Harlow Shapley, disputed both the scale and contents of the universe itself. Shapley believed the Milky Way was so large that it comprised the entire universe, and the spiral nebulae were smaller objects within the Milky Way. Curtis, however, believed the spiral nebulae were far outside the Milky Way and weren't nebulae, but were in fact spiral galaxies all their own! Both men brought their own insight and interpretation to the data. Curtis was correct about the existence of galaxies far outside of our own, while Shapley was right about the size of the Milky Way being much larger than originally believed.*
>
> *It wasn't until 1925–29 when astronomer Edwin Hubble finally determined the distances of objects like the Andromeda Nebula (now called the Andromeda Galaxy), one of the most well-known spiral nebulae at the time. Hubble showed that the distances to these objects were so large, it was impossible for them to exist within the Milky Way. Consequently, today the term* spiral nebulae *is no longer used as we now know that these objects are in fact spiral galaxies.*

Text: _____

Question type	My example
In the Book	
Think & Search	
Author & Me	
On My Own	

Potential Responses:

Text: The Great Debate

Question type	My example
In the Book	*What are spiral nebulae?* *When did Edwin Hubble determine the distances of objects like the Andromeda Nebula?*
Think & Search	*Compare and contrast the views of Heber Curtis and Harlow Shapley.*
Author & Me	*Why is the "Great Debate" considered an important milestone in the history of astronomy?*
On My Own	*Describe a time when you and a peer had opposing viewpoints. What did you do?*

The Diverse Learner: Learning Challenges & Differences

Children with poor reading comprehension appear to lack both knowledge of structural features and how to apply such knowledge. . . . [T]his knowledge can be taught successfully to beginner readers (Oakhill et al., 2015, p. 92).

There are multiple reasons why some students may struggle more with text structure than others. These may include language and learning disabilities, differences in structures based on native language, and lack of reading/listening and/or instructional experience with varied text structures particularly expository text. Studies have shown that students with learning disabilities do not always have a well-developed sense of story grammar, particularly as the structure becomes more advanced and abstract, like theme (Williams, 2005). Expository text is more challenging for all students, particularly for the reader who is at risk. These texts often present additional difficulties for the Spanish-speaking ELL students due to their lack of vocabulary knowledge, the topics, and the linguistic complexity of the selections (Wijekumar et al., 2018).

The strategies and activities discussed in this chapter are effective but often require additional explicitness, individualization, intensity, and scaffolding. For example, studies indicate that visual scaffolds such as graphic organizers, story webs, and text-based strategies that require close analysis of story structures can be effective in meeting the needs of these at-risk readers (Hennessy, 2020).

Putting It All Together: Text Structure

Take a moment to review and connect again with the instructional focus for narrative and informational texts (see Figures 5.2 and 5.3). Then, consider what evidence-based activities you might use to align with the general guidelines that support teaching each of the identified instructional targets. Script your ideas here.

General Guidelines

- Use of exemplar texts

- Use of visual representations

- Use of text structure strategies

- Attention to signal devices

- Planning for effective teacher and student questioning

Voices From the Field

Knowing how texts operate has clear implications for text comprehension. I am wondering if knowledge and understanding around navigating text structures are assumed.

—A Blueprint Book Study Participant

Reflect & Connect!

In what ways will these lessons and activities influence your instruction?

Viewing Link

A 20th Year Celebration of Scarborough's Reading Rope—Literacy Knowledge (Session 9)

Dr. Deborah Reed

https://www.youtube.com/watch?v=Wbtup_bRYK0&t=2227s

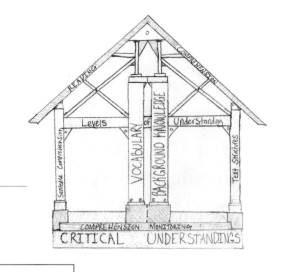

6

Implementing the Blueprint

Knowledge

The focus of this chapter is background knowledge including the what, why, and how of this critical contributor, with multiple instructional examples based on the Reading Comprehension Blueprint instructional framework. Check in and surface current connections to this topic.

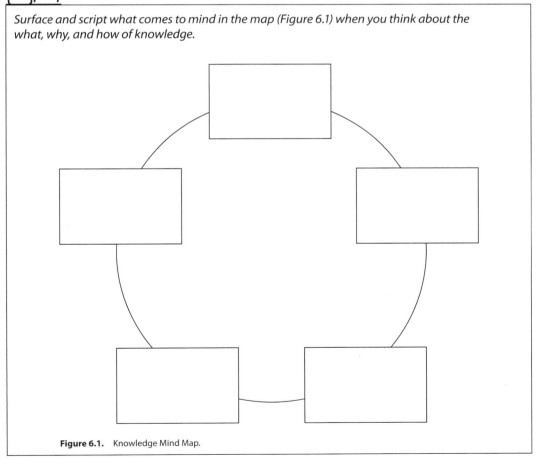

CHECK IN: Connect to current knowledge and practices!

Surface and script what comes to mind in the map (Figure 6.1) when you think about the what, why, and how of knowledge.

Figure 6.1. Knowledge Mind Map.

What: Description & Definition

The word *knowledge* raises varied questions related to the contributions of knowledge to learning, the clarity of terms used to discuss knowledge, and its connections to instruction and student performance. The National Research Council (2000, p. 236) stated, "All learning involves transfer from previous experiences. Even initial learning involves transfer that is based on previous experiences and prior knowledge." Our focus in this text is skilled reading, that is, the ability to read words and make meaning simultaneously. This demands linguistic, phonological, semantic, syntactic, morphological, orthographic, and general knowledge (Castles et al., 2018). Of particular importance to this discussion is an understanding of what we mean when we reference the reader's background knowledge. While a part of general knowledge, background knowledge is specific to the situations, problems, and concepts presented in targeted texts used in an academic setting. It has been referred to as "concepts, experiences, information, and text structures that are relevant to a text under study" (Brody, 2001, p. 241).

Why: The Science

> "A writer must always rely on the reader's knowledge to some degree. There is no text comprehension that does not require the reader to apply: lexical, syntactic, semantic knowledge, domain knowledge, personal experience, and so on." (Kintsch, 1998, p. 313)

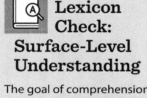

Lexicon Check: Surface-Level Understanding

The goal of comprehension is an overall understanding of the text that includes not only what authors explicitly tell us through their exact words and sentences (surface level) but also what is implicit within the text.

In other words, knowledge is fundamental to comprehension (Castles et al., 2018). Of particular importance to comprehension is linguistic and background knowledge. A reader's domain or topic knowledge works in concert with vocabulary, sentence comprehension (language structures), and literacy knowledge (text structures) to directly contribute to their construction of a coherent representation of complex texts. Comprehension demands background knowledge because language is full of semantic breaks in which knowledge is assumed and, therefore, comprehension depends on making correct inferences (Neuman & Kaefer, 2018, p. 15). If the reader activates little knowledge beyond what is provided in the text, then the reader is likely to be left with a less coherent and surface level of understanding (Elleman et al., 2022). Background knowledge is one of the critical strands of language comprehension denoted in Scarborough's (2001) Reading Rope and a key competency for reading comprehension.

How: The Design of Instruction

Introduction

While all of the contributors discussed thus far are critical instructional targets, it is important to recognize that background knowledge is necessary for the reader to understand what the author of the text does not directly state, that is, the ability to infer what is implied. We all have worked with students who can answer literal questions but do not understand the underlying meanings of the text.

Working with our readers to develop necessary background knowledge and to effectively design and deliver instruction requires a knowledge of both general guidelines and questions targeted at identifying informed instructional tools.

General Guidelines for Acquiring Background Knowledge

Literacy experts have suggested three ways educators can focus on knowledge more seriously (Jacobsen, 2018). These include consideration of the following:

1. *What kids read matters.*

   Different texts have different purposes. Although decodable texts are essential to acquiring word recognition skills, they are not sufficient to build the language competencies students need to work with the demands of academic language and knowledge. Nor were leveled texts specifically designed for this purpose. Several literacy experts have advocated for reading rich texts, including classical literature and for an increased emphasis on content learning. For example, Marilyn Adams has argued, "Giving children easier texts when they're weaker readers serves to deny them the very language and information they need to catch up and move on" (cited in Wexler, 2018, p. 10). Additionally, *Improving Reading Comprehension in Kindergarten through 3rd Grade* (Shanahan et al., 2010, p. 30) recommended that educators "select texts purposefully for reading comprehension." The authors of this document suggested we choose "a variety of texts that are rich in ideas and information" (2010, p. 31). The Blueprint supports the use of age- and grade-appropriate texts that are interdisciplinary, represent different genres, and focus on enduring understandings.

2. *Kids should learn what they read.*

   Marilyn Adams (2011, p. 9) noted, "To grow, our students must read lots. More specifically, they must read lots of complex texts—texts that offer them new language, new knowledge, new modes of thought." A focus on critical topics and enduring understandings in texts provides a foundation for students to develop deeper knowledge of word meaning and related concepts and ideas necessary for deep understanding. The Blueprint, based on the research, also supports a double outcome for reading—the development of not only critical reading skills but also increased knowledge.

3. *Kids should review and revisit content.*

   Adams (2015) advocated for topical units within each core content area, including reading/ELA, that provide students with the opportunity to acquire deeper domain knowledge. These units of instruction focus on one main concept with varied aspects explored in multiple texts. Catts (2021–2022, p. 30) recommends that:

   > As with other content instruction, reading materials in an integrated ELA program are selected to build knowledge. Instead of reading, for example, about volcanoes one day and Rosa Parks the next, which has often been the case in ELA instruction, reading materials are arranged by topic in a logical and sequential manner and form an integrated, content-rich curriculum. In this way, knowledge is acquired and accumulated over time.

These guidelines provide a framework for thinking about the ongoing integrated acquisition of background knowledge not only as a critical competency that supports comprehension but the overall goal of comprehension that is, learning itself.

The Blueprint

The Reading Comprehension Blueprint itself (Figure 6.2) poses two critical questions that prompt educators to identify instructional opportunities that focus on understanding the demands of the text and how to activate and assess, build, connect, and integrate background knowledge with text.

Blueprint for Comprehension Instruction
TEXT READING **Knowledge** **Background Knowledge** What background knowledge is critical to understanding the text? How and when will you teach students to access, build their knowledge, and integrate it with the text?

Figure 6.2. The Blueprint Questions: Background Knowledge. (*Source:* Hennessy, 2020.)

While considering responses to these questions, educators might also ask themselves the following:

1. What is necessary for understanding the critical topics and understandings represented in this text?

2. What did the author assume readers would bring to the text?

3. What are my students bringing to the text?

4. Given what my students know, what else might my students need to know?

5. What instructional tools (activities and/or strategies) will support the integration and use of background knowledge to understand the text?

These questions, coupled with the educator's knowledge base, lead to the identification of an informed instructional approach and instructional tools.

A Targeted Instructional Approach: ABCs of Background Knowledge

While instructional opportunities for acquiring background knowledge occur incidentally, our focus is to explicitly **A**ctivate & **A**ssess, **B**uild and **C**onnect Background Knowledge by using targeted instructional activities and strategies related to the demands of the text (see Figure 6.3).

Activate and assess background knowledge	Build background knowledge	Connect to background knowledge
Anticipation guides	Multiple topical/themed texts	Anticipation guides
Questions and prompts	Virtual and real-time experiences	Questions and prompts
Charts, webs, maps	Authentic artifacts	Charts, webs, maps
Visual images	Vocabulary connections	Application to other readings

Figure 6.3. The ABCs of Background Knowledge. (*Source:* Hennessy, 2020.)

Intentional Instruction: Lesson Plans & Activities

In this section, we discuss how to create lesson plans and instructional activities that focus on effective explicit approaches that follow these guidelines and include direct explanation and instances of teacher modeling, student practice, and opportunities for application with text. We begin with examples of model lesson plans and then move on to instructional activities that focus on background knowledge.

Remember that each lesson connects to its unit's enduring understandings and essential questions to address the overarching goals of student learning, while also mapping out specific objectives, activities, and assessments to grow students' understanding of literacy knowledge.

Model Lesson Plans

The model lesson plans in this section serve to investigate how educators can use authentic artifacts to build student background knowledge. With this endeavor, teachers exhibit and discuss items related to content including pictures, maps, music, writing, research data, and more. The use of authentic artifacts is an excellent place to use primary and secondary sources. The Library of Congress describes primary sources as "the raw materials of history" and includes the original documents, objects, and firsthand accounts from the time under study. It elaborates, saying, "They are different from secondary sources, accounts that retell, analyze, or interpret events, usually at a distance of time or place" (Library of Congress, n.d.). These documents provide students with insight into the past and promote a deeper understanding of history and humanities-based topics. Furthermore, the ability to analyze and think critically about these articles from the past has become an increasingly important component of historical inquiry using document-based questions (DBQs).

However, the use of authentic artifacts can be employed across subject areas. For example, math students could investigate real-world data on employment, housing, health care, and so on to determine which U.S. city is the best place to live, while students in science may examine a series of graphs that depict population trends for the orangutan. The possibilities for working with authentic artifacts are endless and can be especially engaging for learners of all ages, grades, and abilities.

Authentic Artifacts With First Grade

(textbook pg. 161)

This first lesson plan highlights an exploration of primary sources connected to the first grade unit *All About Me!* Students expand upon their knowledge of classroom communities by comparing those of the past with the present. Notice how this lesson highlights the use of authentic artifacts through the close examination of primary source photographs that depict classroom communities of the past. In addition, students also practice and apply their knowledge of text structure by utilizing the language of compare and contrast.

Name: Classroom Communities: Now and Then

Grade: First

Preparation for Instruction

Enduring Understandings:

- I am part of a family and a classroom community.

Essential Questions:

- What is a community?
- How are communities today different from and similar to the ones in the past?

Content Objectives:

- Students will be able to
  - Describe a community.
  - Compare their classroom community of today to the ones of the past.

Literacy Objectives:

- Students will be able to:
  - Build background knowledge about the topic of community
  - List and expand upon the qualities of a community
  - Compare and contrast classroom communities of the past to their own today.

Resources/Materials:

- Primary source photographs from the Library of Congress:
  - *Freedmen's school, Edisto Island, S.C.* by S. A. Cooley (https://www.loc.gov/item/2010647918/)
  - *School in Session, Pocahontas County, West Virginia* by L. W. Hine (https://www.loc.gov/item/2018678735/)
  - *Elementary school children standing and watching teacher write at blackboard, Washington, D.C.* by F. B. Johnston (https://www.loc.gov/resource/cph.3b36952/)
  - *Playground, baseball, Madison School baseball* (https://www.loc.gov/item/2016851245/)
  - *Playground scene. Irwinville school, Georgia* by J. Vachon (https://www.loc.gov/item/2017717221/)
  - *Five-cent hot lunches at the Woodville public school. Greene County, Georgia* by J. Delano (https://www.loc.gov/item/2017795070/)
- Compare/Contrast T-Chart

Sequence of Events

Purpose: To compare and contrast their school community of today to the ones of the past

Review/Prerequisite Skills: To participate in this lesson students should have the following prerequisite skills:

- Ability to categorize information
- Understanding of similarities and differences

Teacher/Student Instructional Activities:

Lesson opening:

1. Explain to students that we will be investigating classroom communities of the past and comparing and contrasting them to our classroom communities of today.
2. Briefly define and review the terms *similarities* and *differences*. For example, items that share similarities have qualities and traits that make them the same. Things that share differences, however, have qualities and traits that set them apart.
3. Explain to students that they will be identifying similarities and differences between modern classrooms and those of the past.

Teacher modeling:

4. Display a compare-and-contrast T-Chart for students, like the following sample.

School communities of today	Categories	School communities of the past
	Who is in their school community?	
	What does this school community look like? What does it include?	
	What do they do during the day? What did they learn? How did they play?	

5. Begin the activity by asking students what school is like for them today. This can include:
   a. Who is in their school community?
   b. What does this school community look like? What does it include?
   c. What do they do during the day?
   d. What concepts do they learn? Add students' answers to the T-Chart.
6. Display one of the primary source photographs from the Library of Congress collection for students.
7. Model analyzing the photograph to identify similarities and differences.
   a. For example, using the photograph of elementary school children standing and watching the teacher write at the blackboard (https://www.loc.gov/resource/cph.3b36952/), you might provide:
      i. "I notice that in the photograph I see both students and their teacher, and this is the same in our class, as well. The students are also working on writing like we do."
      ii. "However, in this photograph the teacher is using a chalkboard and chalk to write, but in our classroom, we use a whiteboard. The students and the teacher are also dressed more formally."
8. Model adding your thinking to the corresponding category on the T-Chart.

Student-guided practice:

9. Display another image for students to review.
10. Using the following sentence frames, guide students in analyzing the similarities and differences in the image.
    a. Both schools today and in the past share _____.
    b. Both schools today and in the past are alike because _____.
    c. They are different because schools today have _____, while those in the photograph have _____.
    d. Another major difference is _____ and _____.
11. Add students' responses to the corresponding category on the T-Chart.

Independent practice:

12. Have students break into partnerships or small groups. Provide each grouping with one of the remaining primary source photographs.
13. Distribute a copy of the compare-and-contrast T-Chart to each group.
14. Using the sentence frames provided during student-guided practice, students should analyze the images for similarities and differences between schools today and those in the past. They can write or draw their answers in the T-Chart provided as the teacher circulates around the room and provides support to students as needed.
15. Once the activity is complete, students can reconvene in the whole group and share their findings with the class. The teacher can add their ideas to the whole-group, compare-and-contrast T-Chart.

Differentiation/Inclusive Instructional Practices:

- Use of sentence frames to support student language of compare and contrast (frames can also be removed depending upon the readiness of the learners)
- Students can write or draw their responses
- Flexible grouping is used throughout the lesson

Evidence of Student Learning/Informal Classroom-Based Assessment:

- Participation in whole-group lesson
- Participation in partnerships or small groups
- Classroom discussion
- Completed compare and contrast T-Chart

Teacher Reflection in Implementation:

_____

_____

_____

_____

_____

_____

_____

Try This! The Library of Congress is one of the best resources for primary source documents. It offers a variety of classroom materials as well as professional development opportunities for educators. Take a moment to explore its Teacher Resources and Primary Source Sets. What materials did you find, and can they be adapted or used with the topics and units you teach? Reflect in the space provided below.

_____

_____

_____

_____

_____

_____

Authentic Artifacts With the Eighth Grade

This second lesson plan highlights an exploration of primary sources and film media connected to the eighth-grade unit *Who Am I?* Students expand their knowledge of identity formation by exploring the role of society and its impact on identity. This lesson highlights the use of authentic artifacts through the examination of primary source political cartoons and various film clips that depict stereotypes of Asian Americans. Students will discuss the impact of stereotyping and prejudice on author Gene Yang's memoir, *American Born Chinese,* and the role of the character cousin Chin Kee.

Name: Understanding Chinese discrimination in *American Born Chinese*

Grade: Eighth

Preparation for Instruction

Enduring Understandings:
• Societal views can influence individual identity.

Essential Questions:
• How is identity shaped?
• How does society influence our identities?
• How can graphic novels help us analyze complex issues related to social justice, such as stereotypes?

Content Objectives:
• Students will be able to:
  ◦ Reflect on the various ways certain social contexts impact our identities.
  ◦ Examine the topic of identity in a variety of stories.

Literacy Objectives:
• Students will be able to:
  ◦ Understand there are many variations of the narrative genre.

◦ Recognize, from reading and writing, the nature of memoir.
◦ Analyze the impact of an author's literary choices (symbolism) in a memoir.

Resources/Materials:
• *American Born Chinese* by Gene Luen Yang
• *The Only One Barred Out* political cartoon from the Library of Congress
  https://www.loc.gov/item/2001696530/
• Various movie clips. Some good examples include:
  ◦ *Sixteen Candles* (scenes featuring Long Duk Dong), Fu Man Chu movies (starring Christopher Lee), *Gremlins*
• Media Literacy Organizer (example below)

Sequence of Events

Purpose: Students will investigate how certain social contexts including prejudice, racism, and discrimination impact our identities.

Review/prerequisite skills: To participate in this lesson students should have the following prerequisite skills:
• Understanding of the terms *stereotype, prejudice, racism,* and *discrimination*
• Understanding of the elements of story grammar, specifically character
• Understanding that authors create story characters to contribute to plot and help move their stories forward

Teacher/Student Instructional Activities:
• Explore the appearance and actions of the character and why they are considered offensive. Consider why this character exists and what purpose he/she serves in the work.

Lesson opening:

1. Explain to students that today we will be discussing some of the literary choices of author Gene Luen Yang in his graphic novel, *American Born Chinese*, specifically, some of the author's literary choices about the character Chin-Kee.

2. Remind students that the character of cousin Chin-Kee is a symbol that represents Asian American stereotypes in *American Born Chinese.* Share what the author Yang had to say about the character in an interview with PBS: "And then—it hasn't happened in a while—but every now and then somebody will come up to me, usually it's

at a comic book convention, and they'll say, 'You know that Cousin Chin-Kee character? He's so cute. Do you have a T-shirt with him, because he's *so* cute.' And I was not going for cute when I designed that character" (Barajas, 2016). Have students complete a quick-write activity: *What do you think author Gene Yang meant by this?*

3. After students have finished writing, explain that today we will discuss some of the stereotypes in the media and pop culture that Yang considered when creating this character.

Teacher modeling:

4. Display the Media Literacy Organizer for students to see. An example of this chart is shown here. Explain to students that we will be investigating a series of sources today, including primary sources and film clips, to further discuss the influence of stereotypes on identity and how this influenced Gene Yang in the creation of the character Chin-Kee.

Media Review Organizer	
What do I see/notice?	
What is the message communicated?	
What is its purpose?	
What is the point of view?	

5. Display the primary source image, *The Only One Barred Out* (https://www.loc.gov/item/2001696530/). Explain to students that this political cartoon was created as commentary about the Chinese Exclusion Act. Provide some background on this act.

   a. Passed in 1882, the Chinese Exclusion Act was the first ban placed on immigration based on race. It explicitly banned Chinese laborers, but not businessmen, scholars, and so on, from entering the country. During this time, Chinese immigrants experienced increased violence and hatred due to the belief held by many Americans that Chinese workers would "take" jobs from native-born people.

6. Model your analysis of the political cartoon using the Media Literacy Organizer. For example:

   a. **I see/notice** what looks like a Chinese man dressed in more traditional Chinese clothing being locked out of the "Golden Gate of Liberty." However, on the wall it says, "Notice – communist, nihilist – socialist, Fenian & hoodlum welcome but no admittance to Chinamen." Thus, all of these other groups of people (some of which Americans also viewed as "undesirable") can come into the country, but not laborers of Chinese descent. The man is sitting among his belongings labeled "order," "peace," "industry." Thus, despite bringing these qualities with him, he is still prevented from entering America.

   b. **The message communicated is** that Chinese people are no longer welcome in the United States. This is reinforced by the quote provided at the bottom by an "Enlightened American Statesman" who said, "We must draw the line somewhere, you know."

   c. **The purpose** of this political cartoon is to show the anti-Chinese sentiment happening in the country at this time.

   d. The creator of this cartoon shared the **point of view** that despite having many positive qualities, Americans viewed Chinese laborers as "undesirable" due to the belief that they would win jobs over native born people.

Student-guided practice:

7. Explain to students that many of these stereotypes can been seen in more modern media today, as well.

8. Share one short film clip depicting Asian Americans. Guide students in completing the Media Literacy Organizer using questions like:

   a. What did you see/notice in this media portrayal?

   b. Who is the intended audience? What message is being communicated to them?

   c. What is the purpose of this piece of media? What do you think it is supposed to do?

   d. Why do you think the author created this piece of media in this way? Explain.

Independent practice:

9. Have students break into small groups. Distribute one copy of the Media Literacy Organizer to each group.

10. Students can select a film clip to analyze and work together. While groups work together, the teacher can circulate around the room and support groups as needed.

11. After they finish, the groups can reconvene and share their observations.

12. Then have students revisit their quick-write from the beginning of the class period. *Is there anything else they can add/change/revise based on today's class?*

Differentiation/Inclusive Instructional Practices:

- Flexible grouping is used throughout the lesson
- Students work with a variety of media sources including print and film to address multiple ways to take in information
- For independent work, students can select a film clip of their choosing or the teacher can preassign media based on each group's needs.

Evidence of Student Learning/Informal Classroom-Based Assessment:

- Participation in whole-group lesson
- Participation in partnerships or small groups
- Classroom discussion
- Completed media literacy organizer
- Quick write on Gene Yang quote

Teacher Reflection in Implementation:

_____

_____

_____

_____

_____

Try This! As shown in this lesson, media sources, like film clips and videos, can serve as an excellent means for building student background knowledge. Think about a unit or topic you typically teach. Do you utilize various media types to help learners build background? If so, what do you use? And if not, what might you incorporate now based on what you've learned?

_____

_____

_____

Intentional Instructional Activities: Activating and Assessing Background Knowledge

Activating and assessing students' background knowledge on the topic or text to be learned has multiple benefits and helps learners reflect on what they know and use this information to make connections to the text. Thus, the instructional tools discussed in this section provide teachers with a baseline of what relevant knowledge their learners already possess as well as prompts to guide students to reflect on what they already know.

Anticipation guides are an excellent strategy to informally assess students' prior knowledge, challenge or affirm their preconceived notions, and potentially set a purpose for reading. To create an anticipation guide, the teacher should first reflect on the major ideas present in the given reading. For example, if preparing a read aloud for *The Family Book* by Todd Parr (2010), the informed educator would want to consider ideas and themes connected to different types of families. Using this knowledge, the teacher would then create a series of powerful statements related to the book's big ideas. Students would be tasked to agree or disagree with these statements, as in the example shown in Figure 6.4, which targets relevant aspects of first grade students' knowledge about families and family dynamics.

Before reading		Statement	After reading	
Agree	Disagree		Agree	Disagree
		A family often includes children and the grownups who care for them.		
		Families are a loving community.		
		There are different ways to be a family.		
		Family members have the same roles and responsibilities.		

Figure 6.4. Sample statement agree/disagree chart for elementary school students.

Use of anticipation guides should begin with teacher explanation and modeling. Students can then complete the guide individually or in partnerships with the goal that learners will reconvene as a whole group to review their thinking through teacher-led discussion. In addition, while reading the text, the teacher should emphasize connected information, which students would be encouraged to reflect upon when they revisit the organizer after reading.

This strategy can be used across content areas and disciplines and adapted to varying age and grade levels. For instance, the next example in Figure 6.5 targets high schooler's thinking about the Columbian Exchange.

Before reading		Statement	After reading	
Agree	Disagree		Agree	Disagree
		The Columbian Exchange was one of the most influential turning points in world history.		
		The Columbian Exchange had an equal impact on people everywhere, regardless of where they lived or their social class.		
		Increased global connectivity and communication can result in positive and negative outcomes.		

Figure 6.5. Sample statement agree/disagree chart for high school students.

Alternatively, the final example in Figure 6.6 could be used to assist middle school students to reflect on their current understanding of the order of operations.

Before reading		Statement	After reading	
Agree	Disagree		Agree	Disagree
		The order of operations is a sequence of steps to help us solve expressions with multiple operations.		
		The order of operations begins with parentheses.		
		Exponents are a shorthand for multiplication.		
		After exponents, perform multiplication and division, whichever comes first when moving from left to right.		

Figure 6.6. Sample statement agree/disagree chart for middle school students.

Try This!   As we begin this section, let's take a moment to reflect on what we currently know about background knowledge by reading each of the following statements. After reading, decide if you agree or disagree with each. You can even include an adverb to show how much you agree or disagree (e.g., *strongly* disagree, *somewhat* agree). Finally, explain your thinking in the space provided. And be prepared to return to this activity when this chapter comes to a close!

Statement	Agree or disagree?	Explain
Activating student background knowledge helps educators get a sense of what their students know, while prompting learners to make connections to the text.		
Building students' background knowledge can be targeted before reading through direct, explicit instruction.		
Activities used to activate and assess students' background knowledge can also be used to help them make connections and modify or adjust their understandings.		

Use of Questions or Prompts

(textbook pg. 157)

As we discussed previously, questioning is an incredibly powerful strategy to support students in all aspects of comprehension. This applies to working with background knowledge, as well, and the informed educator can create questions and prompts to activate and assess their students' background knowledge. After previewing the text or topic of study, the teacher can create a series of questions to gauge student understanding. Additionally, student response methods can be varied based on student strengths and needs (i.e., in writing, orally, mini quiz). The example questions shown here can also be adapted to include a variety of content areas and disciplines.

Questions and Prompts to Activate & Assess Background Knowledge
What do you already know about [topic/enduring understanding/big idea]?
What experiences have you had related to [topic/enduring understanding/big idea]?
What do you think it would be like to live _____ (place) during _____ time?
Do you know what it is like to be _____ (characteristic or quality)?
Do you remember reading or learning about _____ (connections to other readings)?
Based on what you know about _____ (topic), what might _____ (text, passage) be about?
What type of text is this? Have I seen this type of text before?

For example, to assess student knowledge of the Columbian Exchange, a history teacher might prepare the following questions to ask their students at the start of a unit:

- What do you think it would have been like to live during the Age of Exploration?
- Would you have wanted to live during this time? Why or why not?
- What might be a consequence of introducing a new plant or animal to a new environment?

Try This! Using the model unit *All About Me!* and the concept of *community*, create a series of questions that could be used to activate and assess first grade students' background knowledge. For example, one might ask: *What do you know about participating in a community?* Brainstorm at least three questions, and afterward reflect: how can you vary the response methods to make this activity accessible for all students?

My Questions

1. _____

_____

_____

2. _____

_____

_____

3. _____

_____

_____

Webs, Charts, and Diagrams

(textbook pgs. 157, 159–160)

Another way to activate and assess students' background knowledge is through the use of charts, webs, and diagrams. With this, a teacher selects a graphic organizer to structure student knowledge. One frequently used organizer is the KWL chart. This strategy prompts students to reflect on what they <u>know</u> (K) about a topic, what they <u>want</u> to know (W), and at the end of a lesson or unit, reflect on what they've <u>learned</u> (L). Thus, it initially surfaces student knowledge, but can build upon and connect to students' background knowledge, as well.

K - What do you <u>know</u> about: _____?	W - What do you <u>want</u> to know about: _____?	L - What did you <u>learn</u> about: _____?

The KWL strategy has also been expanded since its initial design by Donna Ogle in 1986. Two other varieties, which can be used with students independently researching a topic, are the KWHL and the KWHLAQ. Use of

KWHL chart tracks what students <u>know</u> (K), what they <u>want</u> to know (W), <u>how</u> students will find the targeted information (H), and, finally, what they have learned (L). In the following completed example, notice that the H, or *how* section, provides a list of steps the student will take to research the Columbian Exchange.

K - What do you <u>know</u> about:	W - What do you <u>want</u> to know about:	H - <u>How</u> will you find out about:	L - What did you <u>learn</u> about:
The Columbian Exchange	The Columbian Exchange	The Columbian Exchange	The Columbian Exchange
Named after Columbus. Happened during the Age of Exploration. Explorers came in boats. Columbus wanted gold and gems. He thought he discovered India.	What was Columbus' purpose for exploration? Why was Columbus credited with "discovering" America? What was exchanged? How did this exchange impact different countries and societies? Was the Columbian Exchange a positive or negative event in world history?	Complete a search on the Internet. Go to the school library. Review resources like my textbook.	

Finally, the KWHLAQ chart is sometimes described as an upgrade that addresses 21st-century skills. This strategy includes all the components of a KWHL but adds in the <u>action</u> students will take (A), and what <u>questions</u> they still have (Q). Thus, students are challenged to reflect on how they will apply their newfound knowledge and why it matters. For example, take a look at the completed KWHLAQ chart in Figure 6.7 for a high school

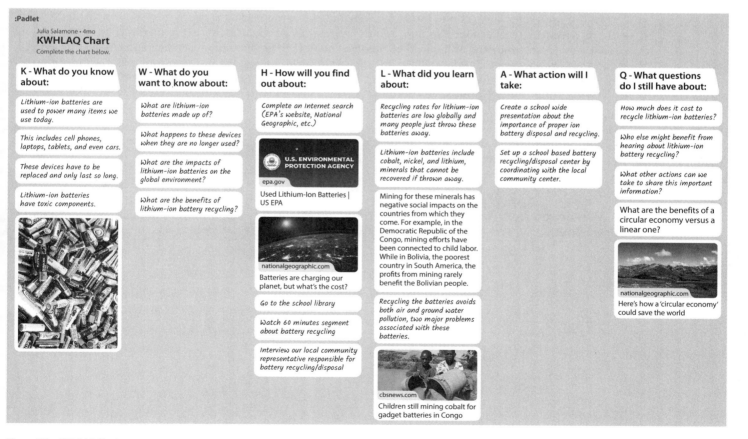

Figure 6.7. KWHLAQ Chart.

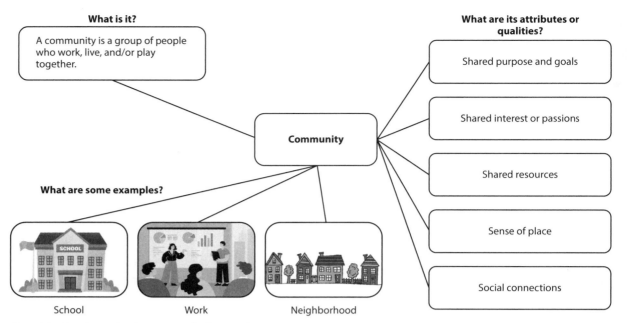

What is it?

A community is a group of people who work, live, and/or play together.

Community

What are its attributes or qualities?

Shared purpose and goals

Shared interest or passions

Shared resources

Sense of place

Social connections

What are some examples?

School

Work

Neighborhood

Figure 6.8. Sample completed concept map for the topic of community.

environmental science project about the impact of lithium-ion batteries on the environment. This chart was completed with the use of Padlet, a digital tool perfect for collaboration. Here students can easily post responses to each category of the KWHLAQ chart and can return to this collective space as they work through an assignment or project. Students are able to collect not only their responses but other resources as well, including images, websites, articles, and videos.

Finally, concept maps can be used to activate and assess student background knowledge, while teaching them to organize information into meaningful categories. For instance, review the concept web in Figure 6.8 created for the word *community* at the start of the *All About Me!* unit. Students brainstormed their initial ideas about the term, which the teacher captured using words and images. As the students explored this concept throughout the unit, new ideas, examples, and qualities could be added to the map to organize their expanded knowledge. Concepts maps are also easily adaptable to any subject or topic, making them a great tool to use across the curriculum. In addition, this strategy can be used with a variety of ages and grade levels as it can be adjusted depending on the complexity of the topic covered.

 Try This! Now it's your turn to try! Using the KWHLAQ chart provided, map out your own action plan for how you will support learners in activating and assessing their background knowledge.

K - What do you <u>know</u> about:	W - What do you <u>want</u> to know about:	H - <u>How</u> will you find out about:	L - What did you <u>learn</u> about:	A - What <u>action</u> will I take:	Q - What questions do you still have about:

Visual images can also be used to activate students' relevant background knowledge. The educator can select pictures, photographs, illustrations, and/or artwork connected to the current unit and understandings. Using these images paired with purposeful questions, the educator can begin to surface students' background knowledge before and during reading.

For example, the images shown in Figure 6.9 could be used to activate student background knowledge about the concept of *community*. The informed educator can pair these images with a series of questions to gauge what students know about how a community works together. Questions could include:

- What do you notice about the people in these images? What do they appear to be doing? How are they working together?
- Can you think of a time you worked together with others? What was it like?
- What do you know about being a member of a community?

This also provides an excellent opportunity for educators to include the use of primary and secondary sources. Figure 6.10 is a primary source photograph, *The First Picket Line* (1917), from the expansive collection housed by the Library of Congress and could be used to activate students' background knowledge about the women's suffrage movement.

Potential questions could include:

- What people and objects do you see? How are they arranged?
- Do you notice any words? If so, what do they say?
- What do you already know about the women's suffrage movement?
- What do you think it would be like to live as a woman during this time?
- What strategies do you think women used to win the right to vote?

Figure 6.9. Sample images to active background knowledge for the concept of community.

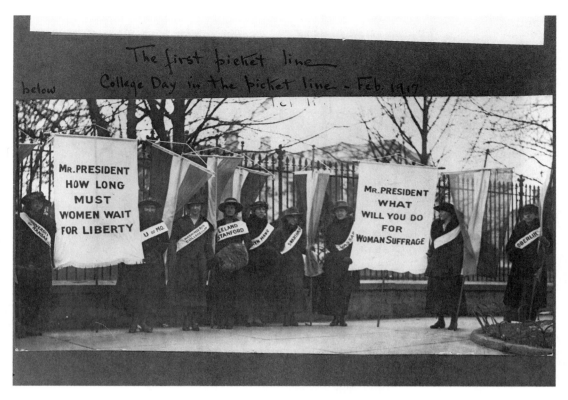

Figure 6.10. *The First Picket Line.* (*Source:* The first picket line: College day in the picket line [photograph]. [1917]. Library of Congress. https://www.loc.gov/pictures/item/97500299/)

Try This! The image in Figure 6.11 accompanies an American History unit on child labor and human rights. It is from the Library of Congress' Lewis Hine collection and depicts a "tipple boy," one of the child laborers who worked the tipple, a structure used to load coal into railway cars. Using this image, brainstorm a series of questions that could be used to activate learners' background knowledge and prepare them to learn more about this topic (Hine, 1921).

My Questions

1.

2.

3.

Figure 6.11. Tipple boy from Library of Congress' Lewis Hine collection. (From Hine, L. W., photographer. [1908]. Tipple Boy, see Photo 150 Turkey Knob Mine, Macdonald, W. Va. Witness E.N. Clopper. Location: MacDonald, West Virginia. Macdonald United States West Virginia, 1908. [Photograph] Retrieved from the Library of Congress, https://www.loc.gov/item/2018673780/.)

Intentional Instructional Activities: Building Background Knowledge

Building students' background knowledge can be targeted through direct, explicit instruction before, during, and after reading. These activities should be purposefully connected to the core knowledge required for understanding and identified prior to starting the unit or lesson. The instructional tools discussed in this section are designed to build background knowledge through multiple topics/themed texts, experiential learning, and connections to vocabulary.

One way the informed educator builds student background knowledge is through the selection of multiple texts connected to the same topic or theme. The table below shows this for the units *All About Me!* and *Who Am I?* With *All About Me!*, first grade students are learning about developing a sense of identity, while the list provided for the *Who Am I?* unit asks eighth-grade students to explore the concept of identity and the role it plays in forming values, ideas, and actions.

All About Me!	Who Am I?
• *Leo the Late Bloomer* by Robert Kraus • *Eyes That Kiss the Corner* Joanna Ho • *Chrysanthemum* by Kevin Henkes • *Frederick* by Leo Leoni • *The Proudest Blue* by Ibtihaj Muhammad • *We Are All Wonders* by R. J. Palacio • *The Best Part of Me* by Wendy Ewald • *It's Okay to Be Different* by Todd Parr • *The Day You Begin* by Jacqueline Woodson • *Fry Bread* by Kevin Noble Maillard • *Hair/Pelitos* by Sandra Cisneros • *The Family Book* by Todd Parr • *Last Stop on Market Street* by Matt de la Peña • *All Are Welcome* by Alexandra Penfold	• *Persepolis* by Marjane Satrapi • *American Born Chinese* by Gene Luen Yang • *El Deafo* by Cece Bell • *A Long Way Gone: Memoirs of a Boy Soldier* by Ishmael Beah • *Red Scarf Girl: A Memoir of a Cultural Revolution* by Ji-li Jiang • *I Am Malala: The Girl Who Stood Up for Education and Was Shot by the Taliban* by Malala Yousafzai • *Brown Girl Dreaming* by Jacqueline Woodson • "The Jacket" by Gary Soto • Various chapters from *The House on Mango Street* by Sandra Cisneros • "Fish Cheeks" by Amy Tan • "When I Was Puerto Rican" by Esmerelda Santiago • "Richard" by Allie Brosh

Theme selection is critical as a strong topic serves to engage students and teachers alike. And as Jennings and Haynes (2018, p. 18) remind us, "When teachers anchor language exercises in interesting real-world topics, students have the chance to review and practice meaningful vocabulary and concepts." Thus, by reading varied texts connected to the same engaging topic or theme, students build both background knowledge and vocabulary, which prepares them to later show what they know in speaking and writing. We will explore this idea later in this section when we discuss connections to vocabulary.

Tips for Success!

Inclusive Instructional Practices

When it comes to the construction of background knowledge, educators have the unique opportunity to purposefully select texts and topics that focus on critical understandings that include varied genres and represent different disciplines. Furthermore, this knowledge should reflect the collective voices and experiences of all Americans and students should see themselves reflected in the texts and topics explored in school. Thus, educators should strive to provide all learners with opportunities to see their lives, experiences, histories, identities, cultures, and perspectives reflected in what they're learning in school (mirrors) as well as opportunities to learn about the lives, experiences, histories, identities, cultures, and perspectives of others (windows). When educators foster background knowledge that is inclusive and connected to topics critical for understanding, they lay a solid foundation on which learning can be built. One excellent tool is the *Reading Diversity Checklist*, which is available for free on the Learning for Justice website. This tool helps educators to assess the diversity of perspectives included in one's reading curriculum and can be accessed at: https://www.learningforjustice.org/magazine/publications/reading-diversity

Reflect & Connect!

Think about a unit of instruction that you typically teach. Do you use multiple themed/topical texts as a component? If yes, take a moment to reflect: how did you arrive at your final book selection? What was your process in selecting thematic texts that connected to topics critical for understanding? If not, in what ways will this discussion of thematic/topical text selection in this chapter change your current instructional practices? Write your thoughts in the space provided.

Experiential Learning

(textbook pg. 161)

Experiential learning is another excellent way to build student background knowledge. This includes the use of authentic artifacts, like the ones highlighted in the model lesson plans, as well as the use of virtual or real-time experiences. Consider our unit, *All About Me!*, which works to expand students' understanding of the concept of *community*. This also offers a wonderful opportunity to capitalize on real-time excursions to build student background knowledge. For example, students could visit a neighborhood bakery, grocery store, or even farm to see where local food comes from. Visits to a nearby train station offer opportunities to see how people travel within a community, while trips to a local post office or fire station provide students with opportunities to meet community workers who provide essential services and help our communities function. All these experiences serve to broaden students' awareness of where people live and work by immersing them in active experiences.

Furthermore, with the advent of advanced technology, virtual experiences are more accessible than ever. These outings are typically low cost, can be aligned to almost any learning goal, and may offer students more intimate experiences than in person excursions. For example, many zoos and aquariums, including San Diego, Cincinnati, and the Monterey Bay Aquarium, offer students opportunities to get a close-up look at animals through the use of live streams or virtual chats with zoo educators. There are also several amazing historical sites that provide students with access to places such as the Sistine Chapel, Machu Picchu, Ellis Island, Gettysburg Battlefield, and even the Great Wall of China. The list in Table 6.1 offers a handful of resources to consider across disciplines, and this is only a small sampling of what can be found online.

Table 6.1. Experiential learning resources

Website	Grades addressed	Description & link
California Academy of Sciences	K–12	This website offers a plethora of resources including access to the academy's scientists, animal live streams, even virtual classroom visits designed to engage learners of all ages. Visit at www.calacademy.org/learn-explore
Global Oneness Project	3–12	This amazing website that features films, interviews, and photo essays to explore cultural, social, and environmental issues across the globe. Visit at www.globalonenessproject.org
Google Arts & Culture	6–12	Google Arts & Culture features images and videos of artworks and cultural artifacts from over 2,000 partner cultural organizations throughout the world. Visit at https://artsandculture.google.com/
Google Maps Treks	6–12	Travel through a variety of amazing destinations worldwide. Explorations include the Grand Canyon, Taj Mahal, and Great Barrier Reef. Visit at www.google.com/maps/about/treks/#/grid
National Geographic Education	Pre-K–12	This top geography website offers student experiences, classroom resources, and professional development opportunities for teachers. Visit at www.nationalgeographic.org/education
National Museum of African American History and Culture	K–12	This website includes powerful content and stories sharing African American experience from the Smithsonian's National Museum of African American History and Culture. Visit at www.nmaahc.si.edu
United States Holocaust Memorial Museum	6–12	This valuable resource is for anyone who teaches about the Holocaust. This site offers a variety of online resources, so be sure to set aside time to review them. Visit at www.ushmm.org

Reflect & Connect!

Think about any experiential learning activities that you utilize with students. Where do you go and what do you typically do? How do these experiences, whether virtual or real time, provide a space to develop student background knowledge? And what might you add or do differently based on what you learned in this chapter? Write your thoughts in the space provided below.

_____

_____

_____

Connections to Vocabulary   (textbook pg. 161)

Making connections to vocabulary can be leveraged to support students' developing background knowledge and writing skills. Semantic mapping, an activity explored in the vocabulary chapter (see Chapter 3), fosters depth of vocabulary knowledge and vocabulary growth as it helps students build connections between words, core content, and related facts and ideas. Authors Jennings and Haynes (2018, p. 28) advocate for the use of _structured semantic mapping_, which "systematically scaffolds students' knowledge by constraining their associations to selected semantic features." This allows learners to organize their background knowledge in a systematic way.

Review the example in Figure 6.12 for the word _identity_, a concept explored in the eighth-grade unit _Who Am I?_ The educator structured this map by choosing specific features to guide student brainstorming. For example, one facet or feature of _identity_ is an individual's talents and abilities, and students would be expected to list their own propensities as a part of the completed map. This process allows learners to show their understanding of a targeted concept more readily as "the more features learners associate with a word, the better their ability to understand and express what they know about that word" (Jennings & Haynes, 2018; p. 28).

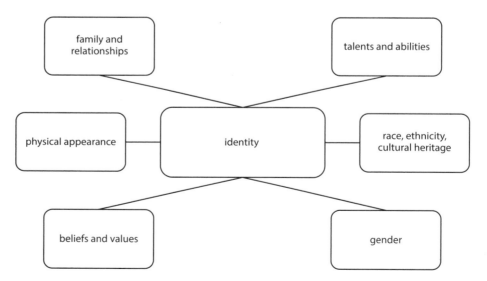

Figure 6.12.   Sample semantic mapping for the concept of identity.

Another benefit of developing background knowledge around topical vocabulary and themes is a reduction of the heavy load placed on student word retrieval and working memory. When students work with thematic/topical content, they build ideas around a connected mental framework instead of "randomly shift[ing] between different mental schema" (Haynes et al., 2019, p. 22). This frees them up to focus their mental efforts on showing what they know in speaking and writing later during assessments. Finally, activities like this can be used across classes and content areas and benefit learners of all abilities, including students with language-based learning differences, those acquiring a second language, and their typically developing peers.

Try This! Think about a theme or topic that you teach. Using the organizer provided, create a structured semantic web to help students build connections between the topical vocabulary and background knowledge explored. Once complete, reflect: how can an activity like this be useful as students begin to share what they've learned in speaking and writing?

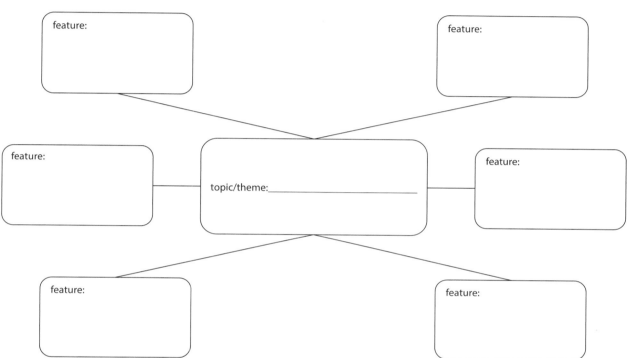

Intentional Instructional Activities: Connecting to Background Knowledge

The activities we discussed previously to activate and assess students' background knowledge can also be used to help learners integrate and connect their background knowledge. For example, as we highlight in this section, anticipation guides and KWL charts can be revisited after learning and modified to reflect new and/or deepened understandings. In addition, educators can help students integrate their background knowledge by applying new background knowledge to other readings. This approach can be used across content areas to help students make connections to topics and themes across disciplines.

The informed educator creates opportunities for students to connect and integrate their background knowledge. For instance, students can revisit anticipation guides explored at the start of a lesson or unit by modifying their responses to show how their thinking has expanded or changed. This is highlighted in the following example, which asks first grade students to reflect on and connect to their learning about families and family dynamics as explored in the *All About Me!* unit.

Statement	My response now	How has my understanding changed?
A family often includes children and the grownups who care for them.		
Families are a loving community.		
There are different ways to be a family.		
Family members have the same roles and responsibilities.		

Thus, after completing the lesson and text *The Family Book* by Todd Parr, students would revisit this document and consider how their understanding has changed.

The same can be accomplished with KWL charts. Here students connect and expand upon their background knowledge by sharing what they *learned* as a result of a lesson or unit. For example, in the following KWL chart, students listed what they learned about the Columbian Exchange as a result of their independent reading and research. Notice how what they learned aligns to the questions they posed at the beginning of the activity.

K - What do you know about: The Columbian Exchange	W - What do you want to know about: The Columbian Exchange	L - What did you learn about: The Columbian Exchange
Named after Columbus. Happened during the Age of Exploration. Explorers came in boats. Columbus wanted gold and gems. He thought he discovered India.	What was Columbus' purpose for exploration? Why was Columbus credited with "discovering" America? What was exchanged? How did this exchange impact different countries and societies? Was the Columbian Exchange a positive or negative event in world history?	Columbus was hoping to find a new route to India, China, Japan, and the Spice Islands, which would allow him to bring back silk and spices. Columbus didn't discover America, and, in fact, landed on islands in the Caribbean. However, he never reached North America, which was already inhabited by the indigenous peoples living there. Some historians also think his son started the rumors of his supposed legacy. Commodities (animals, plants, spices, gold and silver, etc.), people, and diseases crossed the Atlantic during the Columbian Exchange Certain societies and regions benefited more drastically from the Columbian Exchange. For example, many Europeans from the Old World received a rich staple of crops as well as gold and silver from the New World. However, the indigenous peoples of the New World severely suffered from diseases the Europeans brought with them and the transatlantic slave trade led to the enslavement of 10 to 12 million Africans. Though there were some positive effects, the impact of disease was decidedly one-sided and decimated the native population living there. In addition, the exchange led to the enslavement of both the native populations and millions of African men, women, and children. While the sharing of plants and animals led to a diverse food supply, some historians think the exchange did almost as much to upset the biological, economic, and social balance of the New World as the transmission of disease.

Try This!   Using the anticipation guide from earlier in this chapter, take a moment to compare your previous responses with your current thoughts. Can you add to, elaborate on, or alter your initial thinking? Then, explain how your understanding has changed or evolved. What do you notice about your understanding now that you're coming to the end of this chapter?

Statement	My response now	How has my understanding changed?
Activating student background knowledge helps educators to get a sense of what their students know, while prompting learners to make connections to the text.		
Building students' background knowledge can be targeted before reading through direct, explicit instruction.		
Activities used to activate and assess students' background knowledge can also be used to help them make connections as well as modify or adjust their understandings.		

As we have discussed, the use of questioning is an incredibly powerful way to develop and support learners' reading comprehension. The same applies to asking students to connect to and integrate their background knowledge with the author's words. If we consider a commonly used framework for developing questions, Bloom's Taxonomy, we can look at the analysis questions to assist learners in drawing connections between ideas. This framework is categorized into six levels including remembering, understanding, applying, analyzing, evaluating, and creating and moves from lower order to higher order thinking skills. With this in mind, Figure 6.13 features a series of verbs and potential question stems that could be used to help students in this manner. Notice how both the verbs and sentence stems ask students to analyze what they've learned and think critically about how their understanding connects to other learning and perspectives.

Verbs	Sentence stems
analyze	If _____ happened, what might have occurred at the end?
compare	How is this similar to . . . ?
contrast	What do you see as other possible outcomes?
connect	How did _____ changes occur?
deconstruct	Compare your thinking about _____ with what was presented in _____ .
deduce	Distinguish between . . .
differentiate	Differentiate between . . .
distinguish	What evidence supports your thinking of . . . ?
examine	What can you deduce about . . . ?
explore	Link _____ to . . .
link	Organize the parts/features/qualities of _____ by . . .
organize	Determine the factors that . . .
relate	

Figure 6.13. Verbs and sentence stems to activate students' questioning skills.

Questions that ask students to make connections between the stories/texts that they read and their own life experiences, other texts, and world events is another great way to help them integrate the information. Questions can be differentiated based upon the students' level of understanding and/or response mode (oral or written). The following stems serve as a small sampling of question stems designed to help students connect to their own experiences, other stories/texts, and real-world happenings:

- Does this story/text remind you of something from your own life?
- How does this text compare/contrast to/with others you have read?
- What does _____ remind you of in the real world?

These basic prompts can also be elaborated upon to create student writing responses. The following prompt was crafted to help students integrate their knowledge after reading the short stories "Fish Cheeks" by Amy Tan and "The Jacket" by Gary Soto. Notice how this prompt asks students to apply what they know to multiple readings. This sort of writing activity could be used at the end of a unit to help learners to analyze the text and explain and interpret their understanding.

In both "Fish Cheeks" and "The Jacket," Amy Tan and Gary Soto relay a significant event the authors experienced as teenagers, which is then reflected upon as Tan and Soto retell the story as adults. Compare both authors' retellings. How did their thinking as teenagers match up to their understanding as an adult later on? Did their ideas change? If so, how? Provide evidence from the stories to support your thinking.

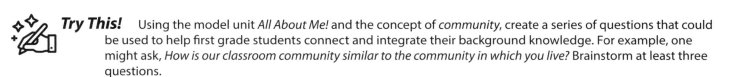

Try This! Using the model unit *All About Me!* and the concept of *community*, create a series of questions that could be used to help first grade students connect and integrate their background knowledge. For example, one might ask, *How is our classroom community similar to the community in which you live?* Brainstorm at least three questions.

My Questions

1. _____

   _____

   _____

2. _____

   _____

   _____

3. _____

   _____

   _____

Tips for Success!

Inclusive Instructional Practices

Students with specific reading comprehension difficulties, those who lack access to text due to word recognition issues like dyslexia, and ELLs may experience difficulty with activating and using prior knowledge. Thus, it is our responsibility as educators to adapt our instruction to meet the needs of all learners. This includes assessing for and building knowledge of academic vocabulary, as this is a critical component of background knowledge needed to understand the text. In addition, teachers should anticipate and preview topics that might be different or unfamiliar to the learners that they teach. For instance, ELLs may have different knowledge of elections and government based on their experiences in their native country. The informed educator looks to build connections between what the learner knows about a topic in the context of their own unique culture and experiences and uses this as a bridge to build upon and expand their understanding. Finally, it is critical to avoid making assumptions about what knowledge students do and do not possess. In this way, we honor the knowledge each learner brings with them and create a welcoming environment for all.

The Diverse Learner: Learning Challenges & Differences

While the ABCs for background knowledge provide direction, effective instruction calls for scaffolding and differentiation based on student needs. The building of background knowledge is dependent on multiple factors. For example, the student with word recognition difficulties may not initially have the opportunity to build knowledge through reading like their peers. Providing access to text as they acquire word reading skills is critical. Knowing others may have the knowledge specific to a question or task but have difficulty accessing and activating knowledge is also important. Providing specific strategies, such as an organizer that prompts the reader to consider what the text says, what they know, and then, what they think, can support their ability to make the necessary connection. While instructional context is an important contributor for all students, our students' experiences reflect the social and cultural influences of a larger environment. Understanding their culture, including history, educational systems, government, and traditions, can inform the educator in building connections between what the student does know and what is necessary for understanding text.

Putting it all Together: Knowledge

Take a moment to review and connect again with the targeted instructional approach for background knowledge. Then, consider what evidence-based tools you might add to the ABCs. Script your ideas here.

Voices From the Field

Background knowledge allows students to activate related information, and then students can make connections to new learning and even extend learning and use it to create something new.
—A Blueprint Book Study Participant

Reflect & Connect!

In what ways will these lessons and activities influence your instruction?

Listening & Viewing Links

Video: Daniel Willingham: Why Teaching Content Is Teaching Reading https://www.youtube.com/watch?v=RiP-ijdxqEc

Filling the Gaps: Text Sets Build Background Knowledge and Improve Comprehension of Informational Texts https://iowareadingresearch.org/blog/text-sets-background-knowledge

Knowledge Matters Campaign: Knowledge Ignites Literacy and Learning https://knowledgematterscampaign.org/

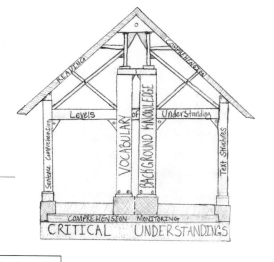

7

Implementing the Blueprint

Levels of Understanding & Inference

The focus for this chapter is the varied levels of understanding and inference, including the what, why, and how of this critical contributor, and features multiple instructional examples, all of which are based on the Reading Comprehension Blueprint instructional framework. Check in and surface current connections to this topic.

CHECK IN: Connect to current knowledge and practices!

Surface and script what comes to mind in the map (Figure 7.1) when you think about the what, why, and how of understanding text at different levels.

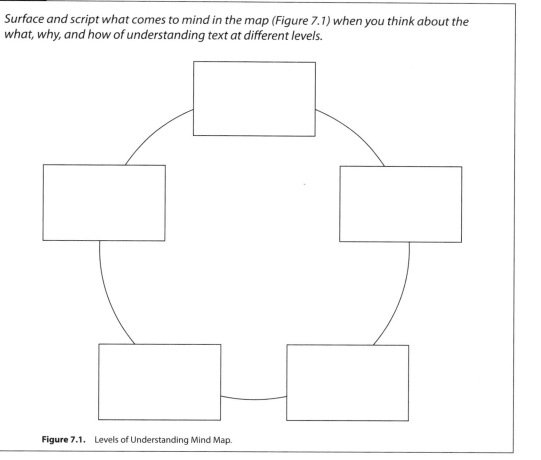

Figure 7.1. Levels of Understanding Mind Map.

What: Definition & Description

Levels of Understanding

What often comes to mind when asked to consider the phrase "levels of understanding" are connections to Bloom's Taxonomy, a cognitive framework for increasingly deeper levels of learning and knowledge (e.g., ability to remember, apply, evaluate, create) or more commonly used descriptions for levels of understanding (e.g., literal and inferential comprehension). While these are related to this discussion, our focus is on the relationship between the role of the language and cognitive processes and knowledge discussed in earlier chapters and three levels of representation of meaning. These levels of representation of meaning include working with the 1) surface code of the text, 2) the underlying textbase, and 3) a mental or situation model (Kintsch, 1988). At the surface code level, the reader initially interacts with the exact words, their meaning and the syntax of the text. Comprehending the textbase requires using the meaning of these words and syntax to literally understand the ideas expressed on the page and then integrating them with what is implied in the text with the author's intended meaning. The author assumes that the reader will recognize the explicit connections between ideas represented on the page and, at the same time, integrate background knowledge to understand what is implied (Kintsch & Rawson, 2005). To fully gain the intended meaning from a text, a reader must go beyond the surface level, work with the textbase, and integrate related knowledge to create a coherent mental representation or mental model that is an overall understanding of the situation expressed in the text. (Kintsch, 1988). See Figure 7.2.

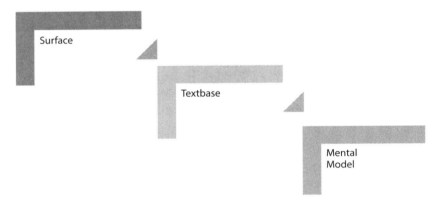

Figure 7.2. Levels of Representation.

During this construction of meaning, the skilled reader continues to use language and cognitive processes and their knowledge to integrate successive units of meaning and infer what is not explicitly stated. At the heart of this process is inference generation, the process by which a reader integrates information within or across texts using their background knowledge to fill in information not explicitly stated (Elleman, 2017, p. 4).

Inferences

Based on what we know about the levels of representation of meaning, inferences are critical for the reader to ultimately construct their overall understanding of the text. This requires making inferences that 1) connect ideas within and between sentences and 2) prompt the reader to integrate text information with relevant background knowledge. While there are varied ways of describing inference, a comprehensive definition takes into account the role inference plays at different levels of understanding. Consider this definition: ". . . [Inference is] the identification of meaningful relations between the various parts of the text, and between those parts and the reader's background knowledge" (Kendeou et al., 2008, p. 259). This description directly acknowledges that generating inferences involves identifying connections between parts of the text (e.g., sentences) and relationships between the text and background knowledge. These inferences allow the reader to construct a coherent representation of text, one in which the explicit and implicit ideas within the text hang together and make sense. This is accomplished through two broad categories of necessary inferences: local and global coherence inferences.

Local coherence inferences are necessary to integrate information from adjacent pieces of text (Language and Reading Research Consortium [LARRC], 2018). Ideas or concepts are linked together within and between sentences using cohesive ties and connectives. Consider these two examples:

1. What words in the following sentence refer to or also mean Thomas Jefferson? The words *he* and *great man* are linking or working as ties between ideas within the sentence.

    Benjamin Banneker was telling Thomas Jefferson that *he* was a *great man*.

2. What word in this sentence is connecting ideas and signaling a relationship between parts of the sentence? The word before connects two clauses that make up this sentence and references time.

    Before the end of the school year, over 1,500 Black demonstrators were arrested.

On the other hand, global coherence inferences are used to fill in details not explicitly stated that are needed to construct a globally coherent representation of text meaning, for example, inferences about themes, morals, and settings (LARRC, 2018). They are knowledge-based and fill in the gaps between explicit information in text and what is stored in memory. Readers use global inferences for varied purposes including to:

*   Understand the cause of events
*   Predict future actions
*   Identify setting
*   Identify characters' motives, beliefs, and traits
*   Understand character relationships
*   Draw conclusions
*   Understand the author's view and/or biases

Consider these examples:

1. Drawing Conclusions:

    Who do you think brought the frog to dinner? Why?

    Frog Goes to Dinner by Mercer Mayer

2. Identifying Setting:

    I live here because I am too much gorilla and not enough human. My domain is made of thick glass, rusty metal and rough cement. Stella's [an elephant] is made of metal bars. The sun bears' domain is made of wood; the parrot's is made of mesh.

    Where is the gorilla? How do you know?

    The One & Only Ivan by Katherine Applegate, p 7.

Lexicon Check: Coherence

When the ideas presented in a text "stick together" or cohere, they are linked in a logical and organized manner. When the text is cohesive, the reader understands how the ideas and relationships presented within a text work together and contribute to understanding.

3. Understanding Cause:

People started coming to North America in the 1600's. They were called colonists. They were from all over Europe, but most came from England. Soon the British had the greatest influence in America. Because of this, America became part of England.

Why did people leave their homes to come to North America?

The Founding of American Democracy by Jessica McBirney, p. 1

Why: The Science

Researchers in linguistics, cognitive psychology and education consider inference as a central component in language comprehension and essential to reading comprehension. (Elleman, 2017, p. 1)

Because inferencing is so central to comprehension, it is a major focus of assessments of comprehension and accounts of comprehension difficulties (Hua & Keenan, 2014, p. 415). Construction of overall meaning of the text results from the reader's aggregating units of meaning that include textual information and related background knowledge. Readers use inference in combination with their knowledge of word meaning and syntax and any relevant background knowledge to understand deeper meanings of text. While it is known that the early predictors of later word reading accuracy are phonological skills, Oakhill and Cain (2012) found that it is inference and integration, along with comprehension monitoring and use of story structures, that predicted later reading comprehension. Not surprisingly, given the nature of standardized measures of comprehension, students who score higher on inference measures perform higher on reading comprehension tests than do those with lower scores (Hall & Barnes, 2017). Studies also affirm the importance of inference-making in reading and listening comprehension over and above other factors such as general ability and memory (Florit et al., 2014; Oakhill & Cain, 2012).

How: The Design of Instruction

Introduction

Given the importance of both local and global inferences, effective instruction should focus on developing students' understanding of word meaning and sentences (surface) as well as the relationships between ideas expressed in the text (textbase) and those that are implied (textbase and mental model). In general, instruction includes strategies and activities that support students by helping them identify clues or key words in the text, activate and integrate background knowledge with text, and ask/answer questions that bridge meaning and surface what is not stated (Hall, 2016).

General Guidelines

As discussed in Chapter 8 of *The Blueprint,* research has revealed several recommendations regarding inference instruction. In fact, teaching inference generation has benefits for both skilled and struggling readers (Elleman, 2017). In this chapter, we focus on activities that use the strategies outlined in Figure 7.3 to support deeper understanding of the text at both the local and global coherence levels.

A combination of techniques is featured readily throughout this section, both within the lesson plans and activities, as this approach is ideal to support student

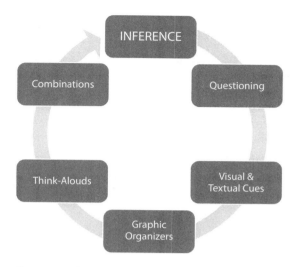

Figure 7.3. Inference Strategies.

comprehension of both local and global coherence. In addition, as with previous chapters, lesson plans and activities for inference making will be linked to what students are reading and learning about. However, supplemental texts (e.g., those with similar themes) can also be used as potential resources for practice and application.

The Blueprint

The questions in the Reading Comprehension Blueprint (see Figure 7.4) provide direction for the educator as they design and deliver instruction that supports their students' ability to express meaning at both literal and inferential levels within the context of texts they are reading.

Blueprint for Comprehension Instruction
TEXT READING
Levels of Understanding & Inference
How will you teach students to construct meaning at different levels of understanding including the surface, textbase, and mental model?
How will you directly teach students to use inference to integrate ideas and background knowledge to the text?
How will you support your students' deep comprehension of text?

Figure 7.4. The Blueprint Questions: Levels of Understanding and Inference. (*Source:* Hennessy, 2020.)

Intentional Instruction: Lesson Plans & Activities

In this section, we discuss how to create lesson plans and instructional activities that focus on effective explicit approaches that follow these guidelines and include direct explanation and instances of teacher modeling, student practice, and opportunities for application with text. We begin with examples of model lesson plans and then move on to instructional activities that focus on background knowledge.

Remember that each lesson connects back to its unit's enduring understandings and essential questions to address the overarching goals of student learning, while also mapping out specific objectives, activities, and assessments to grow students' understanding of literacy knowledge.

LESSON 1

Writing Connection: Editing to Improve Local Coherence   (textbook pgs. 180–183)

This lesson emphasizes the reading and writing connection as it highlights revising one's writing to eliminate repetition and add varied word choice. Here the teacher models using varied cohesive ties as well as sentence combining focused on connectives to avoid redundancy and create a cohesive piece of writing overall. Once again, the exercise is centered on what students are reading and learning about—in this case, *The House on Mango Street* by Sandra Cisneros. In this way, students develop this skill within the texts they are reading in school.

Name: Editing to Improve Local Coherence   **Grade:** Eighth

Preparation for Instruction

Enduring Understandings:

- Individual identities are complex and show themselves in many ways.
- Everyone has multiple identities.
- Societal views can influence individual identity.

Essential Questions:

- What defines our identity?
- How is it shaped?
- Do we keep the same identity throughout our lives?
- How do authors develop character's identity?

Content Objectives:

- Students will be able to:
  - Reflect on the various ways certain social contexts impact our identities.
  - Examine the topic of identity in a variety of stories.

Literacy Objectives:

- Students will be able to:
  - Analyze the impact of an author's literary choices in a memoir.
  - Compare characters and self to create connections and demonstrate understanding of the character within a story.

Resources/Materials:

- *The House on Mango Street* by Sandra Cisneros
- Copy of completed writing prompt (within lesson) for revising. This includes student copies and one for teacher modeling.
- Document camera, Smartboard, or passage rewritten on chart paper (so students can see the revision process)

Sequence of Events

Purpose: Students will be able to revise writing to include varied word choice and sentence structure

Review/prerequisite skills: To participate in this lesson students should have the following prerequisite skills:

- Understanding of what it means to revise
- Knowledge of cohesive ties (pronoun referents, synonyms, & substitutions) and connectives
- Knowledge of appositives

Teacher/Student Instructional Activities:

Lesson opening:

1. Explain to students that good writers revise their writing to include varied word choice and sentence structures.
2. Today we will address this by revising a given passage by focusing on the use of varied cohesive ties (specifically pronoun referents and synonyms and substitutions) and combining simple sentences using connectives.

Teacher modeling:

3. Display the following passage and ask students to read it aloud. Instruct students to share their thoughts and/ or what they notice about this initial draft. The teacher should draw students' attention to repetition in word choice and sentence structure.

> In the first chapter, Esperanza conveys her thoughts about her self-identity as Esperanza describes the family home. Esperanza initially shares some positive features. The house is owned by Esperanza's family. They don't have to share the yard. They don't have to worry about making too much noise. They don't have to pay rent to someone. However, Esperanza says, ". . . it's not the house we thought we'd get" (Cisneros, pg. 3). Esperanza's parents told stories of a "dreamed up" house where Esperanza thought they would live. This house would look like the ". . . houses on T.V." with running water, a basement, and multiple bedrooms and bathrooms. This is not the house Esperanza and her family get. Instead, Esperanza describes the house as ". . . small and red with tight steps in the front . . . bricks crumbling in places . . . no front yard . . . and the house only has one washroom" (Cisneros, pg. 4). Esperanza wants a house to be proud of. Esperanza wants a house she can point to, and not be embarrassed, like when Esperanza lived on Loomis Street. But to Esperanza, the house on Mango Street "isn't it" (Cisneros, pg. 5).

4. Using the first three sentences, the teacher should use think-alouds to model/highlight where repetition in word choice can be noted (highlighted yellow in the image below). For example:

When I look at the first three sentences, I notice that the author uses the name Esperanza four times. I wonder if there is a way I can revise this part of the paragraph to include more varied word choice.

> In the first chapter, <u>Esperanza</u> conveys her thoughts about her self-identity as <u>Esperanza</u> describes the family home. <u>Esperanza</u> initially shares some positive features. The house is owned by <u>Esperanza's</u> family. They don't have to share the yard. They don't have to worry about making too much noise. They don't have to pay rent to someone. However, Esperanza says, ". . . it's not the house we thought we'd get" (Cisneros, pg. 3). Esperanza's parents told stories of a "dreamed up" house where Esperanza thought they would live. This house would look like the ". . . houses on T.V." with running water, a basement, and multiple bedrooms and bathrooms. This is not the house Esperanza and her family get. Instead, Esperanza describes the house as ". . . small and red with tight steps in the front . . . bricks crumbling in places . . . no front yard . . . and the house only has one washroom" (Cisneros, pg. 4). Esperanza wants a house to be proud of. Esperanza wants a house she can point to, and not be embarrassed, like when Esperanza lived on Loomis Street. But to Esperanza, the house on Mango Street "isn't it" (Cisneros, pg. 5).

5. Model for students how you would revise this part of the passage to make it less redundant.

6. For example: *I think I am going to revise the first sentence to use Esperanza only once. I might replace the second usage with the pronoun **she**. Additionally, I want to add an **appositive** here to clearly define who Esperanza is. My new sentence reads: <u>In the first chapter, Esperanza, **a strong willed but insecure young girl**, conveys her thoughts about her self-identity as **she** describes her family home.</u>*

7. Model again for students how sentences 2 and 3 can be revised by replacing Esperanza's name with a pronoun, this time the word **her**. For example:

*I also noticed that the name Esperanza is used twice in a row in sentences two and three. I am going to replace the second time it's used with the pronoun **her** to add some variety. I am also going to add the phrase **for one** to make it flow. My revised writing reads: <u>Esperanza initially shares some positive features. **For one** the house is owned by **her** family.</u>*

8. Draw students' attention to sentences 4–6. Ask them what they notice. Answers may include repetitive use of the word *they*, lack of sentence variety, and so forth.

> In the first chapter, <u>Esperanza, a strong willed but insecure young girl,</u> conveys her thoughts about her self-identity as <u>she</u> describes the family home. <u>Esperanza</u> initially shares some positive features. The house is owned by <u>her</u> family. (They) don't have to share the yard. (They) don't have to worry about making too much noise. (They) don't have to pay rent to someone. However, Esperanza says, ". . . it's not the house we thought we'd get" (Cisneros, pg. 3). Esperanza's parents told stories of a "dreamed up" house where Esperanza thought they would live. This house would look like the ". . . houses on T.V." with running water, a basement, and multiple bedrooms and bathrooms. This is not the house Esperanza and her family get. Instead, Esperanza describes the house as ". . . small and red with tight steps in the front . . . bricks crumbling in places . . . no front yard . . . and the house only has one washroom" (Cisneros, pg. 4). Esperanza wants a house to be proud of. Esperanza wants a house she can point to, and not be embarrassed, like when Esperanza lived on Loomis Street. But to Esperanza, the house on Mango Street "isn't it" (Cisneros, pg. 5).

9. Now model for students how sentences 4–6 can be combined to eliminate repetition and create varied sentence structures. For example:

   *So, I am noticing a couple of things in this passage. First, the author uses the word **they** over and over. Also, these sentences all have a fairly repetitive structure. I am wondering if I can combine ideas to eliminate some of the redundancy. My revised writing is:* **They** <u>don't have to share the yard, worry about making too much noise,</u> **or pay rent to someone.**

Student-guided practice:

10. Next, have students examine sentences 7 and 8. Guide students through the process of revising these sentences to include varied word choice.

> In the first chapter, **<u>Esperanza, a strong willed but insecure young girl</u>**, conveys her thoughts about her self-identity as **<u>she</u>** describes the family home. **<u>Esperanza</u>** initially shares some positive features. The house is owned by **<u>her</u>** family. **<u>They</u>** don't have to share the yard, worry about making too much noise, **or** pay rent to someone. However, <u>Esperanza</u> says, ". . . it's not the house we thought we'd get" (Cisneros, pg. 3). <u>Esperanza's</u> parents told stories of a "dreamed up" house where <u>Esperanza</u> thought they would live. This house would look like the ". . . houses on T.V." with running water, a basement, and multiple bedrooms and bathrooms. This is not the house Esperanza and her family get. Instead, Esperanza describes the house as ". . . small and red with tight steps in the front . . . bricks crumbling in places . . . no front yard . . . and the house only has one washroom" (Cisneros, pg. 4). Esperanza wants a house to be proud of. Esperanza wants a house she can point to, and not be embarrassed, like when Esperanza lived on Loomis Street. But to Esperanza, the house on Mango Street "isn't it" (Cisneros, pg. 5).

11. Guiding questions could include:
    a. What word is overused in these sentences?
    b. What could we do to add variety in word choice here?
    c. Could we add transitional words or phrases to help with the overall flow?
12. Potential revised responses could include:
    a. However, Esperanza says, ". . . it's not the house we thought we'd get (Cisneros, pg. 3). **In fact**, **her** parents told stories of a "dreamed up" house where the **entire family** would live.

Independent practice:

13. Have students work in partnerships or small groups to revise the remainder of the paragraph with an emphasis on eliminating redundancy in overused words and sentence structures.
14. As students work, the teacher can circulate around the room and support students as needed.
15. Once the groups have completed the activity, reconvene as a whole group to share their completed responses with the group. A completed potential response is included here for your reference.

In the first chapter, **Esperanza, a strong willed but insecure young girl,** conveys her thoughts about her self-identity as **she** describes the family home. **Esperanza** initially shares some positive features. The house is owned by **her** family. **They** don't have to share the yard, worry about making too much noise, **or** pay rent to someone. However, **Esperanza** says, ". . . it's not the house we thought we'd get" (Cisneros, pg. 3). **In fact, her** parents told stories of a "dreamed up" house where **the entire family** would live. This house would look like the ". . . houses on T.V." with running water, a basement, and multiple bedrooms and bathrooms. This is not the house **they** get. Instead, Esperanza describes **it** as ". . . small and red with tight steps in the front . . . bricks crumbling in places . . . no front yard . . . and the house only has one washroom" (Cisneros, pg. 4). Esperanza wants a house to be proud of. **One she** can point to, and not be embarrassed, like when **her family** lived on Loomis Street. But to Esperanza, the house on Mango Street "isn't it", **and she continues to dream of a day when she can have a more beautiful and autonomous home of her very own** (Cisneros, pg. 5).

Differentiation/Inclusive Instructional Practices:

- Flexible grouping is used throughout the lesson.
- Highlighting, underlining, and color-coding can be used to draw attention to redundancies in words, phrases, clauses, and sentences.
- Students should be encouraged to read their revised work aloud to help students identify areas in need of improvement.

Evidence of Student Learning/Informal Classroom-Based Assessment:

- Participation in whole-group lesson
- Participation in partnerships or small groups
- Classroom discussion
- Completed revised writing piece to include varied word choice and sentence structures

Teacher Reflection in Implementation:

Try This! Now that you've learned about ways local coherence inference connects to writing and revisions, it's time to put this strategy into action. Read the following passage and consider how you can use your knowledge of cohesive devices, both cohesive ties and connectives, to revise the writing for varied word choice and sentence structure. Once complete, compare your answers with the completed response provided. How did your revisions compare?

In the short story "Fish Cheeks," author Amy Tan retells an event from her teenaged years. The event is when Amy's mother invited the minister's son, Robert, to her house for Christmas Eve dinner. Robert is also her crush. Amy writes about her embarrassment of the Chinese dishes her mother prepared. The dishes include "fleshy prawns . . . a slimy rock cod with bulging eyes . . . [and] tofu, which looked like stacked wedges of rubbery white sponges" (Tan, p. 1). Amy is also embarrassed by her relatives who eat noisily. Her relatives also ". . . licked the ends of their chopsticks and reached across the table, dipping them into the dozen or so plates of food" (Tan, p 1). Amy is embarrassed by her Chinese heritage. Amy wants to be seen as American. When the guests leave, her mother gifts her a miniskirt as a symbol of her American identity. Her mother also tells Amy that she must remain Chinese on the inside. She must be proud of being different. As an adult, Amy reflects back on this memory. Amy realizes that her mother understood more than she originally thought. Amy's mother taught her a valuable lesson. This helped Amy embrace her heritage.

Source: Tan, 1987.

Potential response (revisions in bold):

In the short story, "Fish Cheeks," author Amy Tan retells an event from her teenaged years **when her** mother invited the minister's son, **and crush**, Robert, to her house for Christmas Eve dinner. Amy writes about her embarrassment of the Chinese dishes her mother prepared, **which included** "fleshy prawns . . . a slimy rock cod with bulging eyes . . . [and] tofu, which looked like stacked wedges of rubbery white sponges" (Tan, p. 1). Amy is also **ashamed of** her relatives who eat noisily **and** ". . . licked the ends of their chopsticks and reached across the table, dipping them into the dozen or so plates of food" (Tan, p. 1). **She** is **self-conscious of** her Chinese heritage **and** wants to be seen as American. When the guests leave, her mother gifts her a miniskirt as a symbol of her American identity. Her mother also tells Amy that she must remain Chinese on the inside **and to always** be be proud of being different. **Adult Amy** realizes that her mother understood more than she originally thought. **In fact, her mother** taught her a valuable lesson **and** helped her embrace her heritage.

LESSON 2

Using Graphic Organizers to Support Global Coherence Inference Making

(textbook pgs. 185–186)

This second lesson emphasizes the use of graphic organizers to support students in generating global coherence inferences. This lesson is tied to the unit *All About Me!* and the beautiful picture book *The Proudest Blue* by Ibtihaj Muhammad. Through instances of teacher modeling, guided, and, eventually, independent practice, students are taught to infer character traits based on what a character says, what they do, and what they think. This lesson builds upon student knowledge of adjective use as learners solidify their understanding that these describing words can be used to express a character's personality. However, authors don't always explicitly tell us these traits, so sometimes we need to use evidence from the text and our own background knowledge to infer, or make a good guess, about a character's personality.

Name: Inferring Character Traits With *The Proudest Blue* by Ibtihaj Muhammad

Grade: First

Preparation for Instruction

Enduring Understandings:

- I am unique; there is no one else like me.
- My family is unique.
- All of the people in my class are unique and have their own interests and can do different things.

Essential Questions:

- What characteristics and traits make me an individual?
- What makes my family unique?
- What makes my classmates unique?

Content Objectives:

- Students will be able to recognize that everyone has similarities and differences.

Literacy Objectives:

- Students will be able to:
  - Identify and discuss story elements (characters, setting, events, conclusion)
  - Analyze story character and infer character traits from text
  - Identify words, adjectives, and identity terms that describe story characters, themselves, their families, and their classmates

- Use new vocabulary words in their speaking and writing with prompting and support

Resources/Materials:

- *The Proudest Blue* by Ibtihaj Muhammad
- Inferring character traits chart (student copies and for teacher modeling; see Figure 7.5, which is also available as a blank, downloadable worksheet on the Brookes Download Hub; see front matter for instructions to access the downloads that accompany this book)

Sequence of Events

Purpose: Students will be able to infer character traits from the text.

Review/prerequisite skills: To participate in this lesson students should have the following prerequisite skills:

- Define the term *character trait*
- Understanding that adjectives are used to describe
- Have participated in one read aloud of *The Proudest Blue* by Ibtihaj Muhammad and discussed story elements overall (especially sisters Faizah and Asiya)

Teacher/Student Instructional Activities:

Lesson opening:

1. Explain to students that today they will explore how readers can infer, or make a well-informed guess, specific character traits based on what characters say and how characters think and act.

2. Review the term *character traits* with students (words that describe a character's personality). Remind students that sometimes an author explicitly tells us about a character's personality through use of adjectives. However, other times, we need to infer a character's personality by thinking about what a character says and how they think and act. Today, we will practice this skill with the book *The Proudest Blue*.

Teacher modeling:

3. The teacher should display a copy of the Inferring Character Traits chart as shown here. Explain that a graphic organizer like this one will help us to determine character traits to describe Faizah, one of the story's main characters.

What the character **says**, **does**, or **thinks**	Inferred character trait

4. Using pages 3-4, the teacher can model a think-aloud inferring the character trait of *joyful*. For example:

   a. "I notice that on these pages the author is providing me some clues that Faizah is a joyful person. I can see this in her excitement over her new backpack and light-up shoes. She also loves to twirl. I am going to list these on my chart as pieces of evidence from the author showing that Faizah is joyful."

What the character **says**, **does**, or **thinks**	Inferred character trait
• Excited by her new backpack and light-up shoes; loves to twirl	• Faizah is joyful

5. Next using pages 5 and 6 and 17 and 18, model a think-aloud inferring the character trait *imaginative*. For example:

   a. "On pages 5 and 6, I notice that Faizah describes her sister, Asiya, as a princess and imagines that she is one too. Then, on pages 17 and 18, she draws a picture of two princesses in their hijabs having a picnic. I think this evidence shows that Faizah is imaginative."

What the character **says**, **does**, or **thinks**	Inferred character trait
• Excited by her new backpack and light-up shoes; loves to twirl • Imagines she and her sister are princesses; draws them having a picnic	• Faizah is joyful. • Faizah is imaginative.

Student-guided practice:

6. Next, using examples in the text, guide students in inferring the character trait of *protective*. Some good guiding questions to help students consider this are:

   a. Can you think of a time in the book when Faizah stands up for her sister?

   b. What does Faizah do, say, or think that shows she looks out for her sister?

   c. How might we describe these actions?

7. Add student responses to the chart. Potential responses are included in the following example.

What the character **says**, **does**, or **thinks**	Inferred character trait
• Excited by her new backpack and light-up shoes; loves to twirl • Imagines she and her sister are princesses; draws them having a picnic • Goes to the big kids' side of the recess yard to give her sister an extra hug; is angry with the boys who make fun of Asiya's hijab	• Faizah is joyful. • Faizah is imaginative. • Faizah is protective.

Independent practice:

8. Distribute a copy of the inferring character traits chart to students. Students can work with a partner to discuss evidence in the story that shows Faizah is proud of her sister. They can use words or pictures to show their evidence on their inferring character traits chart.

9. While students talk together, the teacher can circulate around the room and support partnerships as needed.

10. Once the activity is complete, students can come back together as a whole group and share their responses. The teacher can add their ideas to the classroom inferring character traits chart, as well. An example of a completed chart is here for your reference.

What the character **says**, **does**, or **thinks**	Inferred character trait
• Excited by her new backpack and light up shoes; loves to twirl • Imagines she and her sister are princesses; draws them having a picnic • Goes to the big kids' side of the recess yard to give her sister an extra hug; Faizah is angry with the boys who make fun of Asiya's hijab • Faizah describes her sister's hijab like a sky on a sunny day; she wants her first day hijab to be blue, like Asiya's; she shows Asiya the picture she drew of the two of them in school	• Faizah is joyful. • Faizah is imaginative. • Faizah is protective. • Faizah is proud of (and admires) her sister.

Differentiation/Inclusive Instructional Practices:

- Flexible grouping is used throughout the lesson
- Partner work
- Students can write or draw their responses

Evidence of Student Learning/Informal Classroom-Based Assessment:

- Participation in whole-group lesson
- Participation in partner work and turn and talks
- Completed inferring character traits chart

Teacher Reflection in Implementation:

Try This! Now it's your turn to try it. Read the following passage taken from *The Great Gatsby*. Then complete the inferring character traits chart (see Figure 7.5) for the character of Daisy Buchanan. Once you've finished, reflect: how can you use an activity like this one to support your students in making global coherence inferences?

What the character **says**, **does**, or **thinks**	Inferred character trait

Figure 7.5. Inferring character traits chart. (*Source:* Fitzgerald, 1925.)

> *The next April Daisy had her little girl and they went to France for a year. I saw them one spring in Cannes and later in Deauville and then they came back to Chicago to settle down. Daisy was popular in Chicago, as you know. They moved with a fast crowd, all of them young and rich and wild, but she came out with an absolutely perfect reputation. Perhaps because she doesn't drink. It's a great advantage not to drink among hard-drinking people. You can hold your tongue and, moreover, you can time any little irregularity of your own so that everybody else is so blind that they don't see or care. Perhaps Daisy never went in for amour at all—and yet there's something in that voice of hers"* (Fitzgerald, pg. 77).

What the character **says**, **does**, or **thinks**	Inferred character trait

Potential Response:

What the character **says**, **does**, or **thinks**	Inferred character trait
• Daisy moved with a fast crowd but still had a perfect reputation; didn't drink around "hard-drinking people"; maybe she never "went in for amour" with her husband/ pretended to love him.	• Daisy is shrewd and calculating.

Local Coherence Inference Activities

Effective instruction in local coherence inferences starts with students understanding the *why* (purpose), the *what* (cohesive devices), and the *how* (strategies, activities) of local coherence inference making. Teachers can use the following questions provided as general guidance when planning instruction and preparing the text for activities in local coherence inference making. This includes:

- How will I explain the function of cohesive devices?

- Which type will I target based on student understanding of the text itself?

- How will I explain the difference between cohesive ties and connectives?

- Which text examples will I use? Which are the most relevant to my students' needs?

- How will I explicitly teach strategies for acquiring and applying these skills?

- Are there manipulatives, gestures, and/or visuals that could support/scaffold student understanding?

- How will I provide for individual, partner, or small-group interaction?

For this section of the chapter, we will investigate strategies including the use of questioning, visual and textual cues, graphic organizers, think-alouds, and a combination approach from the perspective of intentional instruction centered on cohesive ties and connectives. These types of necessary inferences help students develop local coherence by making sense of individual sentences as well as how these sentences connect and combine to make sense overall. While skilled comprehenders typically have an automatic awareness of cohesive devices and readily make meaning from them, poor comprehenders require intentional on-purpose instruction, focused on the understanding of the role of cohesive ties and connectives in a sentence.

Questioning   (textbook pgs. 180–183)

As we have discussed throughout this book, questioning is an incredibly powerful strategy to support learners' reading comprehension. Questioning can be used to facilitate students' understanding of both cohesive ties and connectives, including their unique functions and differences. And, as mentioned previously, using questioning in combination with other strategies, especially those that allow students to make connections visually or verbally, works to improve learning outcomes for a variety of learners.

Questioning & Cohesive Ties

When instructing students about cohesive ties, it is important to explicitly discuss their function: they are words and phrases that link up units of meaning within and between sentences. Cohesive ties take their meaning from another part of a sentence or sentences. They replace the word or phrase to which it refers within a different part of the sentence or in another sentence. Some examples include, pronoun referents, synonyms and substitutions, repetition of words and phrases, and ellipses. As the attuned educator prepares the text, they are on the lookout for meaningful examples to highlight and explicitly teach the various styles of cohesive ties. Table 7.1, which features the short story "Fish Cheeks" by Amy Tan, highlights how one might pull out specific examples of cohesive ties in the text and link them to targeted questions to clarify their meaning. Remember: It is important that these skills be developed within the context of the texts students are reading rather than being taught in isolation.

Table 7.1. Cohesive ties in "Fish Cheeks"

Cohesive tie	Example from text	Aligned question(s)
Pronoun referents	*My relatives licked the ends of their chopsticks and reached across the table, dipping them into the dozen or so plates of food.*	In this sentence, which pronoun refers to Tan's relatives? To the chopsticks? What do you notice about these pronouns? Why does this usage make this sentence trickier to comprehend?
Synonyms and substitutions	*Then my father poked his chopsticks just below the fish eye and plucked out the soft meat. "Amy, your favorite," he said, offering me the tender fish cheek.*	Which words does the author use here to stand in for or mean the same as *fish cheek*?
Repetitions of nouns and phrases	*What would Robert think of our shabby Chinese Christmas? What would he think of our noisy Chinese relatives who lacked proper American manners? What terrible disappointment would he feel upon seeing not a roasted turkey and sweet potatoes but Chinese food?*	Why do you think the author chooses to repeat the word *Chinese* throughout this passage? Why is this important to note?

Source: Tan, 1987.

Questioning & Connectives

The same use of questioning can be applied to work with connectives, as well. *Connectives* are words or phrases that signal a logical relationship between the parts of a sentence or between separate sentences and paragraphs. Conjunctions can serve as connectives since they connect words, phrases, and clauses within a sentence, but not all connectives are necessarily conjunctions. There are various kinds of connectives including additive, temporal, causal, adversative (contrast), and conditionality. Table 7.2 again features the short story "Fish Cheeks," but with examples and questions targeting the use of connectives.

Table 7.2. Use of connectives in "Fish Cheeks"

Connective	Example from text	Aligned question(s)
Additive	*And then they arrived—the minister's family and all my relatives in a clamor of doorbells and rumpled Christmas packages.*	Which word does the author use to express an addition of ideas or concepts? (*and*)
Temporal	*At the end of the meal, my father leaned back and belched loudly, thanking my mother for her fine cooking.*	Which word in this sentence cues the reader to the passage of time? (*at*)
Causal	*A plate of squid, their backs crisscrossed with knife markings so they resembled bicycle tires.*	Can you find the word that infers a causal relationship? (*so*)
Adversative (contrast)	*And even though I didn't agree with her then, I knew that she understood how much I had suffered during the evening's dinner.*	Which word(s) does author Amy Tan use to signal a contrast in ideas? (*even though*)

Source: Tan, 1987.

It is critical to assess student knowledge of both cohesive ties and connectives and then provide instructional opportunities that directly teach learners how to integrate ideas when needed. The attuned educator scaffolds this process by initially using direct instruction to model the process, often pairing this strategy with visual cues, like highlighting and coding, which we discuss next, but eventually student self-questioning is the goal. It is also important to note that not every story or passage includes examples of every type of cohesive device. For instance, the short story "Fish Cheeks" does not include an example of ellipses (cohesive tie) or a conditionality connective. Thus, it is important to ensure students are offered the opportunity to identify and practice with all types of these devices. In this instance, supplemental resources, or those connected to a related theme, may be considered an appropriate option.

 Try This!   Read through the following examples from the novel *The Great Gatsby* by F. Scott Fitzgerald. Determine which type of cohesive device is featured and then craft a question in the space provided that taps into the function of the underlined device. Finally, check your understanding by reviewing the answer key provided.

1. "<u>After</u> she had obliterated four years with that sentence they could decide upon the more practical measures to be taken" (Fitzgerald, pg. 109).

   Type of connective: _____

   Question: _____

2. "The <u>Carraways</u> are something of a <u>clan</u>, and we have a tradition that we're descended from the Dukes of Buccleuch, but the actual founder of my <u>line</u> was my grandfather's brother, who came here in fifty-one, sent a substitute to the Civil War, and started the wholesale hardware business that my father carries on to-day" (Fitzgerald, pg. 3).

Type of cohesive tie: _____

Question: _____

3. "'Your face is familiar,' he said, politely. 'Weren't you in the Third Division during the War?'

'Why, yes. I was in the ninth machine-gun <u>battalion</u>.'

'I was in the <u>seventh</u> until June nineteen eighteen. I knew I'd seen you somewhere before'" (Fitzgerald, pg. 47).

Type of cohesive tie: _____

Question: _____

Answer Key:

1. Type of connective: *temporal*

   Question: *Can you identify a word that signals the passage of time?*

2. Type of cohesive tie: *synonym/substitution*

   Question: *Which words does the author use to stand in for the Carraways?*

3. Type of cohesive tie: *ellipses*

   Question(s): *Which word does the author remove from this passage? Why do you think the author chose to do so?*

Using Visuals and Textual Clues   (textbook pgs. 180–183)

Oakhill et al. (2015) identified many strategies and activities that help teachers instruct students and allow them to practice to ensure mastery of local coherence. Students can highlight or color-code words and cohesive devices, or use a coding system, to identify and mark up cohesive ties and connectives within a text. For example, they can underline or highlight pronoun referents, draw arrows connecting words to their synonyms or substitutions, and box connectives. Again, as the attuned educator previews the text, they look for passages to highlight this skill.

The images that follow show how highlighting and coding can be used as a visual cue to draw students' attention to these devices. The text featured is taken from the short story "The Jacket" by Gary Soto, which is connected to the larger theme of identity as highlighted in the *Who Am I?* unit. This again confirms that students are working with and developing these skills within the context of texts they are reading and learning about. Notice how the same passage could be used to highlight a variety of these devices. For example, the first image shown asks students to put a box around connectives that signal the reader to the passage of time.

Put a box around the connectives that signal the reader to the passage of time.

That was the first afternoon with my new jacket. The next day I wore it to sixth grade and got a D on a math quiz. During *the morning recess Frankie T., the playground terrorist, pushed me to the ground and told me to stay there* until *recess was over. My best friend, Steve Negrete, ate an apple* while *looking at me, and the girls turned away to whisper on the monkey bars. The teachers were no help: they looked my way and talked about how foolish I looked in my new jacket. I saw their heads bob with laughter, their hands half covering their mouths.*

Source: Soto, 1983.

However, this same passage could be used to examine the role of pronoun referents. Here the teacher has focused the task on identifying the pronouns that refer to the word *teacher* in the last two sentences of the given passage.

Underline the pronouns that refer to the word teachers in the last sentences.

That was the first afternoon with my new jacket. The next day I wore it to sixth grade and got a D on a math quiz. During the morning recess Frankie T., the playground terrorist, pushed me to the ground and told me to stay there until recess was over. My best friend, Steve Negrete, ate an apple while looking at me, and the girls turned away to whisper on the monkey bars. The teachers were no help: <u>they</u> *looked my way and talked about how foolish I looked in my new jacket. I saw* <u>their</u> *heads bob with laughter,* <u>their</u> *hands half covering* <u>their</u> *mouths.*

Source: Soto, 1983.

In the final example, students are asked to draw an arrow connecting the synonyms and substitutions to the words they refer to. Notice how author Soto renames his bully, *Frankie T.*, as the *playground terrorist*. Additionally, his *best friend* is clearly named as *Steve Negrete*.

Draw an arrow connecting the synonyms/substitutions to the words they refer to.

That was the first afternoon with my new jacket. The next day I wore it to sixth grade and got a D on a math quiz.

During the morning recess Frankie T., the playground terrorist, pushed me to the ground and told me to stay there until recess was over. My best friend, Steve Negrete, ate an apple while looking at me, and the girls turned away to whisper on the monkey bars. The teachers were no help: they looked my way and talked about how foolish I looked in my new jacket. I saw their heads bob with laughter, their hands half covering their mouths.

Source: Soto, 1983.

In this manner, students are able to use the visual and textual cues to recognize and understand the cohesive devices in the texts they are reading. This supports their ability to establish local coherence by integrating information within and between sentences.

Oakhill and colleagues (2015) also recommend the use of picture support for developing precise use of connectives. For example, causality can be developed by using images to help students understand the function of this type of connective. Images, like the one here, help students clearly see the causal relationships in action.

Thus, pairing this photo with targeted questions such as "Why did the dog run to its owner?" helps students to visualize the *why*. In this instance, a fitting response might be, "The dog ran to its owner *because* they were playing fetch" or ". . . *because* its owner had the ball." This offers the opportunity to discuss the function of the word *because*: a conjunction that provides a reason for why something occurred.

Try This! Using the passage provided from *The Great Gatsby*, complete the following tasks:

1. Underline the pronouns that refer to Jay Gatsby throughout the passage.
2. Draw an arrow to the synonyms/substitutions that refer to Gatsby, as well.
3. Put a box around the connective that signals the passage of time.

Once you have finished, compare your findings with the answer key. How did you do?

> On Sunday morning while church bells rang in the villages alongshore, the world and its mistresses returned to Gatsby's house and twinkled hilariously on his lawn.
>
> "He's a bootlegger," said the young ladies, moving somewhere between his cocktails and his flowers. "One time he killed a man who had found out that he was nephew to Von Hindenburg and second cousin to the devil. Reach me a rose honey, and pour me the last drop into that there crystal glass."
>
> —Fitzgerald, pg. 61

Answer Key:

> "On Sunday morning while church bells rang in the villages alongshore, the world and its mistresses returned to Gatsby's house and twinkled hilariously on his lawn.
>
> "He's a bootlegger," said the young ladies, moving somewhere between his cocktails and his flowers. "One time he killed a man who had found out that he was nephew to Von Hindenburg and second cousin to the devil. Reach me a rose honey, and pour me the last drop into that there crystal glass."
>
> –Fitzgerald, pg. 61

Global Coherence Inference Activities

The second type of inference we explore in this chapter is global coherence inference, which is necessary for deep comprehension of the text. As with local coherence, teachers can utilize the following questions as general guidance when planning instruction and preparing the text for activities that develop these gap-filling inferences. This includes:

- How will I explain this type of inference?

- How will I explain the importance of using background knowledge?

- Which text examples will I use? Which are most relevant to my students' needs?

- What strategies or activities will I use to engage students in acquiring or applying skills?

- Are there manipulatives, gestures, and/or visuals that could support/scaffold student understanding?

- How will I provide for individual, partner, or small-group instruction?

The development of global inferences is dependent upon student background knowledge, so students must have cultivated the necessary knowledge for working with specific texts first. Once this is established, educators can employ a series of steps as outlined in Table 7.3.

Table 7.3. Teacher and student steps for global inferences

Teacher actions	Student actions
1. Identifies and prepares the text (or picture)	1. Reads the text (or examines the picture)
2. Frames inferential questions/prompts	2. Reads and uses the questions/prompts
3. Models identification of clues and integration of background knowledge	3. Finds clues and connects to background knowledge
4. Models responses to questions and prompts	4. Responds to questions/prompts

This helpful table reminds us that teacher modeling is key here and should be included initially to help students visualize how to generate global coherence inferences. This section explores two strategies, use of visuals and graphic organizers, to support students with this process. These strategies will also be paired with questions and prompts, as using a combined approach is ideal to support learners' comprehension.

As with local coherence inference, use of visuals and textual cues can be powerful ways to tap into global coherence inference making. Visuals are an excellent resource that can be used with students of all ages. Consider the unit *All About Me!*, which is designed for students in first grade. This unit explores the concepts of identity and investigates the concept of family and how each student's family has its own unique celebrations and traditions. This idea is explored in the read-aloud books *Fry Bread* by Kevin Noble Maillard, *Too Many Tamales* by Gary Soto, and *Bee-Bim Bop!* by Linda Sue Park. These picture books provide a wonderful starting point for the discussion of family traditions and the expression of our heritage through the shared act of making food. To help students draw conclusions about the similarities and differences in family traditions, the teacher can select and prepare images of various families engaging in traditions. To help students draw conclusions about the similarities and differences in family traditions, the teacher can select and prepare images of various families engaging in traditions as shown in the following images.

Using targeted questions, the teacher can first model, and then ask students to draw conclusions about the similarities and differences between these family celebrations and traditions. Framed questions and prompts could include:

- Who do you see in these images?
- What are these people doing?
- How might they be related/connected?
- Why are these people doing what you see them doing in the images?

Then a teacher might identify clues in the picture to highlight similarities (e.g., families coming together over food, a span of generations, quality time spent with family) and differences (e.g., role of religion, time of year, food choices, tradition unique to family). Finally, the teacher would draw conclusions about the qualities that family traditions and celebrations share and those areas where they are different.

This strategy can also be used across age and grade levels, as mentioned earlier, and use of visuals, such as political cartoons, is an effective means to help older students unpack complex topics. The questions below, created by The Haverford School Upper School history teacher Jeremy Hart, were crafted to help students engage in political cartoon analysis. Jeremy poses these questions to prime students' thinking about these images, so they can then evaluate and explain them in both speaking and writing.

Source: Meyer, H. (1898). En Chine – le gâteau des rois et . . . des empereurs. *Le Petit Journal.*

Again, images need to be previewed and prepared in advance so that questions and prompts created help students to construct global coherence inferences. Questions might include:

- What was happening when this cartoon was made? Explain the actual history behind the cartoon.
- Do you think it is an accurate representation of history?
- Can you tie the cartoon to any primary sources?
- Who do you think was the audience for this cartoon? Why?
- What techniques, such as symbols, word choice, caricature, exaggeration, and irony, help communicate the overall message?
- What do you think the cartoonist's opinion on this issue is?

This final example, created by The Haverford School Upper School biology teacher Tasha Lewis, highlights how textual cues can be used to help students predict what a cell membrane might look like based on a description of an organism and its environment. Students were taught to look for textual clues, which are circled.

Directions: *Using the information about your organism and cell below, along with your textbook, predict and draw what its cell membrane might look like. You will need to draw a sketch of the membrane, label it, and then include a description that explains how the structure relates to its function. Additionally, for each component listed, explain why you included it.*

Polar bears are found in arctic climates. They are found in various places in the world, but all locations have ice and seals, their main food source. Like other animals they have macrophages that help protect them from foreign invaders. The way they do that is by recognizing the invader through their membrane and bringing it into the cell. This then allows them to complete phagocytosis using their lysosomes to neutralize the "threat." Hypothesize what a polar bear macrophage membrane looks like on a microscopic level.

Example provided with permission of Tasha Lewis

Students would then use their knowledge of animal cells to sketch a cell membrane that shows how cholesterol, which is contained in eukaryotic cells, inserts phospholipids into the cell membrane in low temperatures to protect the cell from environmental elements.

Reflect & Connect!

Think about any learning activities during which you use visuals or textual clues with students. What do you typically do? How can you adapt these activities to explicitly tap into students' abilities to generate global coherence inference making? What might you add or do differently based on what you've learned in this section? Write your thoughts in the space provided.

Using Graphic Organizers   (textbook pgs. 185–186)

Graphic organizers are another effective strategy to support students' ability to make global coherence inferences. Remember, global coherence inference making helps students in a variety of instances including:

• Understanding the cause of events
• Predicting future events
• Identifying setting
• Identifying character's motives, beliefs, and traits
• Understanding character relationships
• Drawing conclusions
• Understanding author's view and/or biases (Westby, 2010)

Use of graphic organizers supports students in these complex tasks as they prompt connections between the text and knowledge in making meaning. Take the following example, which asks students to make inferences about the setting in the graphic novel *Persepolis* by Marjane Satrapi. Students are given selected text from the story and then must use evidence from the text, along with their background knowledge about this period in history, to make an inference about the story setting.

Passage from the book:	"In 1979 a revolution took place. It was later called 'The Islamic Revolution.' Then came 1980: The year it became obligatory to wear the veil at school. We didn't really like to wear the veil, especially since we didn't understand why we had to. And also because the year before, in 1979, we were in a French non-religious school. Where boys and girls were together. And then suddenly in 1980, we found ourselves veiled and separated from our friends" (Satrapi, 2003, pp. 3–4).
I infer the setting:	. . . becomes more restrictive for women after 1979.
I know this because:	. . . the book describes how schools in Tehran separated boys from girls and made the girls and women wear veils. I also know that in 1979, the Shah was overthrown, and the Shia Muslim leader Ayatollah Khomeini took power. Khomeini was a dictator who denied women equal rights and banned all Western culture in Iran.

A similar approach can be used when investigating character relationships in a text. This second example again highlights the story *Persepolis*, but this time investigates the impact of character relationships. Here students are tasked to examine story dialogue, actions, and interactions to infer information about Marjane and her mother's relationship.

Character 1: Marjane's mother (Taji Satrapi) • strong-willed • participates in freedom demonstrations • protective • clever and cunning	Dialogue: "My mother used the same tactics as torturers" (p. 113). "For an Iranian mother, my mom was very permissive" (p. 131). "Anyway it is not for you and me to decide justice. I'd say we have to learn to forgive" (p. 46). Actions: Mom makes changes to her appearance to protect her family after being photographed in a protest. Mom smuggles home rock posters for Marjane in her father's jacket lining after visiting Istanbul. Mom teaches Marjane to be deceitful to protect her family (e.g., taping the windows). Mom wants to take Marjane to protests "to defend her rights as a woman" (p. 76).	Character 2: Marjane Satrapi • also strong-willed • refuses to conform • loves that her parents participate in freedom demonstrations • wants everyone to be treated equally

What types of interactions do these characters have?
Marjane admires her mother in the book, especially her participation in the freedom demonstrations. She talks with her mother about her frustrations regarding the revolution. They can argue, however, and Marjane sees this as a repression of her rights. Taji sees this as wanting to protect her daughter from danger.

What does this information tell you about their relationship?
Like many mothers and daughters, Marjane and her mother's relationship is complex. In many ways, her mother is her hero, and Marjane admires her participation in demonstrations for freedom as well as her cunning and clever nature. However, Taji will also do whatever is needed to protect her family and wants her daughter to not take unnecessary risks. Marjane sometimes sees this as taking away her rights.

In the final example, a graphic organizer is used to help students identify the author's bias in a given text. Here students are provided once again with a structure and guiding questions to help unpack a deeper level of understanding. By cuing the reader to look for positive or negative word choices, students are able to analyze Satrapi's perspective on the impact of Western countries on Iran's development as an independent nation.

Passage:

"In the 20th century, Iran entered a new phase. Reza Shah decided to modernize and westernize the country, but meanwhile a fresh source of wealth was discovered: oil. And with the oil came another invasion. The West, particularly Great Britain, wielded a strong influence on the Iranian economy. During the second World War, the British, Soviets, and Americans asked Reza Shah to ally himself with them against Germany. But Reza Shah who sympathized with the Germans, declared Iran a neutral zone. So the Allies invaded and occupied Iran. Reza Shah was sent into exile and was succeeded by his son, Mohammad Reza Pahlavi, who was simply known as the Shah" (Satrapi, 2003, p. 1).

Positive words:	**Negative words:**
• Reza Shah decided to modernize and westernize the country (Iran).	• . . . with the oil came another invasion
	• the West . . . wielded a strong influence on the Iranian economy
	• the Allies invaded and occupied Iran
	• Reza Shah was sent into exile

Author's bias or viewpoint:

Marjane Satrapi presents a somewhat positive perspective on the rule of Reza Shah, whose leadership is controversial to this day. However, her views on the Allies, specifically Great Britain, Russia, and the United States, are not. She describes them as motivated by oil and control of the Iranian economy. This imperialistic position is in line with how Russia and Great Britain divided Iran into various spheres of influence

Reflect & Connect!

As we have learned, global inference generation, which tasks students with making connections between the text and their own knowledge, supports students in identifying causes, making predictions, and drawing conclusions from the text. Graphic organizers are helpful tools that assist students with this process by providing a structure that incorporates the use of visual supports, guiding questions, and prompts to foster this connection making. Write about a learning activity during which you utilize graphic organizers to help students generate global coherence inferences. How do you use it and in what context? Then, based on what you've learned, write about how this chapter might influence your instruction moving forward.

_____

_____

_____

_____

_____

The Diverse Learner: Learning Challenges & Differences

Students with learning disabilities often have difficulty making both local and global inferences for varied reasons. For example, studies have indicated that less skilled students often do not recognize the need for an inference, make fewer and sometimes, faulty inferences (Barnes et al., 2015; Barth et al., 2015; Denton et al., 2015). The students' knowledge of and exposure to the various types of inferences is often at the heart of this problem. For example, teachers typically have students focus on predictive inference generation where students predict what will happen next based on story context; however, this type of inference is not as important as generating local and global coherence inferences, both of which are necessary to construct a coherent representation of the text (Hall & Barnes, 2017). Hall and Barnes (2017) recommend that educators prepare a text by marking where inference will be needed and explicitly teach the declarative (definitions), procedural (routines), and conditional (background knowledge) knowledge necessary to generate both types of inferences. There is limited research on the effects of inference instruction for ELLs who have comprehension difficulties. However, a recent study did suggest that they benefit from receiving explicit instruction in generating specific inference types, including noticing gaps and/or lack of coherence in text, identifying clue words or phrases, integrating information within the text, activating background knowledge, and using background knowledge to fill a gap in the text (Hall et al., 2020).

Putting it all Together: Levels of Understanding and Inference

Consider the strategies in Figure 7.3 and related examples provided in this chapter. Add a specific example of how any one of the strategies might be used in your setting. Script your response here.

Voices From the Field

I feel that inferencing is sometimes taught in isolation with instructional materials focused on teaching these skills by testing students' inferencing abilities by asking them to respond with the correct multiple choice answer. However, the development of inference making is best addressed within the texts that the students are reading.

—A Blueprint Book Study Participant

Reflect & Connect!

In what ways will these lessons and activities influence your instruction?

Viewing Link

A 20th Anniversary of Scarborough's Reading Rope – Verbal Reasoning (Session 8)
Kate Cain https://www.youtube.com/watch?v=tVO9sWHY6C4&t=942s

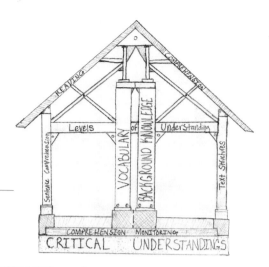

Implementing the Blueprint

Expression of Understanding

The focus for this chapter is the varied opportunities available for expressing understanding of the what, why, and the how that students might use to demonstrate learning. It features multiple instructional examples, all of which are based on the Reading Comprehension Blueprint instructional framework. Check in and surface current connections to this topic.

The multidimensional nature of comprehension presents a significant challenge for assessment. An alternative approach is to test the skills, strategies and specific content-area topics that have been taught.

(Catts, 2021–2022, pp. 32–33)

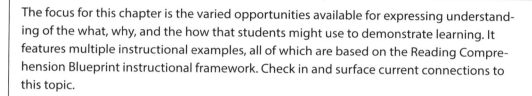

CHECK IN: Connect to current knowledge and practices!

Surface and script what comes to mind in the map (Figure 8.1) when you think about the what, why, and how of ways of expressing understanding of text.

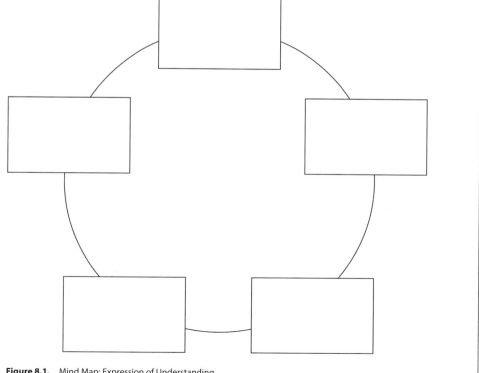

Figure 8.1. Mind Map: Expression of Understanding.

What: Definition and Description

The other chapters in this book have primarily focused on providing instructional tools for acquiring and applying each of the critical contributors necessary for constructing meaning. This chapter continues to explore the varied products or ways students can demonstrate acquisition of skills and understanding of text. While tasks related to assessing understanding are typically formal in nature (e.g., standardized comprehension assessments), this chapter addresses the ways educators can informally assess their students' comprehension on a regular basis. For example, student products may include responses to oral and written prompts/questions as well as multimedia representations of learning (e.g., videos, presentations, images). These can provide valuable information related to the reader's understanding of the text at hand.

Why: The Science

Student response to tasks at varied levels of understanding is critical for multiple reasons. Their responses provide informal assessment data that can be used to identify acquisition of literacy skills and content as well as effectiveness of current instruction and are a vehicle for monitoring the reader's progress and potential need for review. The information from varied tasks may reflect the reader's overall understanding of the text's big ideas and, potentially, their development of a mental model that can be applied to other situations. At the same time, responses may be specific to individual contributors (e.g., word meaning, sentence comprehension) that provide a window into potential sources of difficulties.

How: The Design of Instruction

Introduction

Language is at the heart of reading proficiency. Understanding the meaning of oral or written communication requires facility with receptive language (e.g., listening and reading). The ability to demonstrate understanding requires expressive language skills (e.g., speaking and writing).

As a result, the strategies and activities used to express meaning often include oral and written responses. This chapter briefly addresses oral as well as multimedia responses with the major focus on the connection between reading and writing. The ability to express what is understood through writing is dependent on shared skills as well as skills and strategies specific to writing. The Blueprint poses questions related to expressive language (Figure 8.2); added here is demonstration of understanding through multimedia, which is also reflected in the overview in Table 8.1, which identifies examples of oral and written response as well as multimedia.

Blueprint for Comprehension Instruction
Expression of Understanding
What strategies and activities will you use for students to demonstrate understanding at different levels?   How will you support their oral and written expression of understanding?

Figure 8.2. The Blueprint Questions: Expression of Understanding. (*Source:* Hennessy, 2020.)

Table 8.1. Expression of understanding approaches

Oral response: questions & prompts	Multimedia: visual & audio responses	Written responses
• Question-Answer-Response Approach • Academic Conversations • Socratic Circles	• Pictures • Illustrations • Cartoons • Videos • Podcasts • Songs	• Summaries • Notetaking • Outlining • Charts • Annotating

Oral Response

Expressing understanding orally provides a stepping stone to using writing to demonstrate learning. The informed educator provides multiple opportunities for students to move from talking to writing about text. Questions and prompts are used to foster oral response and support discussion. Jennings and Haynes (2018, p. 12) suggest that open-ended questions that begin with Wh- (e.g., who, what, when, where, why) and H- (how) are initially effective in engaging students in thinking about and responding to the text.

Others have developed specific routines and strategies that can be used to prompt thinking and conversation. These include variations on the QAR (Question-Answer-Relationship), described in Chapter 5, that asks students to think about where the reader can find responses to questions that tap into different levels of understanding. Additionally, approaches such as Academic Conversations (Zwiers & Crawford, 2011) and Socratic Circles/Questions (Fischer, 2019) incorporate the use of open-ended questions to clarify understanding, probe viewpoints, and surface evidence for thinking. These support students' exploration of ideas and the building of deep meaning of text through individual response and discussion.

Media and Multimedia Response

Varied media sources including symbols, images, pictures, audio, video, and animations supported by technology can serve the purpose of enhancing understanding (Guan et al., 2018). Using visual modes such as pictures or illustrations, videos, cartoons, or audio approaches such as songs or podcasts provides an alternative way of interpreting and representing text. They are a bridge between oral and written response and may incorporate either or both.

Written Response

As noted, writing is an important vehicle for constructing and expressing understanding for multiple reasons. Have you considered that reading and writing use many of the same language and cognitive processes and skills? The shared-knowledge model (Fitzgerald & Shanahan, 2000) "conceptualizes reading and writing as two buckets drawing water from a common well or two buildings built on the same foundation (Graham et al., 2016), p. 33." Consider the crossovers in terms of word and sentence choice, text structure knowledge, and background knowledge. For example, the reader uses their knowledge of word meaning to understand the author's use of precise words. Similarly, the reader needs access to multiple vocabulary words to clearly express their own meaning in writing. Shanahan (2017b) stated, "About 70% of the variation in reading and writing abilities are shared."

Graham and Hebert, in their seminal work *Writing to Read,* found that writing about what one is learning about improves comprehension (2010). For example, there is a reciprocal relationship between reading comprehension and writing, that is, one strengthens the other. They identified three instructional practices that capitalize on the reading and writing connection to improve students' reading comprehension. Their findings were based on a large-scale statistical review of research that examined writing techniques that improve students' comprehension. These instructional practices include:

- Have students write about the texts they read

- Teach students the writing skills and processes that go into creating text

- Increase how much students write (Graham & Hebert, 2010, p. 5)

In this section, we unpack these recommendations and discuss how to utilize the reading and writing connection to help students express what they know.

Intentional Instruction: Lesson Plans & Activities

In this section, we discuss how to create learning activities that focus on effective explicit approaches that include direct explanation and instances of teacher modeling, student practice, and opportunities for application with text. We begin with examples of model lesson plans and then move on to instructional activities that support the expression of understanding in varied modes.

Model Lesson Plans

Write Summaries of a Text

Teaching students to respond to a text through summary writing is one of the recommendations discussed in the *Writing to Read* report. Graham and Hebert (2010, p. 14) explain that "[summary writing] requires additional thought about the essence of the material, and the permanence of writing creates an external record of this synopsis that can be readily critiqued and reworked." Thus, it makes sense that this recommendation would serve to improve learner's reading comprehension. This lesson plan section examines two different approaches to summarizing, one aligned to narrative and one aligned to expository text.

Summarizing Narrative Text With Somebody-Wanted-But-So-Then

When summarizing text, it is important to consider the text structure and the genre of writing featured. As we discussed in the text structure section, narrative text has a unique purpose, structure, features, and signal words. Thus, it is important to provide explicit instruction in these characteristics and cue learners to consider them when summarizing. One strategy that helps learners summarize the features of narrative text is the *Somebody-Wanted-But-So-Then* (SWBST) strategy (Beers, 2003; Macon et al., 1991). This strategy allows students to summarize the elements of a story into a short summary as is highlighted in the following lesson plan.

Name: Summarizing *Chrysanthemum* with Somebody-Wanted-But-So-Then   **Grade:** First

Preparation for Instruction

Enduring Understandings:

- I am unique; there is no one else like me.
- All of the people in my class are unique and have their own interests and can do different things.

Essential Questions:

- What characteristics and traits make me an individual?
- What makes my classmates unique?

Content Objectives:

- Students will be able to recognize that everyone has similarities and differences.

Literacy Objectives:

- Students will be able to:
  - Identify and discuss story elements (characters, setting, events, conclusion)

  - Identify words, adjectives, and identity terms that describe story characters, themselves, their families, and their classmates
  - Use new vocabulary words in their speaking and writing with prompting and support
  - Summarize a narrative story using the Somebody-Wanted-But-So-Then strategy

Resources/Materials:

- *Chrysanthemum* by Kevin Henkes
- Somebody-Wanted-But-So-Then organizer (see Figure 8.3, which is also available as a blank, downloadable worksheet on the Brookes Download Hub; see front matter for instructions to access the downloads that accompany this book)
- Assortment of well-known fairy tales

Sequence of Events

Purpose: Students will be able to summarize a narrative story.

Review/Prerequisite Skills: To participate in this lesson students should have the following prerequisite skills:

- Understanding of the story elements of narrative text (character, setting, plot, conclusion)

Teacher/Student Instructional Activities:

Lesson opening:

1. Explain to students that today we will be investigating a strategy to help us summarize a story.
2. A summary is a condensed version of a longer story that we write in our own words. Today we are going to practice summarizing the story *Chrysanthemum* by Kevin Henkes.
3. Review the story elements (story grammar) of narrative text featured including character, setting, plot, and conclusion.

Teacher modeling:

4. Display the following Somebody-Wanted-But-So-Then (SWBST) chart for students. This chart helps us to summarize narrative stories by remembering what the main character wanted, what problem or roadblock they encountered, and how they ultimately resolved the issue.

Somebody	Wanted	But	So	Then

5. Before using the SWBST chart for *Chrysanthemum,* use a familiar fairytale and teacher think-aloud to model for students how to complete this organizer. For example, if using the fairytale Hansel and Gretel, the teacher could go through the following:

   a. "The first category is *Somebody.* This refers to the story characters. In this fairy tale, the main characters, who face a problem, are Hansel and Gretel."

   b. "Next, I need to think about what Hansel and Gretel *wanted.* Well, they were taken to the forest by their evil stepmother and wanted to return home to their father."

   c. "*But* then Hansel and Gretel see the witch's house made entirely out of candy! She tricks them into coming inside and captures them."

   d. "After that, Hansel and Gretel learn that the witch wants to eat them, which is a big problem! *So,* Gretel tricks the witch and pushes her into the oven."

   e. "*Then*, at the end of the story, Hansel and Gretel escape the house and make their way home to their father."

A sample completed table is provided for your reference:

Somebody	Wanted	But	So	Then
Hansel and Gretel, who were lost in the woods	to return home to their father	a witch with a house built out of sweets lured and captured them to eat	Gretel tricked the witch and pushed her into the oven	the children escaped and journeyed home

6. The teacher can then model using the completed SWBST organizer to say the summary aloud and then write it on the board. For example: *Lost in the woods, Hansel and Gretel wanted to return home to their father, but they were lured with sweets and captured by a witch. So, Gretel cleverly tricked the witch by pushing her into an oven, and then she and her brother escaped and went home.*

7. Point out to students that with a summary, writers condense a longer text into a short, concise explanation. Thus, not every story detail is included. That differentiates a summary from a retell.

Student-guided practice:

8. Explain to students that we will now use the SWBST organizer to summarize the story *Chrysanthemum.*

9. Using the following questions, guide students in completing the SWBST graphic organizer as a group. It can be displayed on chart paper (or on the white board) and filled in throughout this portion of the lesson. Guiding questions include:

   a. Who is the *somebody* in this story? (Chrysanthemum)

   b. What does Chrysanthemum *want*? (she wants to fit in at school)

c. *But* what happens? What is her problem? (the kids make fun of her name)

d. *So* how did she try to solve the problem? (she felt sad and talked to her parents)

e. *Then* what happens in the end? (Mrs. Twinkle shared her name, Delphinium, and that she was considering the name Chrysanthemum for her baby)

A sample completed table is provided for your reference:

Somebody	Wanted	But	So	Then
Chrysanthemum	to fit in at school	the other children made fun of her name	she felt sad and talked to her parents about it	Mrs. Twinkle shared her name (Delphinium) with the class and that she loved the name Chrysanthemum

Independent practice:

10. Students (in partners) should practice saying the summary aloud. They can then write their summary sentence to be collected by the teacher at the end of class.

11. The teacher can circulate around the room and support partnerships as needed.

12. Students can read their completed sentence summaries to the class.

Differentiation/Inclusive Instructional Practices:

- Depending on their handwriting, provide students with more space on the page to write or allow them to dictate to an adult.
- Flexible grouping is used throughout the lesson.
- Partner work

Evidence of Student Learning/Informal Classroom-Based Assessment:

- Participation in whole-group lesson
- Participation in partner work
- Completed SWBST summary sentence

Teacher Reflection in Implementation:

Somebody	Wanted	But	So	Then

My Summary Statement:

_____

_____

_____

_____

_____

Figure 8.3. Somebody-Wanted-But-So-Then (SWBST) organizer.

Try This! Using the well-known fairy tale Goldilocks and the Three Bears, complete the following Somebody-Wanted-But-So-Then (SWBST) organizer provided (Figure 8.3). Once this is complete, write a short summary of one to three sentences providing a brief overview of the story. Afterward, reflect: how can a strategy like SWBST be useful in your teaching practice? You can also compare your answer with the one provided in the answer key!

Somebody	Wanted	But	So	Then

My Summary Statement:

_____

_____

_____

_____

_____

Answer Key:

Somebody	Wanted	But	So	Then
Goldilocks	to see what was inside the house	no one was home	she went inside anyway and tried the porridge, sat in the chairs, and finally, slept in the smallest bed	the bears came home, discovered what Goldilocks had done, and she ran away

My Summary Statement:

Goldilocks wanted to see what was inside the house, but no one was at home. So she decided to go inside anyway and tried the porridge, sat in the chairs, and finally, fell asleep in the smallest bed. Then the three bears came home, discovered what Goldilocks had done, and she ran away.

LESSON 2

Summarizing Expository Text With WINDOW

In this model lesson, we shift our attention to summarizing expository text using the mnemonic WINDOW (Asaro-Saddler et al., 2018; Saddler et al., 2019). This self-regulated strategy teaches students the guidelines for expository summarization, including: **W**rite a topic sentence, **I**dentify important information, **N**umber the pieces of identified information, **D**evelop sentences, **O**rganize sentences using transition words, and **W**rite an ending sentence. Self-regulated strategy development, also referred to as SRSD, is an instructional approach that combines writing and self-regulation strategies. Through a gradual release of responsibility, students adopt the skills and strategies utilized by skilled writers, with the utmost goal being student independence. We will learn more about the SRSD approach later in this chapter. For now, read through this lesson, which applies the WINDOW strategy to a *New York Times* article about the Iran Revolution. This news article is used in conjunction with the graphic novel *Persepolis*, by Marjane Satrapi, and provides students with context for the book, as it discusses the impact of the Iran Revolution then and now.

Name: Summarizing Expository Text with WINDOW   **Grade:** Eighth

Preparation for Instruction

Enduring Understandings:

- Individual identities are complex and show themselves in many ways.

- Societal views can influence individual identity.
- It's important to see my identities as well as the identities of others reflected in the world around me.

Essential Questions:

- What defines our identity?
- How is it shaped?
- Do we keep the same identity throughout our lives?

Content Objectives:

- Students will be able to reflect on the various ways certain social contexts impact our identities.

Literacy Objectives:

- Students will be able to summarize an expository text using the WINDOW mnemonic.

Resources/Materials:

- Access to the *New York Times* article "The Iran Revolution at 40: From Theocracy to 'Normality'" WINDOW mnemonic written out on chart paper and provided as a resource for student use

Sequence of Events

Purpose: Students will be able to effectively summarize an expository text using the WINDOW mnemonic.

Review/Prerequisite Skills: To participate in this lesson students should have the following prerequisite skills:

- Understanding of the features of expository text
- Understanding of both sentence and paragraph construction
- Awareness of expository transition words (namely description)

Teacher/Student Instructional Activities:

Lesson opening:

1. Explain to students that today they will be investigating a strategy to help us summarize expository text.
2. Review with students that a summary is a condensed version of a longer piece of text that we write in our own words. Today we are going to practice summarizing a newspaper article to help us build background knowledge about the Iranian Revolution. Remind students that this will help them have context for the graphic novel *Persepolis*, which is set during this time.
3. Review some of the elements of expository text, especially text features like headings, images, and captions, which students can use to navigate the news article.

Teacher modeling:

4. Distribute the article "The Iran Revolution at 40: From Theocracy to 'Normality.'"
5. Display the WINDOW mnemonic for students to see. Explain that today we will be using this strategy to help us summarize this text. WINDOW stands for:
   i. **W**rite the main idea.
   ii. **I**dentify important information.
   iii. **N**umber the pieces of identified information.
   iv. **D**evelop sentences.
   v. **O**rganize sentences using transition words.
   vi. **W**rite an ending sentence.

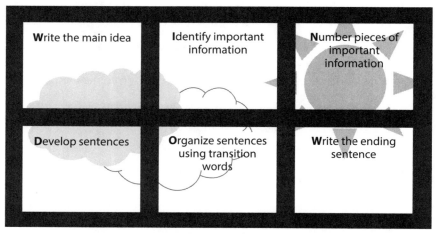

Asaro-Saddler et al., 2018; Saddler et al., 2019

6. Start with **W**rite the main idea. Explain that a strategy used by skilled readers is to identify the main idea by previewing the text's headings, images, and captions. Model this for students. For example:

   a. "I'm noticing that this article has many images. If I look at them and read through the captions, I can see how Iran was at the time of the revolution (1979), all the way until the present (2019). These images show how Iran has changed gradually and become more progressive than in the past. For example, one of the earlier images shows women being separated from men on the subway, while a more recent image shows women and men together at a ski resort and a couple holding hands in the park."

   b. "The title of this article is also called "The Iran Revolution at 40: From Theocracy to 'Normality.'" I can also predict that the main purpose of this piece is to show how Iran changed has changed somewhat from a strict 'theocracy,' a government whose leaders and laws are guided by religion, to a country/government that features more 'normality.'"

   c. "Based on this information, I think the main idea of this article is: *Iran has changed a great deal in the 40 years since its revolution.* I am going to jot that down as my 'working' main idea or topic sentence."

   d. "We will confirm or revise this main idea after reading."

7. "Now we will **I**dentify important information as we read. I want to read this passage carefully to understand. As I do, I am on the lookout for **F**acts, **R**easons, and **I**deas (FRI) from the author. I am going to list them out."

8. Begin reading through the first part of this article, which focuses on Iran after the Iranian Revolution, with students. **F**acts, **R**easons, and **I**deas to identify are:

   a. Ayatollah Khomeini took control in 1979; the Iranian government was built of his ideological choices.

   b. He placed regulations on the media to eliminate western influences.

   c. Women had many regulations, such as wearing head scarves, couldn't ride bikes, separated from men.

   d. However, when behind closed doors people were different (secret parties, pop music).

Student-guided practice:

9. As you transition to the second part of the article, have students help you identify the **F**acts, **R**easons, and **I**deas to note. This includes:

   a. Now, many of these social restrictions have softened.

   b. Women now ride bikes and motorcycles, dye their hair pink, wear nose rings.

   c. Music: while still prohibited on TV, musicians perform on the streets in Tehran.

   d. People have access to internet and satellite TV.

   e. Couples can be seen together in public.

   f. Government (theocracy) and politics have remained the same.

10. Next, have students number these pieces of information in a way that makes sense and is easy to understand. Guide students in understanding that since this article features a shift in time, from then to now, ordering the items in a chronological order will help with readability. We can group them this way:

    a. Ayatollah Khomeini took control in 1979; the Iranian government was built of his ideological choices (1).

    b. He placed regulations on the media to eliminate Western influences (2).

    c. Women had many regulations → wearing head scarves, couldn't ride bikes, separated from men (3).

    d. However, when behind closed doors people were different: secret parties, pop music (4).

    e. Today many social restrictions have softened (5).

    f. Women → ride bikes and motorcycles, dye their hair pink, wear nose rings (6).

    g. Music → while still prohibited on TV, musicians perform on the streets in Tehran (7).

    h. People have access to Internet and satellite TV (8).

    i. Couples can be seen together in public (9).

    j. Government (theocracy) and politics have remained the same (10).

11. Next, guide students in taking these ideas and **D**evelop sentences. For example:

    a. "I'm going to start by placing the main idea of the article in my topic sentence. For example: The article "The Iran Revolution at 40: From Theocracy to 'Normality,'" <u>describes</u> how social regulations in Iran have changed in the past 40 years."

    b. "Notice how I used the word *describe* here. This taps into the text structure/purpose of this article: to describe the changes in Iran."

12. You can then guide students in translating sentences connected to ideas 1 through 4. You can use the following example as a guide. Additionally, point out examples of where students can **O**rganize sentences using the appropriate description transition words. These are underlined in the visual for your reference.

> **Topic sentence (express main idea):** *The article, "The Iran Revolution at 40: From Theocracy to 'Normality,'" describes how social regulations in Iran have changed in the past 40 years.*
>
> **Detail 1:** *In 1979, Ayatollah Khomeini took control, and the Iranian government was built around his ideological choices.*
>
> **Detail 2:** <u>*For example*</u>, *he placed regulations on the media to eliminate Western influences.*
>
> **Detail 3:** <u>*Additionally*</u>, *women had many regulations and were made to wear headscarves, were not permitted to ride bikes, and were separated from men in many places.*
>
> **Detail 4:** *However, behind closed doors people were different.* <u>*For instance*</u>, *people held secret parties with pop music even though this was illegal.*

Independent practice:

13. Allow students to work on translating the remaining details into sentences either individually or in groups of two. Remind them that they must **W**rite an ending sentence to wrap up the piece.

14. As students work, the teacher can circulate around the room and support students as needed.

15. Once the activity is completed, students can share their finished summaries with the group. Again, a completed example is shown here for your reference.

> **Topic sentence (express main idea):** *The article "The Iran Revolution at 40: From Theocracy to Normality'" describes how social regulations in Iran have changed in the past 40 years.*
>
> **Detail 1:** *In 1979, Ayatollah Khomeini took control, and the Iranian government was built around his ideological choices.*
>
> **Detail 2:** <u>*For example*</u>, *he placed regulations on the media to eliminate Western influences.*
>
> **Detail 3:** <u>*Additionally*</u>, *women had many regulations and were made to wear headscarves, were not permitted to ride bikes, and were separated from men in many places.*
>
> **Detail 4:** *However, behind closed doors people were different.* <u>*For instance*</u>, *people held secret parties with pop music even though this was illegal.*
>
> **Detail 5:** *Today many of these social restrictions have softened.*
>
> **Detail 6:** <u>*For example*</u>, *Iranian women dye their hair pink, wear nose rings, and ride bicycles and motorcycles as highlighted in the article. Couples can also be seen together in public and are not separated as rigidly.*
>
> **Detail 7:** <u>*Furthermore*</u>, *while music is still prohibited on TV, one can find musicians performing on the streets in Tehran.*
>
> **Detail 8:** *Part of this shift came with the country's access to Internet and satellite TV.*
>
> **Detail 9:** *However, despite these social changes, the government itself, a theocracy has remained mostly the same.*
>
> **Concluding sentence:** *This makes people wonder if government officials in Iran will eventually begin to change their political practices to match the shift in social regulations.*

Differentiation/Inclusive Instructional Practices:

- WINDOW mnemonic can be utilized to help support students' strategy use.
- WINDOW visual can be displayed to promote student recall.
- Students can handwrite or type their responses.
- Flexible grouping is used throughout lesson.

- Have a teacher read-aloud of the *New York Times* article so all learners have access.
- Facts, Ideas, and Reasons can be highlighted, underlined, and numbered during reading.

Evidence of Student Learning/Informal Classroom-Based Assessment:

- Participation in whole-group lesson
- Participation in partner work
- Identification of facts, reasons, ideas listed in the article
- Completed WINDOW summary

Teacher Reflection in Implementation:

Try This! Select a piece of expository text that you use or would like to use with students. Practice using the WINDOW mnemonic to summarize the text. Remember WINDOW stands for:

Write the main idea

Identify important information

Number the pieces of identified information

Develop sentences

Organize sentences using transition words

Write an ending sentence

Once you've read through the text, use the outline provided to help you write your summary. Finally, reflect: how was completing this expository summary different from using the SWBST strategy for narrative? What challenges might your learners encounter when summarizing expository text?

Topic sentence (expresses main idea):

Detail 1:

Detail 2:

_____

_____

Detail 3:

_____

_____

Detail 4:

_____

_____

Detail 5:

_____

_____

Detail 6:

_____

_____

Concluding sentence:

_____

_____

Intentional Instructional Practices

Have Students Write About the Texts They Read

The first recommendation highlighted in the *Writing to Read* report is to have students write about the texts they are reading in class. Writing about a text enhances students' comprehension as it offers opportunities "to think about ideas in a text, requires them to organize and integrate those ideas into a coherent whole, fosters explicitness, facilitates reflection, encourages personal involvement with texts, and involves students transforming ideas into their own words" (Applebee, 1984; Emig, 1977; Klein, 1999; Smith, 1988; Stotsky, 1982, as cited by Graham & Hebert, 2010). This allows students to deeply process texts read because it provides a concrete means of "permanently recording, connecting, analyzing, personalizing, and manipulating key ideas in text" (Graham & Hebert, 2010, p. 712). The researchers then looked at specific instructional practices connected to responding to a text in writing. Thus, in this section explore activities that teach students to write personal reactions, analyze and interpret text, and to take notes. The additional recommendation, writing summaries, was discussed in the model lesson plan section explored previously.

Respond to a Text in Writing

Graham and Hebert (2010) categorize responding to a text in writing as writing personal reactions and analyzing and interpreting text. Writing personal reactions to a text involves crafting a personal response to a story or relaying a personal connection, while analysis and interpretation incorporate a close examination of the text in order to draw conclusions and explain story characters, events, and happenings. Writing personal reactions is an excellent entry point for responding to a text in writing as it allows the student to draw upon their personal thoughts about the text and/or experiences they've had that may be related. For example, after reading the story *Chrysanthemum* by Kevin Henkes, which is a part of the *All About Me!* unit for first grade, students may be tasked to respond to the following personal reaction:

> In the story *Chrysanthemum*, by author Kevin Henkes, we learned about a young mouse who has very special qualities that makes her unique. Each of us has our own special qualities and individual character traits. In the space provided, write about the traits and qualities that make you special. Use at least two adjectives (describing words) to share your special features.

Use of sentence stems can be an excellent tool for creating personal responses to a text. Figure 8.4 includes a sampling of sentence stems that can be used to help students craft their own personal responses connected to text. Additionally, to incorporate student choice these stems can be provided as a menu of writing options to learners which fosters both excitement for and ownership of writing activities.

> This story reminded me of . . .
>
> The character, _____, reminded me of . . .
>
> I like/dislike this story because . . .
>
> I agree/disagree with . . .
>
> If I were _____ I would . . .
>
> I think the setting is important because . . .
>
> I felt _____ when . . .

Figure 8.4. Personal Response Sentence Stems.

Text analysis and interpretation form a more sophisticated skill as they involve examining the text from a critical lens, collecting evidence, and then drawing conclusions about story evidence or translating ideas in the text into recognizable and authentic applications. For example, character analysis is an instructional practice commonly employed in connection with narrative text. Here students are tasked to find evidence in the story including character actions, motivations, and feelings, to create a full picture of this individual, chart their change over time, and consider who they are AND who they are not. A good example of a character analysis question connected to the story *Persepolis* is:

> Throughout the graphic novel *Persepolis*, the character of Marji grows and changes. We first meet Marji at age 10 and follow her to age 14, when she departs

Iran for school in Vienna to escape the repressive regime. That being said, how would you describe Marji at the beginning of *Persepolis*? How does she change as the story goes on? Cite specific evidence from the text to support your thinking.

Text interpretation, however, involves using one's writing to apply or explain what is read to others. For example, writing an essay that describes how certain historical events took place or explaining a process in science or math are both examples of interpretation. In these instances, the student must know the content deeply in order to communicate their understanding to others. Again, sentence stems are a good way to help students craft written responses across the disciplines. The following chart includes examples aligned to English language arts, history, math, and science.

Subject area	Sentence stem
English language arts	_____ is a symbol of _____ because . . . _____ is a figurative way to explain . . . The author wrote this to illustrate . . . The author uses this style of writing/word choice to communicate . . .
History	These actions/events changed history because . . . These actions/events had future implications. For example, . . . In modern times, this compares to or could mean that . . . If we examine this event through the perspective of _____, we might find . . .
Math	This answer is reasonable/correct because . . . I solved the problem by . . . I can check my work by . . . This problem is asking me to _____ because . . .
Science	The data I collected shows . . . An example of _____ is . . . One reason _____ may occur is . . . One thing that helped me understand this graph/diagram/visual is . . .

Try This! Using one of the sentence stems provided, take a moment to write your own personal response about what you've learned so far in this chapter. Then reflect: how did crafting a personal response help you make a connection to the text and enhance your comprehension of what you've read?

> This chapter makes me think about . . .
>
> I agree/disagree with . . . because . . .
>
> When I read this chapter, I felt . . . because . . .
>
> _____
>
> _____
>
> _____
>
> _____

Write Notes About a Text

Taking notes about a text is another way to enhance students' comprehension (Kiewra, 1989; Peverly et al., 2007, as cited by Graham & Hebert, 2010). Note-taking is important for a variety of reasons. When students sift through a text as a part of the note-taking process, they actively engage in determining relevant information and reduce ideas read into key phrases and words (Graham & Hebert, 2010). This process not only helps students to boost comprehension, but promotes absorption and retention of information, as well (Hochman et al., 2017). There are various note-taking methods available to students. Graham and Hebert (2010) categorize note-taking methods as structured approaches like the Cornell notes or charting methods, which provide students with a clear direction to follow, or a concept map approach where words and phrases are linked to emphasize their relationships. In this section, we review each of these approaches, as well as outlining, briefly and then address the use of student annotations for both narrative and expository text.

Structured note-taking methods provide students with a framework or direction to follow when capturing notes (Hebert, 2019). One popular structured method is Cornell notes, which is shown in Figure 8.5 (Pauk & Owens, 2010). With this method, students write down important ideas, details from the text, or unknown words and phrases in the right-hand column of their notes. Then, on the left-hand side, students reflect on their thoughts in the form of questions, confusions, and/or personal reactions to the text. Finally, after reading the text and collecting their initial thoughts, students review their notes and write a summary of the information on the bottom portion of the note-taking page.

In the example provided in Figure 8.5, notes on the first chapter of the graphic novel *Persepolis* are shown. Important ideas, details, and unknown words are captured as one reads, with the reduction of information completed shortly afterward. This promotes comprehension and retention of what is read.

Charting is another effective way to capture notes, especially when a student is tasked with listing facts and categorizing and/or comparing information. Figure 8.6 examines the impact of various animals exchanged during the Columbian Exchange. Using a note-taking method like this, students can carefully analyze the origin of each exchange and how each animal changed or was changed by its new landscape.

Important ideas, details, or unknown words and concepts:	My thoughts and personal reflections:
• Called "The Veil" • The year is 1980. Ten-year-old Marjane "Marji" Satrapi is living with her mom and dad in Iran. • The Islamic revolution has happened; Marji's mother protests against it. • Marji wants to be a prophet and is deeply spiritual. Her school thinks this is strange.	• Titled this b/c Marji now must wear a veil because of the revolution—something she and her friends don't like and are confused by. • Marji's mother changes her appearance after she is photographed protesting. She must be incredibly scared of being caught! • Marji hides her religious ways from her parents to keep them from worrying about her.

Summary of what I read:
Marji and her parents' lives are upended by the Islamic Revolution, which causes drastic changes for everyone. Since Marji is only 10 at the time, she fails to fully understand the situation, but continues to be her own person as evidenced by her self-selected career choice (to be a prophet) and independent personality.

Figure 8.5. Sample Cornell notes for *Persepolis*.

Animal	Origin	Environmental/biological impact	Cultural impact
Horses	*Old World to New World (reintroduced)*	*Impacted native plant populations negatively; crushing and eating plants, etc.*	*Used for hunting and travel; incredibly useful for Native Americans*
Turkeys	*New World to Old World*	*Domestication by Europeans caused the turkeys to grow larger, making it harder for them to fly*	*Easy to domesticate; could feed more people; were used for holidays and celebrations*
Pigs	*Old World to New World*	*Free-range pigs destroyed crops and food stocks in the New World*	*Pigs were robust and tough in a variety of conditions; their meat could be preserved*
Llamas	*New World to Old World*	*Originally used for labor, llamas were very close to extinction during the Columbian Exchange*	*Llamas have grown beyond their use as a "beast of burden" and are loved worldwide*
Chickens	*Old World to New World*	*Chickens were able to roam more readily in the New World (free range), which allowed them to spread*	*People could eat not only the meat from the chickens themselves, but also their eggs*

Figure 8.6. Sample charting note-taking method.

Outlining is another commonly employed method of note-taking that tasks students with "taking notes based on the macrostructure of the text" (Hebert, 2019, p. 114). Outlining makes use of headings and subheadings to organize material read and is an effective means to help students organize and plan when writing, as well. Figure 8.7 shows how outlining was used to capture information from a ninth-grade physics reading on Newton's first law.

Chapter 2, Section 1: Newton's First Law

1. **Galileo's Law of Inertia**

    a. Galileo Galilei (1564–1642)

    b. "Thought experiment": ball in motion on a hard, smooth surface will stay in motion

    c. *Law of inertia:* the natural tendency of an object to stay at rest or stay in motion with a constant speed and in a straight line

    d. Realized objects are stopped by *force* (the push or pull against them)

2. **Newton's First Law of Motion**

    a. Isaac Newton (1643–1727)

    b. Used law of inertia to develop Newton's *first law:* an object at rest or in motion will either say at rest or continue moving at the same speed and direction unless force affects it

    c. When force acts on an object, it changes its *acceleration* (velocity over unit of time)

    d. *Mass* is a measure of inertia; greatest mass = greatest inertia

3. **Running Starts (connection to sports)**

    a. Running start: an athlete begins moving before reaching the starting line (i.e., javelin throw)

    b. *Speed* of a javelin (change in distance per unit of time) is the SUM of the athlete *running*, forward speed of the hand and elbow, etc.

    c. Velocity = speed in a given direction (slightly different from speed, but often used interchangeably)

4. **Frames of Reference (connection to sports)**

    a. *Frame of reference* is the vantage point with respect to which position and motion are described

    b. When describing speed, we must always ask "Relative to what?"

Figure 8.7. Sample outlining from a ninth-grade physics reading on Newton's first law.

In Figure 8.7's example, headings of each chapter section are bolded, while important vocabulary terms are italicized. These simple visual cues help students to break readings into their corresponding sections and emphasize important terms.

Finally, concept mapping provides learners with a visual representation of how concepts are linked. The main topic is placed in the center of the map in a circle. From here students are tasked to use words and lines to connect related ideas, subtopics, and information. Graham and Hebert (2010) recommend providing students with examples of exemplar concept maps connected to specific readings. Students can then apply what they've learned by completing partially completed expert maps, working toward independent completion of this task. Hebert (2019) recommends the following steps to support students with concept mapping:

- While reading the text initially, instruct students to be on the lookout for important ideas.

- Place those ideas within a circle in a way that shows their importance. For example, in Figure 8.8—which captures the various themes in the story "Fish Cheeks"—the main themes of identity, belonging, family, and coming of age are placed in larger ovals, while connected examples are included in smaller ovals. This emphasizes the topic-and-subtopic-nature of the map.

- Finally, students can link concepts using lines and words.

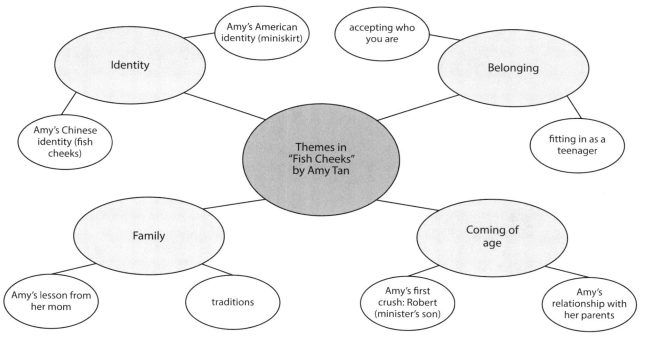

Figure 8.8. Sample concept map for themes in "Fish Cheeks" by Amy Tan.

It is also important to consider text annotations as an avenue to write notes about a text. Text annotations are a reading strategy where students mark the text for relevant information. Sometimes this takes the form of coding and underlining and/or highlighting, but students can also use margin notes to capture key ideas in the text as well. It's important to consider the genre, text structure, and purpose for reading prior to annotating the text. For example, if reading the narrative genre, text annotations should focus on the elements of story grammar including character, setting, plot, and so forth. Figure 8.9 highlights an example of coding aligned to the narrative story, *Me and Marvin Gardens* by S. A. King. Here, Laura Price, a middle school English teacher, created a series of labels for students to use when marking passages. For example, whenever the main character, Obe Devlin, is tasked with making a decision, students mark the passage with the label "Ob." This marking system helps students to stay on top of character actions that drive the plot.

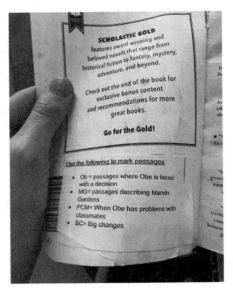 

Figure 8.9. Sample coding for *Me and Marvin Gardens* by S. A. King. (Used with permission of Laura Price.)

When reading expository text, students may annotate based on the discipline or content area of focus and use the available text features to help them guide their thinking. For example, if annotating a chapter in a science textbook, students may incorporate coding that involves identification of headings and subheadings as well as a lookout for procedural words and phrases and equations or formulas (Zywica & Gomez, 2008). While text features like headings and subheadings are standard text features of any textbook, procedural words/phrases and equations and formulas are more specific to the discipline of science. Thus, it is important to help students build an awareness of essential literacy features when working in the four main disciplines.

Author and literacy expert Joan Sedita (2023) recommends the following tips to help students annotate a text including:

- Only highlight or underline information relevant to the purpose of reading.

- Consider the use of more than one highlight color to emphasize specific information (e.g., main ideas = blue, supporting details = yellow).

- Use arrows to connect related ideas.

- Use a symbol system to code relevant information. For example, a star or asterisk can be used to mark important ideas, while a question mark can be used to identify a confusing passage.

- Margin notes can be used to clarify one's thinking, pose questions, or make personal connections.

- Key words and phrases can be boxed or circled and then paraphrased. This helps students to demonstrate understanding of the text as they must translate key concepts into their own words while maintaining the concept's essence.

Reflect & Connect!

Think about your own process when capturing notes on a text. What types of notes do you take? Do you capture notes with paper and pencil or electronically? And do you use annotations with both narrative and expository texts? Reflect on these questions in the space provided. Then consider your teaching practices. How can you use what we've discussed in this section to help your students take notes to support and reinforce their understanding of what they read?

_____

_____

_____

Teach Students About Creating Text

While reading and writing involve the same cognitive processes—including attention, word retrieval, working memory, and executive functioning—and draw upon shared knowledge, these skills also differ (Graham & Hebert, 2010). As Shanahan writes, "Readers and writers have to be able to start from different places," and while "readers follow the author's lead" and use their background knowledge to draw conclusions about the author's intended message, *writers* begin with an idea to communicate which they must secure on the page (2019, p. 310). This "requires a greater degree of explicitness and a more thorough and complete grasp of the same information" (Shanahan, 2019, p. 310). Thus, combining these differing perspectives can help learners develop a broader awareness of reading and writing, and in turn, strengthen both skills. In this section, we explore activities that teach students the writing skills and processes that go into creating text including 1) the writing process, connections to text structures, and genre; 2) paragraph and sentence-construction skills; and finally, 3) word-level skills.

The Process of Writing, Genre, and Text Structures

Teaching students about the writing process, or how writers compose text, helps to demystify the work of authors and builds an understanding of all that goes into skilled writing. Typically, in schools the writing process includes:

- Planning: requires determining a plan and setting goals, generating relevant ideas and content, and organizing ideas logically in order to successfully produce coherent text

- Drafting: involves translating ideas into words and sentences to produce written language

- Sharing: involves sharing one's work with others to gather feedback and/or suggestions

- Evaluating: includes self-evaluation, peer, or teacher review to consider whether the work meets the evaluation criteria and student goals

- Revising: involves a composite of critical reading and reflection to make changes to writing content. This includes the writer's understanding of overall revision goals and evaluation criteria.

- Editing: requires making changes to punctuation, grammar, and spelling

- Publishing: includes finalizing one's work to share it widely with others

Students can then be taught to apply this process to varied genres of writing. A genre is a specific type of writing aligned to a particular topic, purpose, and audience. The *Common Core State Standards* (National Governors Association Center for Best Practices & Council of Chief State School Officers, 2010) and other rigorous state standards require students to write in three genres: narrative, expository/informative, and opinion/argumentative. Students can be introduced to genre elements and text structures using read-alouds and access to other classroom texts. For example, in the *Who Am I?* unit, which explores understandings connected to identity and selfhood, students read various exemplar memoirs including short stories such as "Fish Cheeks" by Amy Tan and graphic novels like *Persepolis* by Marjane Satrapi. After reading several of these exemplar texts, students are then tasked to write their own personal narratives that develop a real experience or event in their lives. The attuned educator can draw parallels between memoir and personal narrative, which share many of the same elements, but also discuss the nuances between the two as shown in Figure 8.10.

Memoir	Both	Personal narrative
• Many moments; covers a period of time • Author reflections and lessons learned are embedded throughout the story	• Both are written about the author's own life • Both include the elements of story grammar including characterization, conflict, dialogue, etc.	• Single moment in time • Recounts the moment as it occurred and includes the author's thoughts and feelings

Figure 8.10. Comparison between memoir and personal narrative.

Students should always be provided extensive opportunities to read a specific genre, identify its elements and text structures, and then discuss the aligned evaluation criteria prior to writing. While beginning writers may initially practice writing for one genre at a time, they eventually become more aware of the demands, purposes, and goals of writing and "begin to blend them in the way experienced writers often do" (Hochman et al., 2017).

Students should also be taught specific writing strategies aligned to the writing process to help them become effective writers (Graham et al., 2012). One means to achieve this is through the use of self-regulated strategy development (SRSD). The SRSD is an evidence-based approach to writing instruction, which has been studied extensively as a way to help students acquire specific strategies aligned to each part of the writing process. Figure 8.11 highlights several examples of SRSD strategies as well as those recommended in the Institute of Education Sciences (IES) practice guide *Teaching Elementary School Students to Be Effective Writers* (Graham et al., 2012).

Component of the writing process	Strategy	Strategy description	Connections between reading and writing
Planning	POW (SRSD)	P: **Pick** an idea O: **Organize** my thoughts W: **Write** and say more	Skilled authors use planning as a first step in the writing process. This helps them generate ideas and develops their knowledge of basic genre structures, which can act as a road map to organize their thoughts.
	PLAN (SRSD)	P: **Pay** attention to the prompt L: **List** main ideas A: **Add** supporting details N: **Number** the major points	
	Outlining	Identify your topic and thesis. Brainstorm connected main ideas and supporting details. Organize these main ideas and details into an outline.	
Drafting	Use of exemplar texts and sentences for imitation	Teachers can identify exemplar sentences, passages, and texts to highlight elements of the genre. Once the elements have been taught, sentences and passages can be selected for sentence imitation. Students must have a solid foundation in basic sentence writing and composition before moving onto this skill.	During the drafting phase, skilled writers use their plans to craft cohesive text. Here writers use their knowledge of sound-symbol relationships and spelling, vocabulary, syntax, and genre to translate their ideas on the page.
Sharing	Teacher conferring	Immediate and frequent feedback is best, although not always possible. Utilizes rubrics and checklists as tools to guide sharing process.	Skilled authors utilize and incorporate feedback to improve their writing. Sharing writing is one means to achieve this. Additionally, sharing writing enhances the reading-writing relationship as a form of communication since this feedback process allows for the identification of errors and incorporation of suggestions to improve overall readability.
	Peer sharing	This is an option for providing more frequent feedback. Expectations for sharing process MUST be modeled and practiced in advance. Utilizes rubrics and checklists as tools to guide sharing process.	
Evaluating	Self-evaluation	Skilled writers ask themselves: *Does my writing align to the evaluation criteria?* *Does my reader need more information to understand my message?* *What can I add/delete/change to improve my work?*	Skilled authors understand the criteria of good writing. They are able to use the evaluation criteria, which align to the various genre structures, to self-evaluate. This helps authors make meaningful revisions to their work.
	Self-monitoring	Skilled writers self-assess their ability to: Establish and achieve goals for writing Sustain attention on the task at hand Successfully implement strategies, and if not, determine a plan to adapt	

Figure 8.11. Examples of self-regulated strategy development (SRSD) strategies.

(continued)

Figure 8.11. *(continued)*

Component of the writing process	Strategy	Strategy description	Connections between reading and writing
Reviewing, Revising & Editing	Peer revision	Peers can provide each other with feedback by: *Does the writing align to the evaluation criteria?* *What is effective about this piece of writing?* *What suggestions can I make to improve my partner's work?*	Skilled authors use reviewing, revising, and editing to consider whether or not their text communicates effectively to their audience. They effectively put themselves into the reader's shoes and reread their work from this perspective. This allows them to truly assess the effectiveness of their message.
	SCAN (SRSD)	S: Does it make **sense**? C: Is it **connected** to my belief? A: Can you **add** more? N: **Note** errors?	
	COPS (for editing)	C: Did I check for correct **capitalization** (first word in sentences and proper names)? O: How is the **overall** appearance of my paper? P: Did I use commas and ending **punctuation**? S: Did I **spell** each word correctly?	

Tips for Success!

SRSD instruction provides one approach to writing that is effective for typically developing learners and those with learning disabilities, as well (De La Paz & Graham, 2002). It consists of six stages including:

- *Develop Background Knowledge*
- *Discuss It*
- *Model It*
- *Memorize It*
- *Support It*
- *Establish Independent Practice*

For more information check out the following resources:

- Powerful Writing Strategies for All Students, *by Karen Harris, Steve Graham, Linda Mason, and Barbara Friedlander.*
- Developing Strategic Writers Through Genre Instruction, *by Zoi A. Philippakos, Charles MacArthur, and David L. Coker, Jr.*
- Building Comprehension in Adolescents: Powerful Strategies for Improving Reading and Writing in Content Areas, *by Linda H. Mason, Robert Reid, and Jessica L. Hagaman*
- Releasing Writers: Evidence-Based Strategies for Developing Self-Regulated Writers, *by Leslie Laude and Pooja Patel*
- thinkSRSD's website at: https://www.thinksrsd.com/

Furthermore, students need to understand that writing is a flexible process and is recursive in nature. Figure 8.12, The Writing Cycle Model, is based on the theoretical models by Hayes and Flower (1980) and Berninger and Winn (2006) and is a more explicit model representing writing as a combination of cognitive and writing processes.

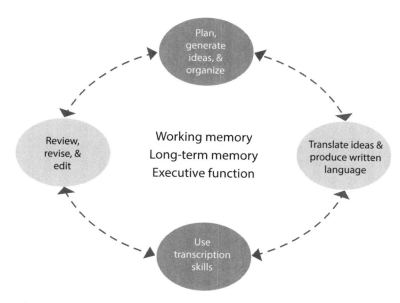

Figure 8.12. The Writing Cycle Model. (*Sources:* Berninger & Winn, 2006; Hayes & Flower, 1980.)

The four writing processes include 1) planning, generating, and organizing ideas; 2) translating ideas and producing written language; 3) transcription skills; and 4) reviewing, revising, and editing.

These four components are influenced by the cognitive factors of working memory, long-term memory, and executive functions, located in the center of Figure 8.12. The bidirectionality of the arrows in this model indicate that writing is not a linear process, and, in fact, it is recursive in nature. Thus, writers move back and forth between the various components as they work to develop text, keeping in mind the influence of audience and purpose throughout. Educators can use knowledge of these skills and processes as well as the influence of cognitive abilities to design and implement effective writing instruction. Furthermore, when students struggle with writing, this knowledge helps teachers to pinpoint which component of the Writing Cycle is in need of review, reteaching, or additional practice.

 Lexicon Check

Transcription refers to the skillful and automatic use of handwriting, spelling, and mechanics to written products.

Translation refers to ability to access and use knowledge of word meaning and sentence and text structure to communicate ideas.

Reflect & Connect!

Understanding the writing process is an integral part of becoming a skilled writer. In this section, we explored the writing process through two different means. First, we discussed the series of student-facing actions, including the writing process components: planning, drafting, sharing, evaluating, revising, editing, and publishing. Then, we examined the Writing Cycle, a teacher-facing model that educators can use to inform their own knowledge and practices of writing. Now reflect on what you've learned. How can you use both of these tools to inform your practice with learners? What are some of your takeaways based on what you learned in this section?

Paragraph or Sentence Construction Skills

Graham and Hebert (2010) also recommend providing students with systematic and explicit instruction in sentence construction, paragraph composition, and longer papers and essays. As we discussed previously, and as experts Judith Hochman and Betsy MacDermott-Duffy remind us, "One of the most fundamental skills a good writer should have, an essential element of writing, is the ability to develop a good sentence" (2015). Thus, teaching students strategies like sentence combining and expansion, which we discussed earlier, are excellent ways to help learners craft more sophisticated sentence structures. Additionally, students can be introduced to the variety of sentence structures through use of a sentence hierarchy. This allows sentence instruction "to be incremental and sequential, moving from simple to more complex (Haynes et al., 2019, p.23). Figure 8.13 is based on the work of Jennings and Haynes (2018) and features a sample sentence hierarchy for simple sentences that feature adjectives and adverbs. These sample sentences align to the read-aloud *Frederick* by Leo Leoni, highlighted in the *All About Me!* unit.

Simple sentence	Example
noun + verb *(who?) (do?)*	The mice labored.
adjective + noun + verb *(Which one?)* *(What kind?)* *(How many?)*	The hardworking mice labored.
noun + verb + adverb *(where?)* *(when?)* *(why?)* *(how?)*	The mice labored tirelessly.
adjective + noun + verb + adverb	The hardworking mice labored tirelessly.

Figure 8.13. Sample sentence hierarchy for simple sentences. (*Source:* Haynes & Jennings, 2018.)

 **Tips for Success!**

To learn more about teaching sentence variety through the use of a sentence hierarchy, check out *From Talking to Writing* by Terrill Jennings and Charles Haynes (2018). For learners who struggle with writing and expressive language skills, this book is an excellent resource that offers educators a plethora of strategies including vocabulary, sentence structure, and composition of narrative and expository text.

You can learn more at: landmarkoutreach.org/product/2nd-ed-talking-to-writing/

Thus, students would start with the simplest construction and add on from there. Additionally, using the question words can prompt students to recall the function of the parts of speech.

Once students are able to craft a variety of sentences and have an understanding of genre, they can use this knowledge to build paragraphs and longer pieces of text. This is where outlining comes into play. An outline serves as a roadmap, which learners can follow to craft longer pieces of text. In their text, *The Writing Revolution*, writing experts Judith Hochman and colleagues (2017) describe the many benefits of outlining including:

- Providing students with a clear structure (beginning, middle, end) to follow

- Assisting students in staying on topic and avoiding repetition by allowing them to see the overall structure of their writing

- Promoting students' ability to distinguish between relevant and irrelevant information and quotes

- Helping students sequence their ideas in a logical manner

- Promoting analytical thinking as learners must critically consider the information they want to include and how to structure it coherently

What does the story "Fish Cheeks" tell us about identity?

Topic sentence: *The story "Fish Cheeks," by Amy Tan, shows that one's identity is complex and changes over time.*

Detail 1: *beginning of story → Amy is embarrassed by her Chinese heritage + wants to be "seen" as American*

Detail 2: *end of story → Amy's mother gifts her with a miniskirt (symbol = American identity) BUT also tells her to have pride in her Chinese heritage*

Detail 3: *as an adult → Amy understands her mom's message*

Concluding sentence: *Identity is multifaceted and its continuity changes from adolescence to adulthood.*

Figure 8.14. Sample outline for "Fish Cheeks" by Amy Tan. (*Source:* Tan, 1987.)

Figure 8.14 shows a sample outline connected to the story "Fish Cheeks" by Amy Tan. In this example, students were asked to respond to the question, *What does the story "Fish Cheeks" tell us about identity?* However, prior to independently crafting their own outlines and paragraphs, students need to develop the necessary prerequisite skills. These foundational skills include how to differentiate a topic sentence from supporting details, how to identify and eliminate redundant information, and finally, how to craft a concluding sentence that echoes "the idea of the topic sentence but not repeat it verbatim" (Hochman et al., 2017, p. 98). Students can develop and build these skills by using examples connected to the texts and concepts they are learning about. This provides students with the opportunity to work from high-quality models, which helps them develop a deeper understanding of structure and organization and serves as a reference point for their writing goals.

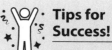

Tips for Success!

To learn more about using outlining as a plan to help learners draft paragraphs and longer pieces of writing, check out the text *The Writing Revolution* (TWR) by Judith Hochman and colleagues. This method, which can be used across subjects and grade levels, is grounded in building students' writing skills including sentence construction, planning, drafting, revising, and editing, using specific strategies taught via explicit instruction.

You can also visit TWR's website at: thewritingrevolution.org

Try This! Read through the randomly ordered sentences that follow. After reading, sort and place each sentence into the correct category on the organizer provided. This includes identifying the topic sentence, supporting details, and concluding sentence. When you are finished reflect: how is an activity like this one useful for both reading comprehension and writing?

1. However, the introduction of new diseases, like smallpox, decimated the New World's Native American populations and led to the "Great Dying" as well as a devastating loss of indigenous culture and heritage.

2. The Columbian Exchange was the transfer of plants, animals, and diseases from the Old World (Europe and Africa) to the New World (the Americas).

3. For example, crops, such as maize and potatoes, expanded food production and helped feed growing populations in Europe and Africa, while animals, such as horses, cattle, and pigs, played a significant role in supporting agriculture and economies in the Americas.

4. This two-way exchange forever changed the course of world history and had a profound impact on the world's ecology and culture.

5. Overall, this transfer of plants, animals, and germs had positive and negative consequences worldwide.

Topic sentence:	
Detail 1:	

Detail 2:	
Detail 3:	
Concluding sentence:	

Answer Key:

Topic sentence:	The Columbian Exchange was the transfer of plants, animals, and diseases from the Old World (Europe and Africa) to the New World (the Americas).
Detail 1:	This two-way exchange forever changed the course of world history and had a profound impact on the world's ecology and culture.
Detail 2:	For example, crops, such as maize and potatoes, expanded food production and helped feed growing populations in Europe and Africa, while animals, such as horses, cattle, and pigs, played a significant role in supporting agriculture and economies in the Americas.
Detail 3:	However, the introduction of new diseases, such as smallpox, decimated the New World's Native American populations and led to the "Great Dying" as well as a devastating loss of indigenous culture and heritage.
Concluding sentence:	Overall, this transfer of plants, animals, and germs had positive and negative consequences worldwide.

Tips for Success!

Connections to Disciplinary Literacy

Graham and Hebert's (2010) final recommendation is to increase how much students write. Thus, all educators must create opportunities for students to write throughout the school day, across all subjects and disciplines. This is where *disciplinary literacy* comes into play. Disciplinary literacy refers to the specialized way we read, write, and communicate in a discipline. Shanahan and Shanahan (2012) describe it as the ways of thinking, the skills, and the tools that are used by experts who create, communicate, and use knowledge in the disciplines. This differs from *content-area literacy*, which focuses on skills and strategies that can be used to approach text across disciplines and assist with comprehension, but ultimately, are not sufficient for an in-depth understanding of a specific discipline. Despite these differences, both content-area and disciplinary literacy provide students with opportunities to write across the school day, something we as educators have the responsibility to provide because this serves to improve learners' comprehension as student writers "can gain insights about reading by creating a text for an audience to read, even when the student is the intended audience" (Nelson and Calfee, 1998, as cited by Graham & Hebert, 2010). One excellent resource on disciplinary literacy is the CEEDAR Center through the University of Florida. Its mission is to prepare learners for college and career readiness through teacher education and outreach and can be accessed at: ceedar. education.ufl.edu/cems/disciplinary-literacy/

The Diverse Learner: Learning Challenges & Differences

When thinking about writing in a culturally and linguistically diverse (CLD) classroom, educators must carefully consider the context of students' participation, their identities, and instructional practices to support their development as writers. Kinloch and Burkhard (2016) describe context as *where* students from CLD backgrounds write (e.g., home, school, work) and for *what purposes*. When planning writing tasks, the informed educator provides opportunities for learners to draw from their "complex and varied language repertoires" and share their unique voices (University of Illinois, n.d.). They are also mindful to avoid a deficit-oriented approach which views these factors as challenges to be overcome (Kinloch & Burkhard, 2016). Identity is another critical factor in the CLD classroom. Students should have the opportunity to see themselves as writers and understand that writing is a tool to "explore how they view themselves" (Kinloch & Burkhard, 2016, p. 386). Educators can support this process by providing students with "culturally relevant" instructional practices. Examples include crafting written responses to culturally relevant literature and poems as well as writing assignments where students can share their "collective and individual experiences about their trans-national identities" (Kinloch & Burkhard, 2016, p. 386). It is also important to keep in mind that students with language-based learning disabilities often struggle with writing. The foundational skills of handwriting and spelling and strategies for planning, translating oral language into written, and then revision often requires more explicit instruction and practice.

Finally, educators must be aware of their own assumptions about language when responding to CLD students' writing. Unfortunately, research has shown that many learners from linguistically diverse backgrounds including "second language writers and speakers of non-mainstream dialects routinely receive feedback that leaves them feeling overwhelmed, unmotivated, frustrated, and anxious about their academic abilities" (University of Illinois, n.d.). One effective practice is to provide feedback that encourages writing growth as opposed to critique that emphasizes correctness (Dobbs & Leider, 2021). Educators can do this by providing feedback that targets students' writing development and purpose as well as the use of language in relation to the intended audience (Dobbs & Leider, 2021). Framing feedback in this manner emphasizes student capability and that writing improvement can be attained as part of the review process.

Putting it all Together

Add a specific example of how any one of the approaches described in the overview chart (Table 8.1) or chapter might be used in your setting. Script your response here.

Voices From the Field

It's your turn to represent the field and comment on your experiences with this and other chapters in the book.

Reflect & Connect!

In what ways will these lessons and activities influence your instruction?

Viewing & Listening Links

The Reading-Writing Connection—Steve Graham https://www.youtube.com/watch?v=tA7QU2s8VSQ

How Can We Take Advantage of Reading-Writing Relationships? https://www.shanahanonliteracy.com/blog/how-can-we-take-advantage-of-reading-writing-relationships-:~:text=Research finds that writing about, and positive impact on learning

References

Adams, M. (2010–2011). Advancing our students' language and literacy. *American Educator, 34*(4), 3–11.

Adams, M. J. (2015). *Knowledge for literacy: Literacy ladders.* http://www.shankerinstitute.org/resource/literacy-ladders

Adlof, S. M., & Catts, H. (2015). Morphosyntax in poor readers. *Reading and Writing, 28,*1051–1070.

Anderson, L. W., & Krathwol, D. (Eds.). (2001). *A taxonomy for learning, teaching and assessing: A revision of Bloom's taxonomy of educational objective.* Longman.

Applegate, K. (2015). *The one and only Ivan.* Harper Collins Publishers.

Asaro-Saddler, K., Muir-Knox, H., & Meredith, H. (2018). The effects of a summary writing strategy on the literacy skills of adolescents with disabilities. *Exceptionality, 26*(2), 106–118.

Austen, J. (2003). *Pride and prejudice* (V. Jones, Ed.). Penguin Classics. (Original work published 1813).

Balthazar, C. H., & Scott, C. M. (2018). Targeting Complex Sentences in Older School Children With Specific Language Impairment: Results From an Early-Phase Treatment Study. *Journal of speech, language, and hearing research: JSLHR, 61*(3), 713–728. https://doi.org/10.1044/2017_JSLHR-L-17-0105

Baker, S., Lesaux, N., Jayanthi, M., Dimino, J., Proctor, C. P., Morris, J., Gersten, R., Haymond, K., Kieffer, M. J., Linan-Thompson, S., & Newman-Gonchar, R. (2014). *Teaching academic content and literacy to English learners in elementary and middle school* (NCEE 2014-4012). National Center for Education Evaluation and Regional Assistance (NCEE), Institute of Education Sciences, U.S. Department of Education. http://ies.ed.gov/ncee/wwc/publications_reviews.aspx

Barnes, M. A., Ahmed, Y., Barth, A., & Francis, D. J. (2015). The relation of knowledge-text integration processes and reading comprehension in 7th- to 12th-grade students. *Scientific Studies of Reading, 19*(4), 253–272.

Barth, A. E., Barnes, M., Francis, D. J., Vaughn, S., & York, M. (2015). Inferential processing among adequate and struggling adolescent comprehenders and relations to reading comprehension. *Reading and Writing, 28*(5), 587–609.

Barajas, J. (2016, September 30). This Chinese American cartoonist forces us to face racist stereotypes. *PBS News Hour.* https://www.pbs.org/newshour/arts/this-chinese-american-cartoonist-forces-us-to-face-racist-stereotypes

Beaty, A., & Roberts, D. (2013). *Rosie Revere, engineer.* Abrams Books for Young Readers.

Beck, I., McKeown, M. G., & Kucan, L. (2002). *Bringing words to life.* Guilford Press.

Beers, K. (2003). *When kids can't read-what teachers can do: A guide for teachers 4–12.* Heinemann.

Berninger, V. W., & Winn, W. D. (2006). Implications of advancements in brain research and technology for writing development, writing instruction, and educational evolution. In C. A. MacArthur, S. Graham, & J. Fitzgerald (Eds.), *Handbook of writing research* (pp. 96–114). Guilford Press.

Biemiller, A. (2010). Words worth teaching: Closing the vocabulary gap. In E. H. Hiebert & M. L. Kamil (Eds.), *Teaching and learning vocabulary: Bringing research into practice* (pp. 223–242). Lawrence Erlbaum Associates.

Brimo, D., Apel, K., & Fountain, T. (2015). Examining the contributions of syntactic awareness and syntactic knowledge to reading comprehension. *Journal of Reading Research, 41*(1), 57–74.

Brody. S. (2001). *Teaching reading: Language, letters & thought* (2nd ed.). LARC Publishing.

Cain, K., & Oakhill, J. (2007). *Children's comprehension problems in oral and written language: A cognitive perspective.* Guilford Press.

Cárdenas-Hagan, E. (2015). Evidence-based vocabulary instruction for English learners. *Perspectives on Language & Literacy, 41*(3) 34–39.

Cárdenas-Hagan, E. (2020). *Literacy foundations for English learners: A comprehensive guide to evidence-based instruction.* Paul H. Brookes Publishing Co.

Carnine, D. W., Silbert, J., Kame'enui, E. J., & Tarver, S. J. (2010). *Direct instruction reading.* Pearson.

Castles, A., Rastle, K., & Nation, K. (2018). Ending the reading wars: Reading acquisition from novice to expert. *Psychological Science in the Public Interest, 19,* 5–51.

Catts, H. W. (2021–2022). Rethinking how to promote reading comprehension. *The American Educator, 45*(4), 26–33.

Catts, H. W., & Kamhi, A. G. (2017). Prologue: Reading comprehension is not a single ability. *Language, Speech, and Hearing Services in the Schools, 48*(2), 73–76.

Catts, H., Nielsen, D. C., Bridges, M. S., & Liu, Y. S. (2014). Early identification of reading comprehension difficulties. *Journal of Learning Disabilities, 49*(5), 451–462.

Cooley, S. A. (1862–1865). *Freedmen's school, Edisto Island, S.C.* [Photograph]. Library of Congress. www.loc.gov/item/2010647918/

Coyne, M. D., McCoach, D. B., Ware, S. M., Loftus-Rattan, S. M., Baker, D. L., Santoro, L. E., & Oldham, A. C. (2022). Supporting vocabulary development within a multitiered system of support: Evaluating the efficacy of supplementary kindergarten vocabulary intervention. *Journal of Educational Psychology, 114*(6), 1225–1241.

Coxhead, A. (2000), A new academic word list. *TESOL Quarterly, 34*, 213–238.

Cunningham, J. W. (1982). Generating interactions between schemata and text. In J. A. Niles & L. A. Harris (Eds.), *New inquiries in reading research and instruction* (pp. 42–47). National Reading Conference.

Darling-Hammond, L., Hyler, M. E., & Gardner, M. (2017). *Effective teacher professional development.* Learning Policy Institute.

Denton, C. A., Enos, M., York, M. J., Francis, D. J., Barnes, M. A., Kulesz, P. A., Fletcher, J. M., & Carter, S. (2015). Text-processing differences in adolescent adequate and poor comprehenders reading accessible and challenging narrative and informational text. *Reading Research Quarterly, 50*(4), 393–416.

De La Paz, S., & Graham, S. (2002). Explicitly teaching strategies, skills, and knowledge: Writing instruction in middle school classrooms. *Journal of Educational Psychology, 94*(4), 687–698. https://www.doi.org/10.1037/0022-0663.94.4.687

Delano, J. (1941). *Five-cent hot lunches at the Woodville public school. Greene County, Georgia. June* [Photograph]. Library of Congress. www.loc.gov/item/2017795070/

Dobbs, C. L., & Leider, C. M. (2021). A framework for writing rubrics to support linguistically diverse students. *English Journal, 110*(6), 60–68. https://www.proquest.com/scholarly-journals/framework-writing-rubrics-support-linguistically/docview/2553865163/se-2

Duke, N. K., & Bennet-Armistead, V. S. (2003). *Reading and writing informational text in the primary grades.* Scholastic.

Dumas, A. (1997). *The Count of Monte Cristo.* Wordsworth Editions. (Original work published 1888)

Dymock, S. (2005). Teaching expository text structure awareness. *The Reading Teacher, 59*(2), 177–181.

Ebbers, S. M. (2011). *Vocabulary through morphemes: Suffixes, prefixes, and roots for intermediate grades.* Cambium Learning Group.

Edwards, E. C., Font, G., Baumann, J. F., & Boland, E. (2012). Teaching word-learning strategies word meanings. In J. F. Baumann & E. J. Kame'enui (Eds.), *Vocabulary instruction: Research to practice* (2nd ed., pp. 139–159). Guilford Press.

Elleman, A. M. (2017). Examining the impact of inference instruction on the literal and inferential comprehension of skilled and less skilled readers: A meta-analytic review. *Journal of Educational Psychology, 109*(6), 761–781.

Elleman, A. M., Lindo, E. J., Morphy, P., & Compton, D. L. (2009). The impact of vocabulary instruction on passage-level comprehension of school-age children: A meta-analysis. *Journal of Research on Educational Effectiveness, 2*(1) 1–44.

Elleman, A. M., Oslund, E. L., Griffin, N. M. & Myers, K. E. (2019). A review of middle school vocabulary interventions: Five research-based recommendations for practice. *Language Speech Hearing Services in the Schools, 50*(4), 477–492.

Elleman, A. M., Steacy, L. M., Gilbert, J. K., Cho, E., Miller, A., Coyne-Green, A., Pritchard, P., Fields, R. S., Schaeffer, S., & Compton, D. L. (2022). Exploring the role of knowledge in predicting reading and listening comprehension in fifth grade students. *Learning and Individual Differences, 98*(3), Article 102182.

Farstrup, A. E., & Samuels, J. S. (2008). *What research has to say about vocabulary instruction.* International Reading Association.

Fischer, C. A. (2019). *The power of the Socratic classroom: Students, questions, dialogue, learning.* Siena Books.

Fitzgerald, F. S. (1925). *The great Gatsby.* C. Scribner's Sons.

Fitzgerald J., & Shanahan T. (2000). Reading and writing relations and their development. *Educational Psychologist, 35*, 39–50.

Florit, E., Roch, M., & Leverato, M. C. (2014). Listening text comprehension in preschoolers: A longitudinal study on the role of semantic components. *Reading and Writing, 27*(5), 793–817.

Gandhi, A., & Hegedus, B. (2012). *Grandfather Gandhi.* Atheneum Books for Young Readers.

Graham, S., & Harris, K. R. (2003). Students with learning disabilities and the process of writing: A meta-analysis of SRSD studies. In H. L. Swanson, K. R. Harris, & S. Graham (Eds.), *Handbook of learning disabilities* (pp. 323–344). Guilford Press.

Graham, S., & Hebert, M. (2010). *Writing to read: Evidence of how writing can improve reading.* Alliance for Excellent Education.

Graham, S., Bollinger, A., Booth Olson, C., D'Aoust, C., MacArthur, C., McCutchen, D., & Olinghouse, N. (2012). *Teaching elementary school students to be effective writers: A practice guide* (NCEE 2012-4058). National Center for Education Evaluation and Regional Assistance, Institute of Education Sciences, U.S. Department of Education. http://ies.ed.gov/ncee/wwc/publications_reviews.aspx#pubsearch

Graham, S., Bruch, J., Fitzgerald, J., Friedrich, L., Furgeson, J., Greene, K., Kim, J., Lyskawa, J., Olson, C. B., & Smither Wulsin, C. (2016). Teaching secondary students to write effectively (NCEE 2017-4002). National Center for Education Evaluation and Regional Assistance (NCEE), Institute of Education Sciences, U.S. Department of Education. http://whatworks.ed.gov.

Graves, M. (2009). *Teaching individual words: One size does not fit all.* Teachers College Press.

Greene, J. W., & Coxhead, A. (2015). *Academic vocabulary for middle school students: Research-based lists & strategies for key content areas.* Paul H. Brookes Publishing Co.

Guan, N., Son, J., & Li, D. (2018). On the advantages of computer multimedia-aided English teaching. *Procedia Computer Science, 131*, 727–732.

Hall, C., & Barnes, M. (2017). Inference instruction to support reading comprehension for elementary students with learning disabilities. *Intervention in School and Clinic, 52*(5), 279–286.

Hall, C., Vaughn, S., Barnes, M. A., Stewart, A. A., Austin, C. R., & Roberts, G. (2020). The effects of inference instruction on the reading comprehension of English Learners with reading comprehension difficulties. *Remedial and Special Education, 41*(5), 259–270.

Hall, C. S. (2016). Inference instruction for struggling readers: A synthesis of intervention research. *Educational Psychology Review, 28*, 1–22.

Harris, K., Graham, S., Mason, L., & Friedlander, B. (2008). *Powerful writing strategies for all students.* Paul H. Brookes Publishing Co.

Hayes, J. R., & Flower, L. (1980). Identifying the organization of writing processes. In L. W. Gregg & E. R. Steinberg (Eds.), *Cognitive processes in writing: An interdisciplinary approach* (pp. 3–30). Lawrence Erlbaum.

Haynes, C., Smith, S. L., & Laud, L. (2019). Structured literacy approaches to teaching written expression. *Perspectives on Language and Literacy, 45*(3), 22–30.

Hebert, M. (2019). Writing from source material. In C. A. MacArthur, S. Graham, & M. Hebert (Eds.), *Best practices in writing instruction* (pp. 108–135). Guilford Press.

Henkes, K. (2009). *Chrysanthemum*. Greenwillow Books.

Hennessy, N. L. (2020). *The Reading Comprehension Blueprint: Helping students make meaning of text*. Paul H. Brookes Publishing Co.

Henry, M. K. (2015). *Unlocking literacy: Effective decoding and spelling instruction* (2nd ed.). Paul H. Brookes Publishing Co.

Hickey, P. J., & Lewis, T. (2013). The Common Core, English learners, and morphology 101: Unpacking LS.4 for ELLs. *Language and Literacy Spectrum, 23*, 69–84.

Hine, L. W. (1908). *Tipple boy, (see Photo 150) Turkey Knob Mine, Macdonald, W. Va. Witness E.N. Clopper. Location: MacDonald, West Virginia.* [Photograph]. Library of Congress. www.loc.gov/item/2018673780/

Hine, L. W. (1921, October 7). *School in Session – (Sunset school). See Photo No. 18. Location: [Pocahontas County—Marey, West Virginia* [Photograph]. Library of Congress. www.loc.gov/item/2018678735/

Hochman, J., & MacDermott-Duffy, B. (2015). Effective writing instruction: Time for a revolution. *Perspectives on Language and Literacy, 41*(2), 31–37.

Hochman, J., Wexler, N., & Lemov, D. (2017). *The writing revolution: A guide to advancing thinking through writing in all subjects and grades.* Jossey-Bass.

Hoover, W. A., & Tunmer, W. E. (2020). *The cognitive foundations of reading and its acquisition: A framework with applications connecting teaching and learning.* Springer.

Hua, A. H., & Keenan, J. M. (2014) The role of text memory in inferencing and in comprehension deficits. *Scientific Studies of Reading, 18*(6), 415–431.

Irwin, J. W. (2007). *Teaching comprehension process* (3rd ed.). Allyn & Bacon.

Jacobsen, L. (2018, April 11). Policymakers, educators look for reasons behind NAEP results. K–12 Dive. https://www.k12dive.com/news/policymakers-educators-look-for-reasons-behind-naep-results/521042/

Jennings, T. M., & Haynes, C. W. (2018). *From talking to writing: Strategies for scaffolding narrative and expository writing* (2nd ed.). Landmark School Outreach Program.

Johnston, F. B. (ca. 1899). *Elementary school children standing and watching teacher write at blackboard, Washington, D.C.* [Photograph]. Library of Congress. www.loc.gov/item/96516051

Kendeou, P., Bohn-Gettler, C., White, M. J., & Van Den Broek, P. (2008). Children's inference generation across different media. *Journal of Research in Reading, 31*(3), 259–272.

Kinloch, V., & Burkhard, T. (2016). Teaching writing in culturally and linguistically diverse classrooms. In C. A. MacArthur, S. Graham, & J. Fitzgerald (Eds.), *Handbook of writing research* (2nd ed., pp. 377–394). Guilford Press.

Kintsch, W. (1988). The role of knowledge in discourse comprehension: A construction integration model. *Psychological Review, 95*(2), 163–182.

Kintsch, W. (1998). *Comprehension: A paradigm for cognition.* Cambridge University Press.

Kintsch, W., & Rawson, K. A. (2005). Comprehension. In M. J. Snowling & C. Hulme (Eds.), *The science of reading: A handbook* (pp. 209–226). Blackwell.

Kraus, R., & Aruego, J. (1971). *Leo the late bloomer.* Windmill Books.

Kurto, K., & Salamone, J. (2021). "Working With Word Meanings." Right to Read: The Science of Reading and Structured Literacy Awareness, 2021. https://www.mtssri.org/course/view.php?id=113.

Language and Reading Research Consortium. (2018). The dimensionality of inference making: Are local and global inferences distinguishable? *Scientific Studies of Reading, 22*(2), 117–136.

Learning for Justice. (2023). https://www.learningforjustice.org/

Leidig, T., Grünke, M., Urton, K., Knaak, T., & Hoff, S. (2018). The effects of the RAP strategy used in a peer-tutoring setting to foster reading comprehension in high-risk fourth graders. *Learning Disabilities: A Contemporary Journal, 16*(2), 231–253.

Leonard, L. B. (2014). Children with specific language impairment and their contribution to the study of language development. *Journal of Child Language, 41*(1) 38–47.

Lesaux, N. K., & Harris, J. R. (2015). *Cultivating knowledge, building language: Literacy instruction for English learners in elementary school.* Heineman.

Leslie, F. (1882). *The only one barred out Enlightened American statesman – "We must draw the line somewhere, you know"* [Digital file from original periodical]. Library of Congress. www.loc.gov/item/2001696530/

Library of Congress. (2023). www.loc.gov

Library of Congress. (n.d.). *Research guides: Using the Library of Congress Online: A Guide for Middle and high school students: Types of sources.* Types of Sources - Using the Library of Congress Online: A Guide for Middle and High School Students - Research Guides at Library of Congress. https://guides.loc.gov/student-resources/types

Lionni, L. (1967). *Frederick.* Pantheon.

Maillard, K. N., & Martinez-Neal, J. (2019). *Fry bread: A Native American family story.* Roaring Brook Press.

Mayer, M. (2003). *Frog goes to dinner.* Penguin Books.

Macon, J. M., Bewell, D., & Vogt, M. (1991). *Responses to literature.* International Reading Association.

McBirney, J. (2016). *The founding of American democracy.* CommonLit. https://www.commonlit.org/texts/the-founding-of-american-democracy.

McCabe, A. (1997). Cultural background and storytelling: A review and implications for schooling. *Elementary School Journal, 97*(5) 453–473.

Mesmer, H. A., Cunningham, J. W., & Hiebert, E. H. (2012). Toward a theoretical model of primary-grade text complexity: Learning from the past, anticipating the future. *Reading Research Quarterly, 47*(3), 235–258.

Meyer, B. J. F. (1985). Prose analysis: Purposes, procedures, and problems. In B. K. Britton & J. B. Back (Eds.), *Understanding expository text* (pp. 11–65). Erlbaum.

Meyer, H. (1890). *En Chine—le gâteau des rois et . . . des empereurs* / H. Meyer. Library of Congress.

Muhammad, I., Ali, S. K., & Aly, H. (2019). *The proudest blue: A story of hijab and family.* Little, Brown.

Nation, K. (2005). Children's reading comprehension difficulties. In M. J. Snowling & C. Hulme (Eds.), *The science of reading: A handbook* (pp. 248–265). Blackwell.

Nation, K. (2019). Children's reading difficulties, language, and reflections on the simple view of reading. *Australian Journal of Learning Difficulties, 24*(1), 47–73.

National Governors Association Center for Best Practices & Council of Chief State School Officers. (2010). *Common Core State Standards for English language arts and literacy in history/social studies, science, and technical subjects.*

National Research Council. (2000). *How people learn: Brain, mind, experience, and school.* National Academies Press.

National Institute of Child Health and Human Development. (2000). *Report of the National Reading Panel: Reports of the subgroups. Teaching children to read: An evidence-based assessment of the scientific research literature on reading and its implications for reading instruction* (NIH Publication No. 00-4754). Washington, DC: Government Printing Office.

Neuman, S. B., & Kaefer, T. (2018). Developing low-income children's vocabulary and content knowledge through a shared book reading program. *Contemporary Educational Psychology, 52,* 15–24.

Newell, G. E., Beach, R., Smith, J., Van DerHeide, J., Kuhn, D., & Andriessen, J. (2011). Teaching and learning argumentative reading and writing: A review of research. *Reading Research Quarterly, 46*(3), 273–304.

Oakhill, J., & Cain, K. (2012). The precursors of reading ability in young readers: Evidence from a four-year longitudinal study. *Scientific Studies of Reading, 16*(2), 91–121.

Oakhill, J., Cain, K., & Elbro, C. (2015) *Understanding and teaching reading comprehension: A handbook.* Routledge.

O'Connor, R. E. (2007). *Teaching word recognition: Effective strategies for students with learning difficulties.* Guilford Press.

Otsuka, J. (2002). *When the emperor was divine: A novel.* Knopf.

Palmer, P. J. (2019). *The courage to teach: Exploring the inner landscape of a teacher's life.* Jossey-Bass.

Park, L. S., & Lee, H. B. (2020). *Bee-Bim Bop!* HarperCollins.

Parr, T. (2001). *It's okay to be different.* Little, Brown and Company.

Parr, T. (2010). *The Family Book.* Little, Brown and Company.

Pauk, W., & Owens, R. J. Q. (2010). Chapter 10: The Cornell system: Take effective notes. In *How to study in college* (10th ed.). Wadsworth.

Playground, baseball, Madison School baseball, 5/20/1914 [Photograph]. (1914). Library of Congress. www.loc.gov/item/2016851245/

Poulsen, M., & Gravgaard, A. K. (2016). Who did what to whom? The relationship between syntactic aspects of sentence comprehension and text comprehension. *Scientific Studies of Reading, 20*(4), 325–338.

Pyle, N., Vasquez, A. C., Lignugaris-Kraft, B., Gillam, S. L., Reutzel, D. R., Olszewski, A., & Pyle, D. (2017). Effects of expository text structure interventions on comprehension: A meta-analysis. *Reading Research Quarterly, 52,* 469–501.

Raphael, T., & Au, Kathryn. (2005). QAR: Enhancing comprehension and test taking across grades and content areas. *Reading Teacher, 59,* 206–221.

Rapp, D. N., van den Broek, P., McMaster, K. L., Kendeou, P., & Espin, C. A. (2007). Higher order comprehension processes in struggling readers: A perspective for research and intervention. *Scientific Studies of Reading, 11*(4), 289–312.

ReadWorks. (2018). Six mass extinctions in 440 million years. American Museum of Natural History. https://www.readworks.org/article/Six-Mass-Extinctions-in-440-Million-Years/e2c70485-3fd1-46fc-b7e3-350dc6a9a588#!articleTab:content/

ReadWorks. (2022). The Green Book: Traveling the Jim Crow South. International Quilt Museum, University of Nebraska–Lincoln. https://www.readworks.org/article/The-Green-Book-Traveling-the-Jim-Crow-South/b4359659-d5be-45af-90a1-80871938e660#!articleTab:content/

ReadWorks. (2015). The New Deal. The Gilder Lehrman Institute of American History. https://www.readworks.org/article/The-New-Deal/bf8cafaa-f647-4e1b-be20-deb8d73f30e4#!articleTab:content/

Reutzel, D. R., Smith, J.A., & Fawson, P.C. (2005). An evaluation of two approaches for teaching reading comprehension strategies in the primary years using science information texts. *Early Childhood Research Quarterly, 20*(3), 276–305.

Saddler, B., Asaro-Saddler, K., Moeyaert, M., & Cuccio-Slichko, J. (2019). Teaching summary writing to students with learning disabilities via strategy instruction. *Reading & Writing Quarterly, 35,* 572–586.

Satrapi, M. (2003). *Persepolis.* Pantheon Books.

Scarborough, H. (2001). Connecting early language and literacy to later reading (Dis)abilities: Evidence, theory and practice. In S. B. Neuman & D. K. Dickinson (Eds.), *Handbook of early literacy research* (pp. 97–110). Guilford Press.

Schumaker, J. B., Denton, P. H., & Deshler, D. D. (1984). *Learning strategies curriculum: The paraphrasing strategy.* University of Kansas.

Scott, C. (2004). Syntactic contributions to literacy development. In C. Stone, E. Silliman, B. Ehren, & K. Apel (Eds.), *Handbook of language and literacy: Development & disorders* (pp. 340–362). Guilford Press.

Scott, C. M. (2009). A case for the sentence in reading comprehension. *Language, Speech, and Hearing Services in Schools, 40*(2), 184–191.

Scott, C., & Balthazar, C. (2013). The role of complex sentence knowledge in children with reading and writing difficulties. *Perspectives on Language and Literacy, 39*(3), 18–30.

Sedita, J. (2023). *The Writing Rope: A framework for explicit writing instruction in all subjects.* Paul H. Brookes Publishing Co.

Shanahan, T. (2013). *Grammar and comprehension: Scaffolding student interpretation of complex sentences.* https://www.shanahanonliteracy.com/blog/grammar-and-comprehension-scaffolding-student-interpretation-of-complex-sentences

Shanahan, T. (2017a). *Is building knowledge the best way to increase literacy achievement?* https://www.shanahanonliteracy.com/blog/is-building-knowledge-the-best-way-to-increase-literacy-achievement-sthash.Pm1kc0jP.dpbs

Shanahan, T. (2017b). *How should we combine reading and writing?* https://www.shanahanonliteracy.com/blog/how-should-we-combine-reading-and-writing

Shanahan, T. (2019). Reading-writing connections. In C. A. MacArthur, S. Graham, & M. Hebert (Eds.), *Best practices in writing instruction* (pp. 309–333). Guilford Press.

Shanahan, T., Callison, K., Carriere, C., Duke, N. K., Pearson, P. D., Schatschneider, C., & Torgesen, J. (2010). *Improving reading comprehension in kindergarten through 3rd grade: A practice guide* (NCEE 2010-4038). National Center for Education Evaluation and Regional Assistance, Institute of Education Sciences, U.S. Department of Education.

Shanahan, T., & Shanahan, C. (2012). What is disciplinary literacy and why does it matter? *Topics in Language Disorders, 32*(1), 7–18.

Sinclair, U. (1906). *The jungle.* Grosset & Dunlap.

Snow, C. E. (2002). *Reading for understanding: Toward an R&D program in reading comprehension.* RAND Corporation.

Soto, G. (1983). "The Jacket." In *The effects of Knut Hamsun on a Fresno boy: Recollections and short essays.* Persea Books

Soto, G., & Martinez, E. (1993). *Too many tamales.* Putnam.

Tan, A. (1987). "Fish cheeks." In *The opposite of fate: A book of musings.* Putnam.

The first picket line - College day in the picket line [Photograph]. (1917, February). Library of Congress. www.loc.gov/item/97500299/.

The only one barred out Enlightened American statesman. We must draw the line somewhere, you know. (1882). [Photograph]. Library of Congress. www.loc.gov/item/2001696530/.

University of Illinois. (n.d.). *Teaching linguistically diverse writers.* Illinois Writer's Workshop. https://writersworkshop.illinois.edu/resources-2/instructor-resources/teaching-linguistically-diverse-writers/

Vachon, J. (1938, May). *Playground scene. Irwinville school, Georgia.* [Photograph]. Library of Congress. www.loc.gov/item/2017717221/

Vaughn, S., Roberts, G., Klingner, J., Swanson, E., Boardman, A., Stillman-Spisak, S., Mohammed, S., & Leroux, A. (2013). Collaborative strategic reading: Findings from experienced implementers. *Journal of Research on Educational Effectiveness, 6,* 137–163.

Verhoeven, L. T. W., & Perfetti, C. A. (2011). Introduction to the special issue: Vocabulary growth and reading skill. *Scientific Studies of Reading, 15,* 1–7.

Westby, C. (2010). Multiliteracies: The changing world of communication. *Topics in Language Disorders, 30,* 64–71.

Wexler, N. (2018). Why American students haven't gotten better at reading in 20 years. *The Atlantic.*

Wexler, N. (2019). *The knowledge gap: The hidden cause of America's broken system and how to fix it.* Penguin Random House.

Wharton, E. (2012). *The house of mirth.* Penguin Classics. (Original work published 1905)

Wiggins, G., & McTighe, J. (1998). *Understanding by design.* Association for Supervision and Curriculum Development.

Wijekumar, K., Meyer, B. J. F., & Lei, P. (2018). Improving content area reading comprehension of Spanish speaking English learners in Grades 4 and 5 using web-based text structure instruction. *Reading and Writing, 31*(9), 1969–1996.

Williams, J. (2005). Instruction in reading comprehension for primary-grade students: A focus on text structure. *Journal of Special Education, 39,* 6–18.

Williams J. P. (2017). Teaching text structure improves reading comprehension: Text structure should be taught starting in the primary grades. *PsychEd.* https://www.psychologytoday.com/us/blog/psyched/201703/teaching-text-structure-improves-reading-comprehension

Williams, J. (2018). Text structure instruction: The research is moving forward. *Reading and Writing, 31,* 1923–1935.

Williams, J. P., & Pao, L. S. (2011). Teaching narrative and expository text structure to improve comprehension. In R. E. O'Conner & P. F. Vadasy (Eds.), *Handbook of reading interventions* (pp. 254–278). Guilford Press.

Woodson, J. (2018). *The day you begin.* Penguin Random House.

Zipoli, R. (2017). Unraveling difficult sentences: Strategies to support reading comprehension. *Intervention in School and Clinic, 52*(4) 218–227.

Zwiers, J., & Crawford, M. (2011). *Academic conversations: Classroom talk that fosters critical thinking and content understandings.* Stenhouse.

Zywica, J., & Gomez, K. (2008). Annotating to support learning in the content areas: Teaching and learning science. *Journal of Adolescent & Adult Literacy, 52*(2)6, 155–165.

Index

Note: Page numbers followed by *f* and *t* indicate figures and tables, respectively